FOR FEAR OF THE FIRE

FOR FEAR OF THE FIRE

JOAN OF ARC *and the Limits of Subjectivity*

Françoise Meltzer

THE UNIVERSITY OF CHICAGO PRESS
CHICAGO & LONDON

Françoise Meltzer is chair of the Department of Comparative Literature and professor in the Department of Romance Languages and Literatures, the Divinity School, and the College at the University of Chicago. She is the author of several works, including *Hot Property* and *Salome and the Dance of Writing,* as well as a coeditor of *Critical Inquiry.*

The University of Chicago Press, Chicago 60637
The University of Chicago Press, Ltd., London

Printed in the United States of America
10 09 08 07 06 05 04 03 02 01 5 4 3 2 1

ISBN (cloth): 0-226-51981-3
ISBN (paper): 0-226-51982-1

Library of Congress Cataloging-in-Publication Data

Meltzer, Françoise.
For fear of the fire : Joan of Arc and the limits of subjectivity / Françoise Meltzer.
p. cm.
ISBN 0-226-51981-3 (cloth) — ISBN 0-226-51982-1 (pbk.)
1. Joan, of Arc, Saint, 1412–1431. 2. Christian women saints—France—Biography. 3. Virginity. 4. France—History—Charles VII, 1422–1461. I. Title.
DC103 .M45 2001
944'.026'092—dc21

2001001083

♾ The paper used in this publication meets the minimum requirements of the American National Standard for Information Sciences—Permanence of Paper for Printed Library Materials, ANSI Z39.48-1992.

For Claudie's Chou Maé,
Jeanne Dumilieu
(who was never called Jeanne),
and for those who loved her

CONTENTS

ACKNOWLEDGMENTS

Too long in the making, this book has constantly benefited from innumerable friends, colleagues and students. I can only list the most obvious here. They are all, of course, all to be held entirely responsible for any mistakes or limitations from which this project frequently suffers.

First, my patient and taxed assistants over these several years: Peter Struck, Mahnaz Fancy, Cindy Klestinec, David Simmons, and (magnificent at the finish line) Joshua Yumibe. Between their faxes and photocopies to France, frantic and disparate forms of communication, technological wizardry, and general high standards of erudition that kept me focused, they are to be pitied and admired at once. I am most grateful.

Thanks are long in coming as well to Margaret Jewett Burland, Arnold Davidson, Jean-Luc Marion, and Yuri Tsivian. Their conversations and bibliographic input have helped to make this book not only possible but more plausible as well. Also to my friends Maureen Mclane and Susan Schreiner, special thanks for brilliantly reading, comforting, and correcting at the eleventh (and a half) hour.

Various parts of this book have been given as lectures at, among other places, the University of London, the Chicago Humanities Institute, the Colloquium on Religion and Literature at the University of Chicago, Yale, Western Ontario, Harvard, the University of Tel Aviv, the Einstein Forum in Potsdam, Germany, and the International Comparative Literature Association. I have, to put it mildly, greatly profited from all of the discussions that ensued.

Previous, somewhat different, or related aspects of this study have appeared or will appear in the following: "Der Diskurs der Jungfräulichkeit, oder von der Geschlechtlichkeit des Heiligen," in *Die Ungewisse Evidenz: Für eine Kulturgeschichte des Beweises*, ed. Gary Smith and Matthias Kross (Berlin, 1998); "Re-embodying: Virginity Secularized," in *God, the Gift and Postmodernism*, ed. John Caputo and Michael Scanlon (Bloomington, Ind., 1999), 260–281; "Joan of Arc and the Celtic Tree: A Fairy Tale," in *Religion as Story*, ed. Ingrid Schafer (Bloomington, Ind., forthcoming); "Mysticism Denied: The Trial of Joan of Arc," in *Mystics: Presence and Aporia*, ed. Michael Kessler and Christian M. Sheppard

(Chicago, forthcoming); "Joan of Arc in America," special issue of *Sub-Stance,* ed. Robert Barsky (forthcoming).

Elizabeth Kominska gets a special thanks for everything; and Jackie Simmons is to be constantly commended for tirelessly attempting to keep me in shape. Kat Beaulieu read an early part of the manuscript and kept me inspired with her humor and conviction.

Robert Natkin, the painter, not only showed great interest in this project but also produced several paintings of Joan of Arc for the book cover. They were not used (to my sorrow), but they remain as testimony to his generosity, friendship, and searing genius of vision.

Philip Gossett, dean of the Humanities Division at the University of Chicago during most of the writing for this book, generously granted me a year's leave to complete the project. Clark Gilpin, dean of the Divinity School, was supportive intellectually as well as financially. Alan Thomas at the Press has, as always, been tireless in his encouragement.

My friend Suzanne Fleischman did not live to see this book completed, but her ardent and wonderfully intolerant spirit has enriched its perspective, as it has my life. I try to live up to her.

My graduate students as always, remain my teachers and most critical audience. They make me go on writing.

Finally (again, as always), Ziva Ben Porat, with all of the impatience and love of a sister, reads, corrects, and galvanizes me into new modes of thinking and arguing. To David Tracy, I owe an immeasurable debt: not only has he read this manuscript, over and over again in all of its stages, but weekly conversations with him, on his work and mine, have kept me passionate in the development of this project, and encouraged—indeed allowed me—to continue. The cliché "without whom this book would never have been possible" is merely a statement of fact with respect to him. Thank you, David.

Claudie, my daughter, has her own vision of Joan of Arc, and I hope that when she is older, she will find a bit of that vision here. Ani and Nick were there for me, even if I wasn't always for them. My husband, Bernie, always my first reader and always my intellectual companion, knows how much I have leaned on him.

Dit outre que tout ce qu'elle avait dit et révoqué, elle l'avait fait seulement par la crainte du feu.

—*Joan of Arc at the Trial of Condemnation*
28 May 1431

INTRODUCTION

THE SNOWS OF YESTERYEAR

Our legends are better than our philosophy.

—Alain (Émile-Auguste Chartier)

IN 1999, THE MUSÉE D'ORSAY in Paris devoted a small exhibit room to a nineteenth-century sculpture of Joan of Arc.[1] Produced in 1870, just as the city of Paris was being threatened by German forces, it is no surprise that the artist turned to Joan: she had become, after all, the symbol of French nationalism, even though she was fifty years away from being declared a saint.[2] The artist, a conservative portrait medalist named Henri-Michel-Antoine Chapu, had won the Prix de Rome in 1855 and subsequently spent five years in Italy. His first triumph, however, was the statue of Joan that he produced fifteen years later. The large statue, placed in the middle of the room at d'Orsay, shows the young

[1] I am grateful to Édouard Papet, curator of sculpture at the Musée d'Orsay, for discussing this exhibit with me. For a full discussion of the museum's Chapu exhibit, see Papet, "La *Jeanne d'Arc à Domrémy* par Chapu (1870–1872)" in *La Revue du Musée d'Orsay* 8, no. 48/14 (1999): 91–95.

[2] In fact, the block of marble was delivered to Chapu on 19 July 1870—the day of the official declaration of war between France and Prussia (ibid., 94).

Joan at Domrémy hearing her voices (fig. 1). Clothed in "typical" feminine peasant garb, she is kneeling on the ground, head slightly tilted, intensely listening (or trying to understand), her hands clasped in prayer or in concentration. The statue is a strong statement in its representational forthrightness: a simple, barefoot peasant girl falls to her knees and tries to understand what is happening to her; the aura of impending historical import hovers like a halo—at least, that is the effect for those who know the story. In a sense, then, the statue produces the effect that Sartre complained was endemic of all biographies: the apparently insignificant events in the early life of the famous are always read back by the reader and biographer to be anything, finally, except insignificant. The girl we see before us is still an obscure peasant girl, but we "read back," in the strong and handsome face that the statue offers us, the courage and tragedy that will be hers. Thus, the very simplicity of the statue belies its meaning, adding to the power of the piece. Surrounding Chapu's statue, in glass cases against the walls of the room, are the artist's sketches for the piece. Here one can see how Chapu worked to create his vision: the potent simplicity of his subject.

On one of the walls is a portrait medal of Joan, done by Chapu several years earlier. It is clearly the same face, at first glance, but here Joan is the warrior, her profile set with the conviction and determination of the famous general. Upon closer scrutiny, it becomes clear that Joan-as-soldier has a larger and slightly aquiline nose, whereas her nose on the statue is straight and smaller. The soldier's lips curve down a bit, in a show of resolution and certainty, whereas those of Joan-as-peasant-girl are thinner and the mouth a bit less set. The portrait shows Joan with short hair, and it would not be clear that she was a woman (or indeed a man) without the description on the label. The statue, on the other hand, shows Joan's hair covered with a kerchief and conveys, with its full and solid arms, a certain modesty and softness in the figure's features.

If one remembers the events that took place in Joan's life between the age of thirteen, when she first heard the voices in her father's garden, and the age of seventeen or so, when she led the French army, it is hardly surprising that the younger Joan would be more vulnerable and the older, more resolute. Nevertheless, Chapu managed to convey a distinct masculinity in the soldier and an equally emphatic femininity in the peasant.[3]

---

[3] As Papet puts it, "If Chapu envisaged at least once a warrior figure, he seems quickly

That is, Chapu marshaled the gender clichés in the development of his images. Such clichés have been amply catalogued without question, not the least by Freud, for example. But let us take another example from the socialist Proudhon, Chapu's contemporary, who wrote that the feminine element is finally a "negative one," which will lead to the destruction of a civilization if left untethered: "The feminine element, notwithstanding the specific quality which results from its very inferiority and makes it recognizable, is in the final analysis a negative element; a diminution or weakening of the masculine element, which alone represents the integrity of the mind."[4] These words, written three years after Chapu won the Prix de Rome, are in themselves platitudes of masculinist ideology. I cite them merely because of the contemporaneity to Chapu: ideas belong to men alone; a civilization that allows too much of a feminine influence will quickly sink into decadence.

There is clearly nothing particularly exceptional about the stereotyping of Chapu's visions (indeed, they are forcefully echoed by the likes of Nietzsche, Freud, and Kierkegaard, to name just three). Nevertheless, the juxtaposition of these two images in the same small room at d'Orsay makes for a certain discomfiture in the viewer; a kind of scopic vertigo. Somehow, these two works present the same face (with its variants), yet the two figures depicted are not the same person. For the gender issues raised by Joan of Arc are entangled in the two most readily recognized aspects of her life: the prototype of femininity, on the one hand (the peasant girl who sewed and prayed at her mother's side), and of masculinity, on the other (the general who led her troops into battle on a charging steed). These are two images that, given the gendered culture in which the West has been steeped, cannot, in fact, be resolved or mediated.

The various and multitudinous depictions of Joan that have come down to us demonstrate the difficulty: she is imagined either as a near-masculine individual such as Chapu's medal portrait or the Minerva-like frontispiece to Schiller's *Die Jungfrau von Orleans* (fig. 2) or as a highly feminine figure completely out of place in battle, complex of clothing and flaccid of gesture. Or she is in a combination feminine / masculine attire

---

to have chosen the register of intimacy, even of modesty, evoking a Virgin of humility beneath the traits of a young peasant girl" (ibid., 93, my translation).

4 Pierre-Joseph Proudhon, *Influence de l'élément féminin sur les moeurs et la littérature française* (Paris, 1957), 5, my translation.

with a certain robustness that is meant, one assumes, to suggest her strength of character. Mark Twain's long book on Joan, for example, was illustrated by Frank Vincent Du Mond (1865–1951), who with near total consistency depicts her wearing a skirt ("petticoats," as one critic put it) over her armor (fig. 3). Twain later objected that Du Mond had produced a Joan who resembled "a strapping middle-aged fishwoman with costume to match" and that her gaze betrayed "the fixed expression of a ham." Twain himself had commissioned, and approved, all of the artist's drawings. But when the author later contemplated them, he was struck by their inadequacy or inappropriateness. Given the gender notions with which we are still fairly burdened, the pervasive conundrum arises of how to depict a woman in the clothing and role of a man, one who asserted under oath that she wore male garb for reasons of expediency and took on a military function because God had ordered her to do so. Du Mond's iconology of Joan highlights the difficulty, and this is what Twain instinctively sensed although he had little notion of how to correct it.

One method of overcoming the gender difficulties posed by Joan is to impose a token other-gender object onto an otherwise thoroughly oriented depiction. For example, in the portrait commissioned by the aldermen of Orléans in 1581, Joan wears high feminine garb but tilts her head prettily in the direction of her sword, which she holds limply and completely unconvincingly in her right hand (fig. 4). This absurd image, as the Johannic scholar Régine Pernoud points out, was to be a prototype for representations of Joan for two succeeding centuries. Another frequent option has been to portray Joan in full armor (usually on her horse, banner flying), thus avoiding any specific gender identification entirely: the metal coverings of her armor completely hide her body (fig. 5) and often much of her face as well. Finally, there is always the solution of portraying the different aspects of her life with different gender emphasis, as if the subject were divorced from herself, which was the solution settled upon by Chapu.

More recent depictions of Joan have shown her as relatively androgynous—such as the raw face of pain we confront in Dreyer's silent film masterpiece, *The Passion of Joan of Arc* (1928) (fig. 6). Here the idea is to erase gender through fusion and to insist on the tragedy of Joan by way of obviating the gender trouble. In a more curious move, Victoria Sackville-West, in her musings on Joan's appearance, decides that she probably most resembled the statue at Domrémy. The statue, she writes, is falsified in many ways, including that it shows Joan with long hair. Discerning the problem, Sackville-West nonetheless immediately embarks upon her own gender assumptions in explaining those of others: "This [the long hair] is quite comprehensible when we reflect that one of the principal accusations against her was that she adopted men's clothes and fashions; naturally, her apologists and rehabilitators, awkwardly embarrassed by her masculine career, aspired to present her under as feminine an aspect as possible."[5] There is something about the statue, Sackville-West decides, with "those thick short thighs, those truncated arms," that evokes "the unattractive peasant girl" whom the saints "so sagaciously selected for their purpose" (fig. 7). She adds, "I think it is not unfair to qualify her as unattractive. Men attempted no rape, nor were women jealous. She made war, but not love. . . . But somehow or other, for all the excitement of her startling notoriety, she clearly aroused neither the natural desire of men nor the competitive mistrust of women." It would not be very difficult to dissect the gender clichés (well intended though they may be) in this passage. Rape, for example, seems to partake of the "natural" desires of men, and an attractive woman must, apparently, always arouse the jealousy of women. Thus, in this mechanical syllogism, a woman who is neither raped nor burdened with the mistrust of other women must logically be "unattractive," complete with thick short thighs and truncated arms. That, in any case, is Sackville-West's unperturbed conclusion.[6]

The fact is, however, that we do not know what Joan of Arc looked like. As Sackville-West herself points out, no contemporary portrait of Joan is known to exist. We do know, however (contrary to what Sackville-West seems to believe), that numerous coins and likenesses of her were made after she freed the city of Orléans. These have all been lost. We have left only a doodle, made by the scribe in the margins of the official document relating the lifting of the siege of Orléans (1429) to the Parliament of Paris (fig. 8). This doodle constitutes the only drawing we have of Joan during her lifetime, although the scribe himself never saw her. Apart from that, we know that when she became a soldier, her hair was "short" and dark. Jean d'Aulon, Joan's squire, described her as "beautiful

5 Victoria Sackville-West, *Saint Joan of Arc* (New York, 1936), 6.

6 In fact, contrary to Sackville-West's assertions, several men testified at Joan's Trial of Rehabilitation that they had been attracted sexually to her but that she had always rebuffed them.

and shapely" (this to underline the surprising fact that no soldier ever tried to touch her and to emphasize her virtue as well). But we do not know whether she was tall or short, heavy or slim, large or small nosed, and so on. We are not sure of the color of her eyes. Several soldiers reported, after her death, that she was a "normal-looking woman." That is not much to go on. The only thing that emerges as certain from her trials concerning her physical being is that she was a virgin. And even here, we have some reason to suspect that she may have been raped by English soldiers during her imprisonment.

Thus, the depictions of Joan of Arc tell us about the assumptions and gender prejudices of each succeeding era, but they tell us nothing about Joan's looks in themselves. They can be read, then, as a semiology of gender: how each succeeding culture imagines the figure whose charismatic courage, combined with her blurring of gender roles, contribute to make her difficult to depict. Each artistic rendition of Joan, then, is yet another fresco in the Imaginary (in Lacan's sense) of the West and yet another attempt to reconcile the variants on patriarchal hegemony with the notions on femininity such a hegemony has generated. Was Joan unattractive? Masculine? Feminine? Androgynous? Hermaphroditic? Or was she "feminine" before she waged war, only to mutate, Orlando-like (but in reverse), into a manly presence when battles were to be won? These are questions that speak more to the inadequacy of gender models and to the insistence on keeping the stereotypes stable. They have, finally, little to do with Joan herself.

As artistic renderings of Joan can be read as semiologies of a given culture, so this book uses the figure of Joan of Arc as an indicator of a series of problematics: the question of feminine subjectivity and of subjectivity itself. Unlike a good deal of contemporary gender theory (including my own), I do not try in this book to appropriate a subjectivity for women but argue rather that subjectivity itself is an illusion grounded in a gendered pattern of self/other. For patriarchy to mark its sovereignty as subject—a need it has consistently demonstrated in the West—it must posit an other that has just as consistently been feminine. Quite apart from the obvious and gendered dyad of oppressor/oppressed that ensues, the adherence to such a dyad has functioned to obfuscate a more dangerous thought: that of the impossible, of death. The fact that the feminine is frequently linked to death is from this point of view not coincidental. The struggle to maintain sovereign subjectivity as a gendered given, furthermore, produces a complete ignorance about gender itself. Thus, the battle for subjectivity is helpful in obfuscating the more frightening notion of the void that may lie behind the facade that subjectivity provides. I will argue that part of the drama underlying the Trial of Condemnation of Joan of Arc is the swift response of the patriarchy (Church, nascent state, army, kingship) when it feels itself to be *conceptually* as well as experientially at risk.

Even when contemporary texts perform the gesture of questioning subjectivity, I believe, the patriarchal hegemony and its philosophy of othering are cautious in their refusal to be genuinely threatened, not to mention rethought. Yet a certain destabilization of categories has been put into place of late, producing an atmosphere (philosophical as well as physical) of uncertainty, with a concomitant ambiguity. Postmodernism (a term, for want of a better one, that I will use throughout as a label) contains what I call a nostalgia for certainty—certainty about ideas and about the body. I have found that in "secular" contemporary texts there is a fascination with figures for whom the gift of the body through death is the logical consequence of conviction—the early Christian martyrs, for example. Contemporary theoretical writings seem to yearn for, even as they are bewildered by, an imagined past when the body and mind were presumed to be unsyncopated—when the body, in other words, whether reviled or seen as a companion, bore upon itself the beliefs of the mind and indeed served as something like a vessel specific to those beliefs. The glance backward toward such an imagined, pre-Cartesian past constitutes what I am calling a nostalgia, one that betrays much about our notions not only of the body but of agency and its gendered configurations. All of this is to be found in the reactions to Joan's story and in the corollary dilemmas it summons.

The story of Joan is pivotal in this sense: On the one hand, many of the obstacles faced by early (female) Christian martyrs are still present in fifteenth-century France. At the same time, Joan's difficulties with the Church and king continue vestigially to the present day. One need but look at the way the notion "woman" is pursued and questioned in contemporary critical discourse.

This book, then, is not only about Joan of Arc, although she is a constant and, I hope, forceful presence. But, like a movie in which the scenery is the foregrounded protagonist, Joan is here the lens that allows for the cultural landscape to unfold around her. Those who are looking for a book on Joan of Arc per se, then, will be disappointed. In some chapters (the first one in particular) she barely appears. On the other hand, hundreds of excellent books have been written about Joan, as the notes to the present study partially attest. I am not attempting here to produce yet another "portrait" of Joan but rather to ask what the theologians, historians, contemporaries, and so forth, who so constantly depicted and scrutinized her (and continue to do so) had and have as *epistemological* baggage and assumptions to inspire (and, just as frequently, to block) them when they considered her case. I look as well into some of the factual aspects of her tragedy: the trials and her execution in particular. For what happens when one is faced with a historical contradiction: a woman who takes on agency, whose divinely inspired voices are politically motivated, who sacrifices her body to fulfill her mission, and who without any education whatever remains strangely conversant in the intricacies of theological, military, and political analyses? The point here, then, is not to look more closely at Joan herself (although this study certainly does that as well), so much as it is to reconsider the various metaphysical conundrums motivated by her story. Why, for example, was virginity such a central concern for her; what was it about female virginity that gave Joan a special status? Why was her virginity probably essential for her to succeed? These are not questions about Joan herself; they are issues relating to the gendering of bodies and the ancillary conviction that ideas (the integrity of the mind, in Proudhon's terms) must remain the purview of masculinity. They are also issues that engage the Church and its own gendered hegemony, its own hold on prophesy.

To begin asking such questions and to approach the "postmodernist" nostalgia that I sense in recent texts, I have necessarily also had recourse to present-day works in critical theory and philosophy. As issues of gender, subjectivity, the body, power, and so on, are debated in contemporary texts, one can begin to tease out the threads that remain from even before Joan's time. When Derrida, for example, argues against gender constructions, he also reveals modern stereotypes even as he struggles against them; and when Foucault delves into rules of chastity in medieval monasteries, he simultaneously suggests how the West sees the body now. So, too, when Levinas speaks of "virility" in a discussion on otherness, he writes with a myriad of assumptions about gender and subjectivity. These are just three of many theorists upon whom I draw to show that the overt cultural and metaphysical codifications of the gendered subject in the France of Joan's day subsist as vestigial and yet tenacious elements in our time now.

Joan is clearly a linguistic subject in the sense of Benveniste. She says "I" and is thus engaging in a linguistic form that assumes a person, as Benveniste will put it. But from a historical and political view, in terms of rights, power, and agency, Joan is a woman and thus clearly not a subject or person before the court. Moreover, philosophically Joan is not a subject because, as I will be reiterating throughout this study, woman as other places the subject position in the masculine; what is feminine is allied to the impossible. Thus, there are three discourses of "subject" that I will be using here: linguistic, historical-political, and metaphysical (which, using the term broadly, occasionally includes psychoanalytic discourse as well). I allow them to blur and collapse into each other at times, to stand in contradiction to each other, precisely as they do for the feminine individual. That is, saying "I" gives one the impression of being a subject, of having agency. But that conviction is annulled by the very nature of the Symbolic (in this case, court proceedings), which—in remaining willfully indifferent to her words and desire, in possessing her speech, and in always defining her according to a sexed/gendered a priori—works to make Joan a "subject" without agency. She is what I am calling a nonsubject in terms of political personhood as well as ontological category. The polyvalence and contradiction in my use of these terms, and in my mixing of these discourses, is meant to perform the very catachresis that subjecthood for Joan engages. The three discourses I indicate cannot be disentangled, yet they variously nullify each other. And that is the point. Joan's story lays bare the epistemological pleonasm of *subject,* in all of its senses, as the site of the masculine. We will be looking here at the representability of subjectivity itself, not its possibility.

As contemporary texts strain to destabilize subjectivity and to abandon the insistence on individuality inherited from the Enlightenment, there is a subtly contradictory move toward charismatic figures such as Joan. It is particularly paradoxical given that the feminine subject does not, in fact, exist in the texts of Western thought. Moreover, a fascination with historical figures comprises in itself a nostalgia for individuality before the Enlightenment—an anachronism that does not fully admit to the fact that individuality is differently configured and indeed quite an alien concept before the Renaissance in Europe. Virginity itself retains a mystique in present-day texts, as does the overly noted notion of woman as enigma. These are the "threads" that remain, vestigially encrusted in our thinking, even as they are forcefully rejected from the intellect of what for lack of a better word I have been calling "postmodernism." In the writings of Levinas, Kristeva, Foucault, Irigaray, Derrida, Bataille, and others, one continues to see the givens that made for Joan's trajectory. The subtle but pervasive affiliation we have with the past is all the more difficult to trace perhaps precisely because we feel ourselves to be so far away from it and from the cartoonlike notions of gender which Joan had to endure in her world.

The six chapters in this book are motivated by specific issues raised by Joan's story, issues that open out onto the larger question of subjectivity. The first chapter establishes the contemporary nostalgia for an imagined, prelapsarian (that is, pre-Cartesian) time when the body and mind are believed to have been in unison. The example here is Louis Althusser, who longs for a premodern body—a longing quite discrete from his Marxian epistemology. Althusser functions as an exemplum of the nostalgia at issue, but the ways in which he is surprised to discover his body and attempts to remain vigilant of its presence go a long way toward explaining the idealization of bodily certainty we have been seeing in postmodernist texts. In Althusser's memoirs, too, we see a fascination with saints and a belief that for the saintly martyr, body and mind are one. Moreover, in his memoirs there is a fear of the loss of subjectivity and an unspoken desire for unity and revelation. Althusser thus sets up the place from which we look back onto Joan of Arc.

The second and third chapters address female virginity: how is it that Joan knew that to be followed and heard, she had to be a virgin? Why does virginity empower feminine discourse? By looking at notions of female virginity—from both a physical and conceptual perspective—we can begin to see how contemporary metaphors continue to ally feminine virginity and anatomy with death. Like death, moreover, virginity is a paradox: it is annihilated at the moment it is ascertained. The female body itself is seen as that which flees from the light—the light of day but also of thought and *logos*. Thus, the notion of female virginity participates in feminizing alterity and, paradoxically, in placing the "veil" of such otherness before the terror of death. Masculine subjectivity is preserved through the protective shield of the hymen and its contemporary metaphors. It is my belief that such pervasive, conceptual metaphors resonate with the historical specificity of Joan's virginity and the extent to which it was seen as crucial in her trial. Indeed, it can be said that this book works throughout from such an assumption: The philosophical metaphors of femininity that pervade the texts of critical theory today are, in my view, abstractions and distant progeny of the more accessible gender constructs that have delineated "woman" in the West since Plato. I include in this even those contemporary texts that seek to discard the notion of "woman." The historical contingency of Joan of Arc, in other words, is determined by the global metaphors of woman and vice versa. This book insists on the historical moment of Joan's murder, but it also insists that her death is a case in which masculinist metaphysics permits and even informs that death, extending (in a far more muted way, of course) to contemporary texts on "woman." Metaphors of transcendence work to determine historical contingency, even as they provide our backward glance at fifteenth-century France. It is a great and vicious circle.

The fourth chapter deals directly with Joan's trial and the way in which her lack of agency silences her voice at every level. The differing registers of the trial, on the one hand, and Joan's allegiance to her voices, on the other, make for an impasse between her and the ecclesial powers that could only end in her death. Here again, the struggle is one between a patriarchal hegemony (the late medieval Church) and a young woman who, without subject position or agency, speaks from a strange position of personal strength. It is a paradox that I will argue is the place where the modern notion of subjectivity itself is both inaugurated (Joan can be said to be one of the first modern figures) and simultaneously revealed as a fragile illusion constructed on the gendered axis of self/other.

Chapters 5 and 6 continue these issues of subjectivity, first with respect to the impossible (death). What does the crowd see when, after her death, Joan's genitalia are displayed to "prove" that she is a woman? How does the crowd understand her femininity, and how do we re-create that vision ourselves? In that moment, when metaphor becomes real, the two disparate registers that I have argued are parallel—metaphor and event—are clearly shown to be symbiotic. The last chapter shows how the contemporary distancing from the Enlightenment entails a concomitant search for the vestigial remnants of a lost prophetic time. In contemporary critical discourse, femininity is looked to as the place of mystery—

one both to be dispelled and contrarily to provide us with a mystery that cannot be solved, thus comforting a need for the possibility of a transcendent. Modern books on Joan of Arc, whether secular or religious, revel in the mystery of her story. What Simone Weil calls the supernatural is not so far removed from secular postmodernism as its insistent juxtapositions, dismantlings, and debunkings would have us believe. Thus, we return to the initial point about nostalgia.

Let us consider now the aspect of Joan as a cultural phenomenon during this millennial era, for Joan of Arc is surprisingly present. I want to contextualize this facet of Joan as an elaboration of what I called earlier the "vestigial" traces of the issues she complicates. Metaphor and historical context are to be understood here as earlier—symbiotic.

On 13 October 1996, the Associated Press ran the following article:

> A fiery reenactment of Joan of Arc's death—complete with a black-robed executioner burning a statue of the saint—prompted protests along with somber contemplation at Marquette University (in Milwaukee). "In the name of justice, I demand you stop!" a woman shouted as the "executioner" walked up and torched the statue. The burning Sunday night was the culmination of a two-week long commemoration of Joan of Arc's canonization at the private Catholic school. Joan of Arc is a revered figure at the campus, which has a chapel, brought stone by stone overseas, where the teen-aged girl was said to have prayed for guidance before leading the armies of the dauphin Charles into battle against the English in 1429.
>
> The ceremony sparked debate in part because the papier-mache [*sic*] statue was holding a cross. Some called it blasphemous while others objected to the anti-women aspect of the funeral pyre. . . . The school gospel choir refused to participate in the ceremony for "personal and religious reasons." One teacher noted, "I can't believe the things we do at this university in the name of Christianity."

In the ceremony, several corollary events had been organized: an iron cross emerged from inside the papier-mâché effigy as it burned; there followed a sprinkling of water from the baptismal font on the embers; and, finally, a dove was released "to symbolize Joan's soul."

Upon looking more closely at this rather intriguing "happening," one learns that the protests were motivated by four main reasons. In the words of the director of the closing ceremony (Fr. Grant Garinger, S.J.), the reasons are as follows:

1. There is a connection between burning crosses and the Ku Klux Klan.
2. Some people equated the burning of the statue with the burning of southern churches in the United States.
3. By burning a female statue, some people defined this as a symbol of violence toward women.
4. Some people had the idea that the statue was for idolizing.

"Some people," it seems, had a great deal of negative feelings toward this event. The organizers, on the other hand, felt that the burning was properly very emotional. One organizer said, "It was remarkable to see us all with tears pouring down our faces." She added, "We knew what was going to happen; we planned it."

Lurking beneath the four reasons for protest in Milwaukee is a series of assumptions having as much to do with the millennium culture in North America as with (of course) Joan of Arc herself.

After having been nearly forgotten during several centuries (except for a ribald and notoriously outrageous mock epic by Voltaire and a very unflattering depiction by Shakespeare), Joan was revived as an icon by, strangely enough, Schiller. His *Jungfrau von Orleans* (1801) brought praise even from Michelet, who saw that play as the source of Joan's cultural resurrection. After that, the cumulative effect in France was astounding. In the nineteenth century, Michelet obsessed on Joan—particularly in the fifth volume of his *History of France* (1840s). At the same time, a young and skeptical scholar named Jules Quicherat spent nearly ten years of his life (1840–49) establishing the documents from Joan's two trials: that of condemnation (1431) and the posthumous Trial of Rehabilitation (1456). Quicherat's work has become the standard edition for any Johannic study. Banville, Chateaubriand, both Dumas, Hugo, Musset, Vigny, Rimbaud, Renan, Mark Twain, and De Quincey all wrote varying versions of a more or less romantic Joan in the last century. (I am concentrating mainly on the French, but there are many other English and German works on Joan.) Less romantically, the end of the nineteenth century finds Zola, in a fit of naturalist pique, dubbing her a "hysterical peasant girl" whose dreamy-eyed interpreters were ignoring the "scientific truth."

There have also been many biographies in the last two hundred years. The two principal ones of the twentieth century are the huge work by Anatole France (which is largely negative and sees Joan as the "mascot" of the Church) and the response by the Scotsman Andrew Lang the same year (1908). Anatole France wrote serenely that Joan suffered from hallucinations of all the senses, especially hearing, and that her "troubles" began in childhood, from which in his opinion she never emerged. Andrew Lang responded with indignation, attacking France for his small-mindedness.

The best English-language biographies are considered to be that of Francis Cabot Lowell (turn of the twentieth century) and Victoria Sackville-West's *Saint Joan of Arc* (1936), already mentioned. In contemporary scholarship on Joan, the principals are Champion, who updated Quicherat in the 1920s, and, beginning in the 1950s, Régine Pernoud, who has devoted her scholarly life to Johannic studies.

Plays proliferate in our day: the most important is no doubt Bernard Shaw's *Saint Joan* (1924). Moreau's *Jeanne* (1909) was played by an elderly Sarah Bernhardt; Anouilh wrote *The Lark* in 1953; Claudel, *Jeanne d'Arc au bûcher* (1937); Brecht, *Saint Joan of the Stockyards* (1932), which was immediately produced in France. In prose, there is the lifelong and monumental oeuvre of Péguy (from 1910 through the 1930s), as well as Aragon, Bernanos, Julien Green, Maeterlinck, Vercors, and Vermorel. Most recently, there have been novels: Tournier's *Gilles et Jeanne*, Michel Peyramaure's *Jeanne d'Arc: Et Dieu donnera la victoire*, and Mary Gordon's novelistic biography *Joan of Arc*. These are just examples—there are many others.

Moreover, throughout the West (in this context I will again largely limit myself to France and the United States), a staggering number of films have been produced about Joan of Arc, of which I will again note only a few. The first documented film attempt is in 1898 (Georges Hatot's *Jeanne d'Arc*), followed by 1900 (Méliès). In 1917, there is the patriotic reverie of De Mille; in 1927, two films—one by De-Gastyne and the other Dreyer's famous version—diametrically opposed both in ideology and in intent; in 1957, Preminger; 1962, Bresson; 1970, Paniflov; 1990, Herzog; and most recently, *The Messenger* (1999), directed by Luc Besson. In all, counting Besson, there have been at least forty major motion pictures on Joan of Arc since 1898 (I have left out of this count the television versions).

Clearly, the historical discourses surrounding Joan of Arc as source are numerous and at frequent odds. Whereas she has been powerfully depicted as a Resistance fighter in World War II (for example, by Vercors and Vermorel) or as a champion of the working class (Brecht), she has been used as well as the Marianne of the Right in France from 1870 to the present. Indeed, Joan becomes the pervasive icon of nationalism when France is threatened from the outside (in the modern era: 1870, 1914, the period between the two World Wars, and again of course in 1939). The leader of the French Right during World War I, for example, Maurice Barrès, wrote six essays on Joan (1916) in which he sees her as the symbol of France's victory over Germany and as a "model" for young Parisian women. In the same period, the continually abrasive Rightist Léon Bloy railed against the Church even as he violently castigated the Germans ("les brutes") in the name of patriotism. In Bloy's view, it is patriotism that Joan was to "invent" and teach in her late feudal era, long before she was to inspire it in subsequent generations. Bloy has two iconologies of the cross: the wooden one for the Christian martyrs as against the "implacable iron" of Germany (which he blames on Luther). I will return to this dual vision of the cross of iron or wood.

Such a collusion between the Right and the image of Joan has perhaps its most remarkable example in the writings of the World War II right-wing intellectual Robert Brasillach. In *Domrémy* (1943), he compares Joan to Antigone and passionately identifies with Joan. The strange twist is that Brasillach was himself tried and executed in 1945 for collaborating with the Germans.[7] Shortly after the war, De Gaulle is caricatured as Chapu's statue of Joan (fig. 9). Like the statue, De Gaulle is in peasant-woman garb, kneeling and, one is to imagine, straining to hear voices.

7 Brasillach also wrote a fictional version of Joan's trial in 1931, which was reissued ten years later. For a positive review at the time of publication, see *La Nouvelle Revue française* (September 1941). Here Joan is seen as a figure reinstating the values destroyed in the prewar period. For a recent perspective on the Brasillach trial, see Alice Kaplan, *The Collaborator: The Trial and Execution of Robert Brasillach* (Chicago, 2000).

The collusion with the Right continues to this day of course in the xenophobic stance of Jean-Marie Le Pen. Here the threat is seen as coming from *inside* France—that is, the foreigners (particularly North Africans) who are "invading" French territory. Claiming Joan as among the one hundred most important people in the history of the world, Le Pen calls her "a saintly national heroine" from whom he claims to receive his orders. With campaign posters portraying Joan as backdrop to his neomonarchist, hyper-Catholic and reactionary patriotism, Le Pen is using Joan's image in the name of the two institutions he supports. They are in fact, however, the twin hegemonies that murdered her: the Church, which, under the aegises of the Inquisition, tried and condemned her, and the French monarchy, which, in the person of Charles VII, allowed her to be sold and executed.

The discourse formation around Joan of Arc in France, then, participates in a specifically patriotic series of *imagos,* via appropriation. We can safely say that Joan is bound up in the French national Imaginary. But she is a powerful icon that can extend beyond French patriotism to slip (surprisingly easily) into other nationalist myths. For example, a poster from World War I in the United States shows a Joan of Arc in full armor, sword held high, her face a perfect example of the starlet look of early movies (fig. 10). The caption reads, "Joan of Arc Saved France: Women of America Save Your Country. Buy War Savings Stamps." And Winston Churchill, it should be remembered, wrote a highly sympathetic account of Joan, admonishing "every soldier" to read her story. It is possible, in other words, for Joan's personification of *patrie* to transcend specifically French cultural boundaries and to be allied to the Imaginary of another nationalist/intellectual discourse.

French colonialism has also transcended boundaries to impose the image of Joan upon the colonized. As Simone Weil notes, "Had France been conquered by the English in the fifteenth century, Joan of Arc would be well and truly forgotten, even to a great extent by us. We now talk about her to the Annamites and the Arabs; but they know very well that here in France we don't allow their heroes and saints to be talked about; therefore the state in which we keep them is an affront to their honour."[8]

The importation of Joan is not always a gift or always born of the lux-

---

[8] "The Needs of the Soul," in *Simone Weil: An Anthology,* ed. Sian Miles (New York, 1986), 102.

ury of resonating cultural *imagos*. There are times when she is imported as part of the imperialist economy of cultural goods. And there is another problem: As a French textbook for French children puts it, Joan is a delicate case because she belongs to France by way of her military victories and patriotic convictions, but she belongs to the church by way of her faith for which, ironically enough, the same church murdered her. Her story blurs registers, as we have already noted.[9]

The story of the Joan story forms a series of reciprocal contaminants: political discourse with ecclesiastic; nationalist boundaries with Catholic globalization; historical documentation with the backformations of a multitude of personal obsessions with Joan; the medical-scientific discourse (is she hysterical, schizophrenic, hallucinatory, generally deranged, psychotic, and so forth?) with mystical conviction—a combination that in turn engages the confrontation between the epistemological insistence on *evidence*, on the one hand, and the equal insistence on the *jehnseits* of mystery and faith, on the other.

Like the dismantled French chapel reconstructed in Milwaukee, imported goods change with the context, even within the dominant discourse of the so-called first world. Joan of Arc is a different cultural product in America than in, say, Orléans (or Paris), just as Simone de Beauvoir and Derrida are not the same textual phenomena in North America as in France. These differences, despite all of the queering accomplished by Joan's story, remind us of the extent to which boundaries do finally (re)impose themselves on notions of cultural production and on national Imaginaries. Let us return, then, to the chapel in Milwaukee and to the four main reasons for the protest against the burning in effigy.

Granted that the context for the burning in effigy story is a Catholic one at an American university, it nevertheless presents with symptoms more pervasive in the cultural context than at first meets the eye. The first protest was, it will be recalled, the connection between a burning cross and the Klu Klux Klan. (Indeed, the executioner of the Inquisition wore robes not unlike those of that later racist brotherhood.) These are clearly North American associations. Consider, for example, the following detail: for Léon Bloy, we have noted, the iron cross was German and the wooden one that of the martyrs. For the director of the effigy ceremony,

---

9 For a study of Joan in school textbooks, see Roger Odin, *Jeanne d'Arc à l'école: Essai sémiotique* (Paris, 1980).

on the other hand, the burning cross cannot be confused with the KKK because "the cross [we are burning] is iron and not wood, so the symbols are very different." Here wood and iron are exactly reversed in their valences. Significantly, when Joan was put to the stake, she asked for a cross so that her gaze could rest on it until her death. An English soldier made her one out of two *wooden* sticks and gave it to her. Then one of the priests who assisted her to the end brought her one (perhaps of iron, perhaps of wood) from the church nearby and held it up for her to see.

In the fifteenth century, no one comments on the *material* aspect of the cross; meaning is there vested in the cross itself.[10] By the twentieth century, on the other hand, the symbol valence of the cross lies in its substance: an iron cross is not the same as a wooden one. It is as if we have gone, epistemologically (versus theologically, the more usual context here), from tran- to consubstantiation in our perception of symbols. Since Kant, perhaps, we have been unable to think outside metaphors, culminating in Derrida's declaration that all concepts are metaphors—a notion that persists despite the protests of Paul Ricoeur, for example.

So a wooden cross is not the same symbol as an iron one, even for the director of a Catholic school in Milwaukee far from the critical theory fray. The point, then, is that these issues have permeated the culture in such a way that the protests about burning Joan of Arc in effigy are in fact arguments about the way we want to understand representation itself. "Stop in the name of justice!" betrays a different notion of representation than does "We knew what was going to happen; we planned it."

The second reason for protest: Burning the statue of Joan is like the burning of southern churches in the United States. Following post-Freudians who work on feminine subjectivity—such as Lacan, Irigaray, Cixous, Kofman, Wittig, Kristeva, Clément, Montrelay—it is not hard to say that this concern (about the churches in the south) is really a displacement from burning women onto the burning of African-American churches. In other words, there is something about alterity in the burning of Joan in effigy that makes the spectator uncomfortable in a largely unacknowledged way. As we all know, what is excluded from "we" the people

[10] The way medieval people understood allegory and symbol is extremely complicated, and I am not trying to simplify this issue here. Rather, my point is that the meaning of the cross in Joan's time is sufficiently stable to allow for a certain indifference to the material from which the cross is made. We will address this problem later in this study.

(blacks, women, children, slaves, the insane, Jews) makes the reenactment of burning a woman a perhaps overly facile actualization of the cultural unconscious. In other words, burning Joan of Arc in effigy echoes burning black churches in the South in the sense that the anathema of the Inquisition is mirrored by the move to subjugate any alterity. If the mimetic gesture of burning Joan is meant to emphasize the tragedy of her death and the brutality of the Church Militant in her era, there is also a way in which that same mimetic gesture mirrors the *desire* to obliterate alterity and to silence all minority discourse. Anathema poses as retrospective penance, and the ceremony itself becomes an emperor and new clothes scenario in which everyone pretends that what is being enacted is somehow *not* being enacted in the same way as the first time: that we can burn Joan better now, since we understand that it was all a mistake.

What, then, is being reenacted? What is the mimetic desire? To what extent are the spectators constituted as objects in the trace of this displacing fire? How does the hegemony of the modern Church here reify the discourse on the subject in its relation to power? At what point are female agency and voice reobliterated in the re-representation of the fifteenth-century version of the same by doubling the gesture? The whole question can be recast as well within Certeau's brilliant study on possessed women in sixteenth-century Loudun.[11] The teachers and students in Milwaukee need not have read any critical theory to engage in a fierce battle on the nature and power of representation. The gospel choir refuses to participate altogether, while the planners of the ceremony congratulate themselves on their "tears pouring down their faces." And then there is the teacher who screams out that the burning should be stopped "in the name of justice."

The theorists of twentieth-century France have saturated much of Western culture, or, put another way, they have discerned and formulated the suspicions that inform our era. Thus, I need not go much further with protests 3 and 4: that the statue burning comprised violence against women and / or that it amounted to idol worship. Again, these are issues of (the gendering of) alterity and representation. These are, I would argue, the very issues raised by the figure and story of Joan of Arc in this millennial context.

---

[11] Michel de Certeau, *The Writing of History*, trans. Tom Conley (New York, 1988), 244–67.

It is therefore all the more significant that in the Besson film *The Messenger* (1999), the *plot* has to do not with Joan's battles and victories/defeats but rather with her lack of certainty about her faith, even with her own experience (Did she really hear the voices? Did she really see the visions?). Thus, the uncertainty that the Inquisition was trying to foist upon the historical Joan is internalized in the film's depiction of her. She becomes her own Inquisition on herself, her own tribunal against her experience. Her quest mirrors Husserl's for an apodictic; doubt and uncertainty become the protagonists.

What Kristeva calls the open sore of our epoch seems peculiarly suggested in Joan of Arc's source story. Her very certainty is cause for our fascination. We seize upon her moments of doubt only to be relieved (if perplexed) by her final return to an apodictic. We grasp at her transvestism as an amulet of her own ambiguity, even as we learn that she said that she dressed in men's clothing not because she thought she was a man or wanted to be one but because she was a soldier and had to dress accordingly.

Today there are more than one hundred thousand Web site matches in America for the words "Joan of Arc." On one of them, L. Ron Hubbard (former leader of the Scientology movement) announces that in a previous life he was Charles VII and had abandoned Joan. On another site, we learn of a "one woman lesbian theater" called "The Second Coming of Joan of Arc." The author and actress, Carolyn Gage, says (one imagines Janis Joplin's "Bobby Magee" in the background), "Saint is just another word for a woman who got burned." A band that has been described as "dadaist" is called "Joan of Arc," at other times, "Jeanne d'Arc." Leonard Cohen and the group Orchestral Manoeuvres in the Dark have written songs to her. In 1999, there were billboards everywhere in the United States and France advertising *The Messenger,* with the actress Milla Jovovich as Joan. "Right now," said the twenty-two-year-old Jovovich in a 1999 interview about her role as Joan, "a theme that's been coming up in my writing is this feeling of nostalgia. . . . Memories floating around, and time passing." Nostalgia seems to be the side effect for millennial fever. In the apocalyptic mood of this millennium, Joan's certainty is seductive even as her various ambiguities make us want to identify her with our time and thus paradoxically to present her as *un*certain.

The final image in Besson's film is the burning cross. It is as if that object—that geometric shape, object of cultural production, or visual dialectic, heavily charged as it is and has been—it is as if the cross itself had become an emblem of confusion in its postmodern production. In other words, we see it but no longer comprehend how the cross means, although we seem willing to accept representation in this instance because it indicates a complex ambiguity. The cross, which has had a history of specific meaning and has evoked distinct responses (religious, indifferent, hostile, curious, aesthetic, and so on), seems itself in this context to have joined the contemporary black hole of cognitive uncertainty—of *méconnaissance* in Lacan's sense. Thus, what I am calling the nostalgia for an apodictic extends to the legend/history of Joan. In Besson's film she seems to assume a contemporary confusion with which we identify; when she recants, she appears to put her voices and her entire mission into question. This ambiguity is followed, however, by a renewed certainty, and Joan sacrifices her body to her faith. When the burning cross appears at the end, it burns with Joan. We are unable to discern whether the film wants us to believe that the cross has been destroyed with her or that Joan, Christ-like, has experienced a moment of doubt before her glorious ascension to heaven. The cross becomes, then, the geometric figure of uncertainty, while Joan herself is seen as the victim of the cross's false promises. At the same time, the film lets us hope that unlike us, Joan saw the burning cross as a vindication, as the proof of her certainty, as comfort despite the horror of her slow death.

The film depicts her and the cross as uncertain. In what object, one is left to wonder, would the (secular) contemporary, condemned prisoner find comfort? What could be held before our collective eyes at the moment of death (or at the moment of the millennium) to reassure us? In the various recent renditions of the Joan of Arc story—corny or obscene, reverential or ironic, hagiographic or demystifying—there is an abiding perplexed desire that wants to understand how certainty in representation looks; how the imagined transparency between thought and body could be; how feminine agency can have existed when feminine subjectivity did not; how it can have been that the gaze was once not, to return to Althusser's term, futile.

The questions asked in this study have finally to do with what assumptions motivate questioning in the first place. There are, in other words, no answers to questions about the questions, any more than any of Joan's trials definitively answered any genuine queries. But it is my hope that if nothing else, this book will contribute to the contemporary rethinking of gendered subject positions in a way that will call continual attention to how little we have changed since Joan's time and at once (paradoxically) how far from us are her culture and its own subjects. Perhaps we will partially arrive at a better understanding—and suspicion—of what underlies the present nostalgia for a past before Descartes and Kant, a past where we imagine that bodies were experienced as seamlessly connected to thought and the *Verfremdungseffekt* of Continental philosophy had not yet severed "us" from conviction. For this idea that we have called subjectivity needs to be reconsidered so that gender dichotomies do not play a role in anchoring it. One of the arguments of this book is that subjectivity itself may well be the tenuous fantasy born of a fear of what Nietzsche called the abyss, masquerading as nostalgia.

François Villon, who was Joan's contemporary, devotes several lines to her in *Les Dames du temps jadis,* part of his *Grand Testament* (1461). The title of the smaller section evokes nostalgia in itself: *jadis* means of old, in former times, in the olden days. These are ladies, then, of another time: lost to us not only because their day is past but because their era is in itself long-gone. It is in this sequence, after a catalog of great but lost women, that Villon places Joan of Arc. Here he adds nostalgia in the already nostalgic theme:

> Et Jehanne la bonne Lorraine
> Qu'Angloys bruslerent a Rouen,
> ou sont-ilz, Vierge souveraine?
> Mais ou sont les neiges d'antan!
> (And Joan the good woman from Lorraine
> Whom the English burned at Rouen,
> Where are they, sovereign Virgin?
> But where are the snows of yesteryear!)

This passage, which has been so thoroughly analyzed that the last line has become a commonplace idiom in English, is ingenious in its mingling of connotations. Nearly all of the complexities generated by Joan's story are contained in these brief lines. "Yesteryear" is a precise translation of *d'antan,* since the latter comes from the Latin *annum,* thus meaning the year past and, more freely, years past. "La bonne Lorraine" evokes the innocent peasant girl, the simple daughter of a farmer who was "good" like the land where she was born (this is the image that we may assume Chapu wished to evoke). Nascent nationalism and the innocence of nature are blended in the image and made all the stronger through the juxtaposition of the following line's allusion to the "Angloys"—those who had the barbaric audacity to burn Joan at Rouen. The English become, in the poem's tenor, both "othered" (they are foreigners) and by the same token *un*natural (they are cruel, not good, and from an unfamiliar land).

What follows is an apostrophe, but it is not clear whether the poet is addressing the Virgin Mary or Joan herself, whom the French famously simply called the Virgin, "la Pucelle." Joan's sanctity is suggested by the ambiguity of the apostrophe, and the simple peasant has now been layered over with an aura of the divine. Moreover, there is a second ambiguity: *ilz* ("they") is masculine plural, whereas "snows," to which one assumes it refers, is feminine. Thus, "where are they" could as well allude to the English, the point being that for all of their cruelty and power, they, too, have succumbed to time. Or (since gender was not stabilized in the lexicology of late medieval French), *ilz* could of course refer to the snows of yesteryear. Snow itself is evocative of purity and innocence: the poet ends with an exclamation rather than a question. "Where are they!" comes as a cry of anguish more than an interrogative, much like the *ubi sunt* in a Latin *planctus*, or lament for the dead. For what can be more frail than snows of years past, what more muddied and evaporated? What remains of virginity? Even the Virgin (whether Joan or Mary) cannot account for what is lost or for why.

Nationalism, blurred figures of divine inspiration, nostalgia for past times, lost innocence, irrevocable virginity, ambiguous gender constructions, the devastation of otherness, sorrow over the death of a courageous young woman, death itself as the fire's dominance over snow—all of these are suggested by Villon in four brief lines and tangled in a knot that I have only begun to unravel. Joan of Arc's story evokes all of these issues. More important, however, I see Joan's brief mission and trial as a moment in the history of the West in which gendered subjectivity was fleetingly put at risk. Perhaps that is why we continue to return to her story—more and more as subjectivity is examined. As the certainty that has placed otherness in the feminine begins to erode, Joan's story becomes one of a few places where we can see the limits and illusion of any sovereign subjectivity, the insistence of desubjugation.

FIGURE 1

HENRI-MICHEL-ANTOINE CHAPU, *Joan of Arc* (1870).
Photograph courtesy the University of Chicago Libraries.

FIGURE 2
FRONTISPIECE TO SCHILLER'S *Die Jungfrau von Orleans* (1801).
Photograph courtesy the University of Chicago Libraries.

FIGURE 3

FRANK VINCENT DU MOND, *Joan Reprimands the Conspirators* and *The Capture of the Tourelles* (1896). From Mark Twain, *Personal Reflections of Joan of Arc.*

Photographs courtesy the University of Chicago Libraries.

FIGURE 4

FRENCH SCHOOL, *Portrait de l'Hôtel de Ville* (sixteenth century).
Photograph courtesy the University of Chicago Libraries.

FIGURE 5
JULES-PIERRE ROULLEAU, statue of Joan of Arc at Chinon (1893).
Photograph courtesy the University of Chicago Libraries.

FIGURE 6
CARL THEODOR DREYER.
Film still from *The Passion of Joan of Arc* (1928).
Still courtesy of the University of Chicago Film Studies Center.

FIGURE 7

ANONYMOUS, Joan of Arc statue at Domrémy (date unknown).
Photograph courtesy the University of Chicago Libraries.

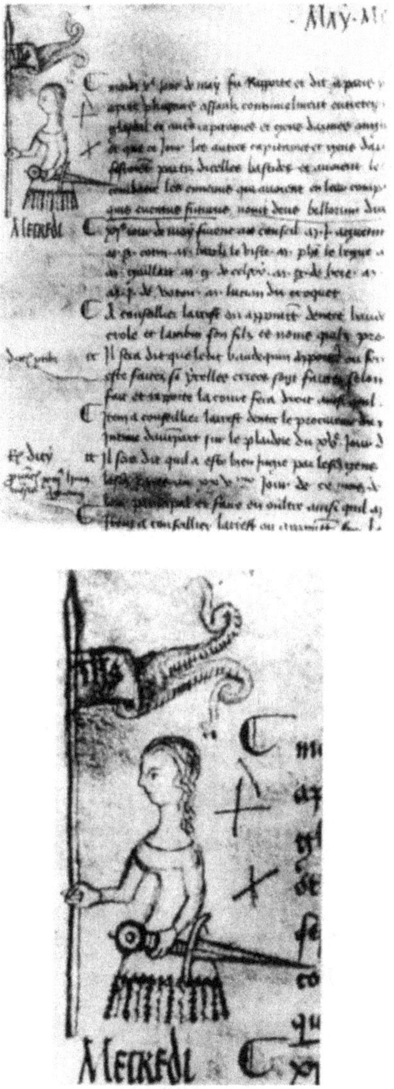

FIGURE 8

CLÉMENT DE FAUQUEMBERGHE, Joan of Arc sketched in the Register of the Counsel of the Paris Parliament, detail of page and sketch (1429). Photographs courtesy the University of Chicago Libraries.

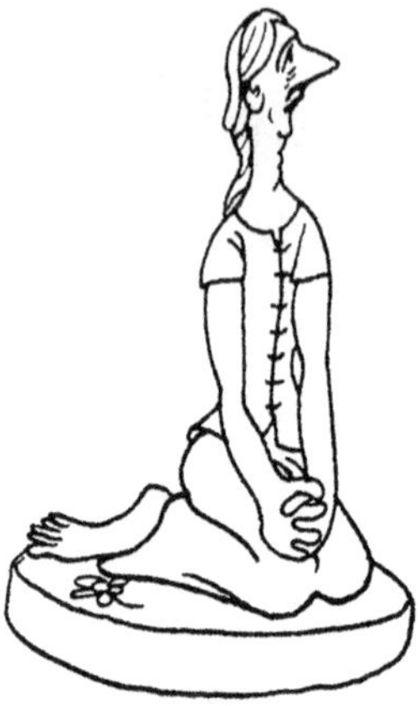

FIGURE 9

JEAN EFFEL, *Le Général de Gaulle en Jeanne d'Arc* (1959).
Photograph courtesy the University of Chicago Libraries.

FIGURE 10

WILLIAM HASKELL COFFIN, *Joan of Arc Saved France.*
United States World War I poster (1918).

CHAPTER ONE

THE BODY REVISITED

To the outer whole, therefore, belongs not only the *original being,* the inherited body, but equally the formation of the body resulting from the activity of the inner being. . . . We have then to consider here how to determine the relation between these two sides and what is to be understood by this "expression" of the inner in the outer.

—Hegel, *Phenomenology of Spirit*

IN THE MIDST of his autobiographical text, *L'Avenir dure longtemps,* Louis Althusser opens a chapter on his relationship to Marxism with a comment on the eye: "The eye is passive," he writes, "at a distance from its object, it receives the image without having to work, without engaging the body in any process of approach, contact, manipulation. . . . The eye is thus the speculative organ *par excellence;* from Plato and Aristotle to Thomas and beyond."[1] As is so often the case in late European capitalism and even modernism (in its broadest sense—that is, since the seventeenth century), the polarity between intellectual and manual labor is foregrounded. What is significant here is that Althusser corporealizes this polarity between speculation (philosophy and theology) and the body's labor into a contrast between the eyes and the hands; the body parts, in other words, already prepare for the privileging of embodiment. The eye is passive and does not "work," whereas contact and manipulation are the

---

1 Louis Althusser, *L'Avenir dure longtemps, suivi de Les faits: Autobiographies* (Paris, 1992), 205. All English translations are my own.

purview of the hands (the word *manipulation* in this passage is followed by a parenthetical remark about why Althusser has always enjoyed having dirty hands). Althusser writes that as a child, he was captured in the realm of the eye "without any contact, or body, for all contact clearly must occur through the body." These comments are followed by a curious statement. Althusser "is told," as he puts it, that in 1975, he pronounced a "terrible sentence": "And then there are bodies, and they have sexes" (206).

That such a sentence should need to be stated, and that it could be uttered as a discovery rather than as a fact too obvious to mention, says as much about "postmodern" thought as it does, ultimately, about Louis Althusser. Indeed, it has been frequently noted that postmodernism is characterized, in part, as a return to materialism. The anthropologist Thomas Csordas has written that "the body is not an *object* to be studied in relation to culture, but is to be considered as the *subject* of culture, or in other words as the existential ground of culture."[2] For Althusser himself, such a move entails the "discovery" of his body, which began when, as a boy, he lived with his grandfather. Walking in the forest, running, riding his bicycle, digging for potatoes—all of this "replaced forever the simple speculative distance of the futile gaze." He adds, "I had nothing in common with the Saint Thomas of theology who still thinks under the sign of the speculative eye, but much more with the Saint Thomas of the Gospels who wants to touch in order to believe. More than that, I was not content with the simple contact of the hand to believe in reality; I had to work it, to transform it to believe—far beyond simple and mere reality—in my own existence, finally conquered" (207). Aquinas's conviction in the compatibility of reason and faith, his scholastic moves to "think" Christianity, are discarded by Althusser in favor of the doubting apostle Thomas who needs tactile proof. For Althusser, however, even contact is insufficient for alleviating doubt concerning one's own existence. What is needed is the transforming work of the hand to believe, in turn, in the body and thus in existence. It is necessary, says Althusser, to "think" with the body in order to apprehend reality; not to speculate with the eye: "That is when I began 'thinking' with my body; and this has stayed with me for good. Thinking, not in the distant and passive dimension of the gaze, of the eye, but rather in the action of the hand, in the infinite play of

2 Thomas J. Csordas, "Embodiment as a Paradigm for Anthropology," *Ethos* 18 (1990): 5.

the muscles, and in all of the body's sensations." The speculating doubt of Descartes (which, it will be recalled, is laced with immense scientific discussions on the eye and its anatomical parts) is here rejected for the outstretched hand of the apostle Thomas's need for proof. If the first is satisfied to establish existence by means of the scopic deductions of an inner, philosophical eye, the second will believe only by the sensory eyes and by the touch of the hand. Descartes's famous move away from Plato's Ideas includes being as nonmaterial and materiality itself as something from which to free oneself. Touch is specifically excluded, for example, as grounds for knowledge: "We can conceive of bodies only by the faculty to understand which is in us, and not by the imagination nor the senses. And we do not know them because we see them, or touch them, but only because we conceive of them through thought."[3]

For Descartes, the way to avoid confusion between materiality and soul is to free oneself from the body. The founder of modern subjectivity, then, proceeds on grounds of what Charles Taylor has called "disengaged reason."[4]

But Althusser wants, as we have seen, to *re*engage the body, and Marxism for him offers the opportunity for embodied thought.[5] Through labor and contact Althusser claims to experience the physicality of thinking and the capacity to recognize the materiality of existence and ideology. It is Spinoza who leads Althusser in this rejection of the *cogito,* principally because Spinoza's substantial monism refutes Descartes's division of the human being into thinking soul and extended body. For Spinoza, the hu-

---

3 "nous ne concevons les corps que par la faculte d'entendre qui est en nous, & non point par l'imagination ny par les sens, & que nous ne les connoissons pas de ce que nous les voyons, ou que nous les touchons, mais seulement de ce que nous les concevons par la pensee." René Descartes, *Oeuvres de Descartes,* ed. Charles Adam and Paul Tannery (Paris, 1973), 9: pt. 1, 26.

4 Charles Taylor, *Sources of the Self: The Making of the Modern Identity* (Cambridge, Mass.: 1989), 143–58ff.

5 I want to be clear here: If Marxism offers the opportunity for embodied thought, it is only insofar as a Marxian practice confers it for Althusser as a pretext to give materiality to his ontological crisis. Marxian thought, or theory, is another question entirely, one that Althusser also (obviously) engages but that is not the issue here. The question, then, is rather how certainty of the body is engendered. It is in this sense that Marxian practice is a useful pretext for Althusser, as will be other practices for different theorists nevertheless similarly haunted by a lack of certainty. In chapter 6, we will return more fully to this question of certainty in contemporary views of Joan of Arc.

man mind is the idea of the body; they are the same thing with different attributes. There is a parallelism between mind and body such that thought cannot be separated from its embodiment. Spinoza, writes Althusser, "is an author who refused all theory of knowledge (of cartesian or later kantian type); an author who refused the founding role of the *cogito* in cartesian subjectivity, and who was content to write 'man thinks,' without drawing any transcendental conclusions" (210). For Althusser, it is clear that Spinoza is important because he reappropriates thought as part of extension after its cartesian exile as mind.

Althusser notes that for Spinoza, the body possesses *mens* (which Althusser translates as "idea," not "spirit" or "soul"), and this "idea" is a *potentia* for Spinoza. It is both a *fortitudo* (surge, character) and an opening onto the world, *generositas,* which Althusser calls a *don gratuit* (an unmotivated gift). The notion of a gift that is unmotivated will help lead Althusser to Marx.[6] *Generositas,* which Althusser will later see as a prefiguration of Freud's libido, becomes the door to hope. Far from being the Cartesian divide of mind/body, *generositas* is in itself the gift of thought to the body; it is the "Desire by which each one strives to aid other men and join them to him in friendship." Such a Desire will lead to joining others in the forming of a political state, and so we arrive at Marx. Equally significant however, is the sense that Althusser has somehow gone full circle by way of a nostalgia for the pre-Cartesian mind, the one that sees, not with instruments and internal scopic deductions but with the eyes of the body.

Althusser's text articulates the postmodern anxiety, concerning not only Cartesian subjectivity but also its transcendental implications. Here "man thinks" has an automatic corresponding mode in thought, and subjectivity is the fragile and fragmentary result of privileged moments when the body is not in doubt because its manual labor permits a fleeting acknowledgment of being. So, too, Simone Weil, in turn following Alain's teachings, had claimed that thought itself must be manual labor if it is to be productive. The resulting syllogism—the body can be felt working; therefore, man can think; therefore, there is (material) existence—is more than the Marxist dictum that work gives meaning to life.

6 For recent discussions on the gift see, for example, Derrida's *The Gift of Death,* trans. David Wills (Chicago, 1995); and Jean-Luc Marion, *Étant donné: Essai d'une phenoménologie de la donation* (Paris, 1997).

For even though Weil and Althusser, both Marxists of varying sorts and both activists, foreground labor as a necessary aspect of materialism, far more than the centrality of labor to human life is at stake. "I was finally happy in my desire," writes Althusser, "that of being a body, of existing above all in my body, in the irrefutable material proof which it gave me that I existed really and at last" (207).

Doubt of being is allayed (but not erased) by bodily activity, not philosophy (or, indeed, theology). Thus, the subject becomes embedded in the body; its sovereignty is not only in question (as in, over and over again, so many of the postmodernist texts)—the very possibility of its existence is captured only in those moments when the body speaks. "And then there are bodies, and they have sexes" is a "terrible sentence" in the sense that what is most obvious, intellectually, to existence—the body—has been lost in our era to such a point that its "rediscovery" is a source of near incredulity. The old Sartrean cliché, then, "Existence precedes essence," can in this light be read as more than a refutation of predeterminism; Sartre, too, is making the body (materiality) the foundation of thought. As Judith Butler has pointed out, in the chapter on the body in *Being and Nothingness* Sartre makes "efforts to expel the Cartesian ghost," but his efforts at "surpassing the body" in themselves presuppose the mind / body dualism. Nevertheless, in Butler's words, "As a condition of access to the world, the body is a being comported beyond itself, referring to the world and thereby revealing its own ontological status as a referential reality. For Sartre, the body is lived and experienced as the context and medium for all human strivings."[7] Although Sartre is concerned with "self-transcendence," unlike Althusser, *Being and Nothingness* nevertheless betrays an ambivalence toward Cartesianism and the embodiment (or not) of consciousness that can be read as an earlier, less radical version of Althusser's concerns. Sartre cannot decide whether consciousness has an ontological status apart from the body; Althusser decides that it does not.

Obvious as this point may seem, Althusser's is a move to ontologize thought in a manner that not only materializes it but also substitutes the fragmentary for the progressive, syllogistic genealogy of being proposed by Descartes. In one of the famous passages on "shock," Walter Ben-

---

[7] Judith Butler, "Variations on Sex and Gender: Beauvoir, Wittig and Foucault," in *Feminism as Critique*, ed. Seyla Benhabib and Drucilla Cornell (Minneapolis, 1987), 130.

jamin articulates this fragmentary aspect of thinking and elides it into the historical materialism Althusser will espouse:

> Thinking involves not only the flow of thoughts, but their arrest as well. Where thinking suddenly stops in a configuration pregnant with tensions, it gives that configuration a shock, by which it crystallizes into a monad. A historical materialist approaches a historical subject only where he encounters it as a monad. In this structure he recognizes the sign of a Messianic cessation of happening, or, put differently, a revolutionary chance in the fight for the oppressed past. He takes cognizance of it in order to blast a specific era out of the homogeneous course of history—blasting a specific life out of the era or a specific work out of the lifework.[8]

It is significant that in this passage, as in that of Althusser, the paradigm of religion serves as metaphor to express a secular conviction. The Messianic "cessation of happening" overcomes the homogeneous course of linear history. Furthermore, the monad, that figure of unity within fragmentation, amplifies a peculiar longing for totality. We will return to this longing.

The quiltlike (or aleatoric and quotational) productions of postmodernism not only are founded on a dismantling of the *cogito* and the speculative empiricism it engages. They also idealize the body as a totality, a kind of otherness within the self not unlike Freud's topographical unconscious, or the mirrored imago in Lacan's Imaginary. Such a totality is suggested even as the body is continually metonymized: "The body, its exuberant exercise . . . all of this life at last found and become mine had replaced forever the simple speculative distance of the futile gaze" (207).

In Althusser's reading, epiphany itself yields awareness, not of numena (as in Kant, for example) but of the material basis for being. *Cogito ergo sum* becomes *le corps put penser.* Both the inflected "I" of the *cogito* and its substantiation, *sum,* are modified clauses of the body. The body must be in parallel mode *with* the mind if there is to be any source of knowledge.

This insistence on the materiality of existence is hardly new. It was,

---

[8] Walter Benjamin, "Thesis on the Philosophy of History," in *Illuminations,* ed. Hannah Arendt, trans. Harry Zohn (New York, 1969), 262–63.

after all, Aristotle who noted that for an entity to exist as an individual, there must be matter. What one senses in postmodernism, however, is a nostalgia for a *mens* before the Enlightenment, before the Cartesian subject, and before modernism. As such, this passage by Althusser, which ostensibly explains his attraction to Marxism, is more a demonstration of the force underlying the postmodernist obsession with critiquing subjectivity. But it is the notion of unity that is at issue and an imagined time before the Cartesian divide, and its doubts, that is longed for.

It is of no surprise then, that Althusser is drawn to Spinoza. As Harry Wolfson has argued, Spinoza "introduces no novelty." For Wolfson, what Spinoza did was to "reinstate, with some modification, the old principles of classical Greek philosophy."[9] If modernism is defined as a repression of the discoveries of the seventeenth century (Wolfson, for example, sees modernism as "a variety of atavism or regression or archaization"; 13), perhaps postmodernism, with its ability to celebrate the technology that some modernisms frequently disdain, has its own agenda of repression, even as it seeks to reconsider seventeenth-century thought. That agenda might be articulated as the attempt to repress the fragmentary nature of its own project, and its ensuing uncertainty, through a different turn. Wolfson sees "the great question in the history of religious philosophy" as having only two alternatives: the Hebrew Scriptures or the Greek philosophers. Postmodernism finds a third: early Christianity.

Theological figures from the premodern period haunt Althusser's texts (the two Thomases, for example). It is worth noting here that Augustine, who, one critic claims, "first recognized and defined the principle of subjectivity,"[10] is obsessed with the divide that was the legacy of the Fall. For him, the Manicheans posit too great a distance between man and universe; Augustine argues for unity and totality. Why does the body obey the mind but the mind does not always obey itself? "Yet the mind is mind," he writes, "and the hand is part of the body."[11] The mind is divided against itself, he notes, only when the soul is not full of God. Once the single course toward God is chosen, there is no more conflict of wills. Thus, for Augustine it is sin that divides the mind from itself. Neil Forsyth writes, "Augustine's theory of sin was, paradoxically, the way in

9 Harry Austryn Wolfson, *From Philo to Spinoza* (New York, 1977), 64.

10 Mark Taylor, *Erring: A Postmodern A/theology* (Chicago, 1984), 38.

11 Augustine, *Confessions,* trans. R. S. Pine-Coffin (London, 1961), 8: sect. 9, 172.

which he learned to understand this wholeness. Like its Manichean counterpart, this theory had to be a complete explanation both of the individual psychology of the believer and of the cosmos in which he found himself."[12] The Fall created a wandering of the self, not unlike that described by Althusser before he discovers the body.

For postmodernism has its own prelapsarian era: before the Enlightenment, but after Augustine. If knowledge is distance, as interpreters of the Fall have frequently noted, the modern Cartesian subject imposes a fall and a distance of its own: mind from body; thought from being; speculation from materiality. Small wonder, therefore, that in the postmodernist agenda to shed the legacy of the Enlightenment, there is a move to critique the Cartesian subject through a "return" to the body. Althusser has to rediscover, almost reenter the body; and in this, he is not alone.[13]

I would argue that our interest today in what I am calling a nostalgia for the thinking body before the Enlightenment constitutes an attempt to participate in what Jean-Luc Marion calls a "saturated phenomenon."[14] Such a phenomenon, for Marion, is one that "an excess of intuition shields from objective constitution." The second type of saturated phenomenon, for Marion, is that of revelation: "an appearance that is purely of itself and starting from itself, which does not subject its possibility to any preliminary determination" (121). There is in secular postmodernism

---

12 Neil Forsyth, *The Old Enemy* (Princeton, N.J., 1987), 396.

13 See, for example, Janet Beizer, *Ventriloquized Bodies: Narratives of Hysteria in Nineteenth-Century France* (Ithaca, N.Y., 1994); Judith Butler, *Bodies That Matter: On the Discursive Limits of "Sex"* (New York, 1993); Peter Brooks, *Body Work: Objects of Desire in Modern Narrative* (Cambridge, Mass., 1993); Peter Brown, *The Body and Society: Men, Women, and Sexual Renunciation in Early Christianity* (New York, 1988); Michel Foucault, *The History of Sexuality*, vol. 1, trans. Robert Hurley (New York, 1980); Jane Gallop, *Thinking through the Body* (New York, 1988); Luce Irigaray, *This Sex Which Is Not One*, trans. Catherine Porter with Carolyn Burke (Ithaca, N.Y., 1985); Thomas Laqueur, *Making Sex: Body and Gender from the Greeks to Freud* (Cambridge, Mass., 1990); Elaine Scarry, *The Body in Pain: The Making and Unmaking of the World* (Oxford, 1985); Susan Sontag, *Illness as Metaphor* (New York, 1988); Susan Rubin Suleiman, ed., *The Female Body in Western Culture: Contemporary Perspectives* (Cambridge, Mass., 1986). This list represents just a small portion of recent books on the body.

14 Jean-Luc Marion, "The Saturated Phenomenon," trans. Thomas A. Carlson, *Philosophy Today* (Spring 1996): 103–24.

a nostalgia for religious (theological, hagiographic) texts of the Middle Ages and before, as any glance at a current bibliography in critical theory will attest. I will be arguing that this is an attempt to witness the witnessing of revelation—to try to see how such a totality was experienced. Indeed, we already find the attempt at depicting such a time when the body was totality in the writings of the eighteenth-century historian Vico: "It is . . . beyond our power to enter into the vast imagination of the first men whose minds were not in the least abstract, refined or spiritualised, because they were entirely immersed in the senses, buffeted by the passions, buried in the body."[15]

Marx himself, it will be recalled, uses religion as an analogy for explaining the fetishization of objects in capitalism:

> We are concerned only with a definite social relation between human beings, which, in their eyes, has here assumed the semblance of a relation between things. To find an analogy, we must enter the nebulous world of religion. In that world, the products of the human mind become independent shapes, endowed with lives of their own, and able to enter into relations with men and women. The products of the human hand do the same thing in the world of commodities. I speak of this as the fetishistic character which attaches to the products of labour, as soon as they are produced in the form of commodities. It is inseparable from commodity production.[16]

We might say that Althusser fetishizes the body (we are back to the "human hand") that is itself curiously objectified as a product of labor. The echoes to Freud are clear (and have been amply noted in recent critical theory). A society that turns the penis into a commodity, for example, and (as in Lacan) "transcendentalizes" it into phallus (his protestations to the contrary notwithstanding) is in an object relations economy with the other and with itself.

---

[15] Giovanni Battista Vico, *The New Science*, trans. T. G. Bergin and M. M. Fisch (Ithaca, N.Y., 1948), para. 378.

[16] Karl Marx, *Capital*, trans. Eden Paul and Cedar Paul, 2 vols. (London, 1930), 1: 45–46.

MOVING TOWARD JOAN OF ARC

The life of almost any early saint in such an economy is particularly evocative.[17] As Edith Wyschogrod and others have shown, the question of saintly corporeality offers a unique example of the problem of the body as both the exemplum and literalization of thought and as a totality whose valence, but not wholeness, shifts. I would put it this way: Postmodernism's longing for its prelapsarian world finds a strange comfort and fascination in the frequent paradox of the saint's body both as a prison obstructing grace and as a possible gift to God through the Christian notion of *caritas*.[18] The body of the saint is fetishized and becomes itself, through what Marx calls the "nebulous world of religion," an object of postmodern cathexis.

A note of clarification: My use of the term *postmodernism* here is for labeling purposes and almost exclusively meant to include texts that see themselves as outside religion and theological concerns, from the point of view of *faith*, in general. Clearly, the kind of nostalgia that I am attempting to articulate has a completely different valence, and telos, in a theological or religious context (questions of faith from the perspective of faith). Secular nostalgia for the time of early saints is to be understood as a move to recuperate the metaphysics and (even) experience of what I

---

17 By "early" I will be meaning here the second through fourth centuries C.E.: in the time of the *Apocryphal Acts of the Apostles*, which tells of the conversion to Christianity by upper-class women; the third-century *Acts of the Christian Martyrs;* and Jacques de Voragine's *La Légende dorée* (written about 1264 C.E. but concerning the early martyrs).

18 My definition of *caritas* relies on David Tracy's "The Catholic Model of *Caritas:* Self-Transcendence and Transformation," in *On Naming the Present: Reflections on God, Hermeneutics and Church* (Maryknoll, N.Y., 1994), 94–106. *Caritas,* or charity, writes Tracy, "[is] since Augustine, the reigning Catholic model: a proposal for a synthesis of human *eros* in the self and the divine *agape* given in Jesus Christ. The particular understandings of both *eros* and *agape* change from one Catholic theologian to another. In every case, however, some synthesis will be formulated; more specifically some transformation of human *eros* (which is basically affirmed) by divine *agape* will be explicated to disclose the concrete and complex experiential reality of *caritas* in Christian lives" (95). For an alternative understanding of *caritas,* see Anders Nygren, *Agape and Eros,* trans. Philip S. Watson (Chicago, 1982). A measure of the centrality of *caritas* to Christian thought is demonstrated by the fact that the *Dictionnaire de la spiritualité: Ascétique et mystique, doctrine et histoire* (Paris, 1953) devotes 185 pages to the concept of "charity." The *New Catholic Encyclopedia,* vol. 3 (San Francisco, 1967), devotes more than thirty.

have argued is seen as a seamlessness between body and idea. As such, therefore, secular postmodernism sees *caritas* (for example) as a philosophical and cultural concept, not as doctrinal or as an issue within the institutionalized faith of Christianity.

While all of this may be seen in itself as a nostalgia for religion, or at least the idea of unity provided by religiosity, the fascination with approaching sacred issues comes in part, and paradoxically, from the fact that secular postmodernism sees itself as rigorously outside religion, outside questions of faith, and unconcerned with issues of divinity except as a cultural, historical aspect. It is then the *otherness* of faith and of the idea of divinity that, from the postmodern view, motivates the fetishization.

It is perhaps Heidegger, one of the *ur*-texts of postmodernism, who formulates the chasm between theology and philosophy the most succinctly. "Being and God," he says, "are not identical and I would never attempt to think the essence of God by means of Being. . . . Faith does not need the thought of Being. When faith has recourse to this thought, it is no longer faith."[19] For Heidegger, the Christian experience is "so completely different that it has no need to enter into competition with philosophy." Theology must hold fast to the view that "philosophy is foolishness," or it will itself become foolish in the eyes of philosophy. Jean-Luc Marion analyzes this passage as follows: "'Foolishness' here indicates much more than an error, a divergence, a conflict; foolishness indicates the irreducibility of two logics that neither can nor must, in any case, comprehend one another: faith cannot comprehend thought, or thought faith; no third position will ever present itself to reconcile them, to the extent that 'in the face of a final decision, the ways part.'"(63).

The otherness of faith from a contemporary perspective, then, lies precisely in the fact that postmodern texts are committed to the problem of being, with its concomitant problematics of thinking the subject (as in the example I have been using, Althusser). Theology, on the other hand, addresses issues of revelation. In Heidegger's words, "The thinker speaks of the 'manifestness' [*Offenbarkeit*] of Being; but 'Being' is an untheological word. Because revelation itself determines the manner of manifest-

---

[19] In *Aussprache mit Martin Heidegger an 06/XI/1951*, privately issued (Zurich, 1952) and now in *Seminare, G.A.*, 15 (Frankfurt, 1986), 436–37. The English translation is by Thomas A. Carlson in Jean-Luc Marion's *God without Being: Hors Texte* (Chicago, 1991), 61.

ness" (Marion, 62). For faith, philosophy is a *Todfeind,* a mortal enemy, says Heidegger.

In Hegel's master / slave confrontation, as in Freud's double ("the harbinger of death," notes Freud), the mortal enemy is of danger precisely because he or she mirrors, in some way, the sovereignty of consciousness. Perhaps these metaphors will help to articulate the predicament of secular postmodernism with, for example, early Christianity and theology: revelation and Being constitute a chasm that, as Heidegger notes, cannot and should not be bridged. And yet we see in many postmodern texts the attempt to do so—in its usual démarche of putting together apparently inappropriate moments (from architecture to texts), postmodernism of the kind we have been considering seems to want to have it both ways: revelation *with* Being.

The idea of *caritas* in this context cannot fail, it seems to me, to intrigue us by virtue of its spontaneous totalization—a move that, I have been arguing, in itself constitutes an intriguing alterity for postmodernism. Totalization belongs to revelation; Being, to division. Even Heidegger falls prey to the nostalgia: "Some of you know," he says in the same seminar, "that I come from theology, that I still guard an old love for it and that I am not without a certain understanding of it. If I were yet to write a theology—to which I sometimes feel inclined—then the word *Being* would not occur in it" (cited in Marion, 61). Postmodernism, too, comes from theology in a certain manner, as we shall see; and it, too, is not without a certain understanding of it. Faith is as if the last taboo and therefore all the more desirable for a culture that fetishizes the body and, even as it interrogates it, Being.

Caritas is understood as the synthesis of *eros* (human longing, striving of the self for happiness) and *agape* (the pure gift of God's love, grace). At its most "literal" (for example, the martyrdom of a saint), *caritas* entails not only self-overcoming, or the erasure of self-love in the face of the divine, but also the erasure or at least denial of the concept of otherness. What I mean by this is that difference is willfully unrecognized in anticipation of the transparency to be achieved between the soul and divinity through the gift of the body.[20] It is this transparency, as Jean

[20] Here I am diverging from Wyschogrod's reading of Merleau-Ponty on the body. "Because the body," writes Wyschogrod, "integral to the manner in which perception occurs, can itself be seen, it is in that respect no different from the house or the cube or any other

Starobinski has so compellingly shown, that haunts Rousseau, that figure whose paranoia positions him outside the ordered categories of the Enlightenment.

In the Christian notion of *caritas* lies the promise of *generositas, le don gratuit,* in Spinoza's sense. Only it is the *don gratuit* of the body in the service of faith, with little if any consideration for "mind." It is this ability to give the body that, I am arguing, fascinates many contemporary texts.[21] From a contemporary view, which is clearly one of backformation, such a gift enacts an agency whose definition falls outside the parameters of the *cogito.* In other words, we may wish to discard the *cogito,* but it has come to be the mental apparatus by which we also attempt to judge it. What Freud said of the unconscious we can also say of the *cog-*

---

visible object that can be inserted into a world of objects. But as Merleau-Ponty suggests, the body is not an object like others because one cannot distance oneself from one's own body so it can give itself as a totality." *Saints and Postmodernism: Revisioning Moral Philosophy* (Chicago, 1990), 17. I am not convinced that this is what Merleau-Ponty meant. Indeed, the quotation Wyschogrod gives from his work to prove her point is, it seems to me, open for a different interpretation in light of the nostalgia we have been discussing here: "Movement is not thought about movement and bodily space is not space thought of or represented. . . . A movement has been learned when the body has understood it. . . . We must avoid saying that our body is in space or in time. It inhabits space and time." *The Phenomenology of Perception,* trans. Colin Smith (London, 1962), 139. In postmodern discussions on the body, it is already experienced as distanced from the self, as we have seen in Althusser. It is precisely the desire to *inhabit* space and time (one thinks here of Heidegger's use of the verb *to dwell* [*wohnen*]), which helps to motivate the fascination in saints who do give the body "as a totality." Certainly, one does not distance oneself from the body in unconscious moments of movement. But the point is that the body has been rendered self-conscious in recent texts in a manner that others it even from its possessor.

21 In Voragine's stories, early Christians are constantly being told to sacrifice animals to the pagan gods, to cleanse themselves of monotheistic tendencies and to demonstrate, through animal sacrifice, that they have returned to a "normal" (and reasonable) religion. Of course, the Christians (most of whom are saints in Voragine) hotly refuse, rejecting animal sacrifice as barbaric and sacrilegious. It is a curious fact, however, that in Voragine these same Christians almost inevitably end up sacrificing their own bodies to God, as if Christianity had not quite thought itself outside of Pagan paradigms (notwithstanding the obvious influence of the crucifixion of Jesus). The point is as well that a body cannot be sacrificed in the martyr tradition unless it is assimilated to thought. For a view of the gendered aspect of sacrifice for the purpose of maintaining patrilineal ties and as a remedy for having been born of woman, see Nancy Jay's *Throughout Your Generations Forever: Sacrifice, Religion and Paternity* (Chicago, 1992). The Voragine edition I am using is *La Légende dorée de Jacques de Voragine,* 3 vols., trans. and ed. Abbot J.-B. Roze (Paris, 1902).

ito: we are both the seeker and the unexplored terrain whose limits are being mapped.

The gift of the body is the most material, concrete form of *generositas* of both mind and body; the divide of mind / body is not only overcome; it is not imagined. What early saints often do is persuade with reason, which they then enact through the body. Consider Saint Catherine of Alexandria, one of the few female saints, as Marina Warner points out, renowned for her intellect.[22] To the pagan king who wanted to kill her if she did not renounce Christianity, Catherine replied, "Whatever the tortures you may imagine for me . . . hurry, for I desire to offer my flesh and my blood to Christ as he did himself for me."[23] She further tells the same king, "If spirit govern you, you will be king; if it is the body, you will be slave" (388). Here the body, as we will be considering at greater length later, is a temple if devoted to God, but it is a husk of defilement if in the service of other human bodies. At once obstacle and vehicle to grace, the body presents this constant paradox in early hagiographic texts (Martyr Acts). The mind expresses and unfolds from this paradox; it is not divided from it. In this sense, then, the martyrs whose stories are told in the *Légende dorée* (including that of Thomas the doubting apostle) are profoundly not subjects in the modern sense. Division and difference play themselves out in the polarized metaphors of body as temple and body as shell of filth, in the longing for grace. A successful saint does not overcome the body; he or she uses it as a pure vehicle for expressing *caritas* through what Voragine continually refers to as "the crown": martyrdom.

Contemporary moves to deconstruct sovereign subjectivity, and to refute therefore any transcendental impulse, are, in a strange way, already achieved through faith in the stories of the writers of the Gospels and Voragine. This may seem like an odd claim. Yet the willed scandal of martyrdom contradicts any possibility of rational subjectivity as we understand it. These stories literalize, or concretize, the realm of the divine, such that what even Kant was willing to grant as "intellectual ideas"

---

22 Marina Warner, *Joan of Arc: The Image of Female Heroism* (New York, 1981), 134.

23 As Kate Cooper notes, taking her point from Bernard Shaw, the enthusiasm of many female Christian martyrs for torture at the hands of a male executioner is almost identical to that of heroines in early Greek romances. The status of the body is not only Christian in this tradition. See *The Virgin and the Bride: Idealized Womanhood in Late Antiquity* (Cambridge, Mass., 1996), 30. See also Page duBois, *Torture and Truth* (New York, 1991).

(noumena) are indistinguishable (by the saint and by the narrative) from phenomena, or the material realm. The nostalgia lurking in Althusser's passage is, I am arguing, motivated by a longing for such a seamlessness, such a radical insistence on the materiality of thought. Or, as Althusser remarks, after a long comment on how prophets neither hear nor understand the word of God, "This filled me with admiration, as did Spinoza's concept of the connection between the religious ideology of the Jewish people and its material existence in the temple, the priests, the sacrifices, observances, rituals, etc. In following him on this last point, as I also did Pascal whom I greatly admired, I was later to insist vigorously on the material existence of ideology, not only on the material *conditions* of existence, but on the *materiality* of its very existence" (210).

Agency flows through, and is realized, by the body. One of the most striking examples for such a claim again engages the saint from the time of the martyrs: the miracle. The miracle of early Christianity is "religious ideology" become "material existence," to use Althusser's terms.[24] The doubting Thomas of the Gospels himself becomes the producer of miracles in the apocryphal book, *The Acts of Thomas*. Again, postmodernism reveals its nostalgia for a time before modernity: Althusser, in siding with this Thomas, is himself longing to touch in order to believe in the miracle of the body speaking as one with itself. A similar impulse can be seen in Roland Barthes's notion of *punctum:* "I have seen the eyes that looked into the eyes of the Emperor," he muses while contemplating a photograph of Napoleon's nephew. *Punctum* is the moment that pierces the modern subject with an imagined memory of full presence.[25] In this metaphor of piercing the body, there is something akin to Althusser's awareness of embodiment through physical toil, as if only a wound (to return to Thomas the apostle) could produce the knowledge of being.

---

[24] For a clear account of the difference between medieval and seventeenth-century notions of the miracle, see Lorraine Daston, "Marvelous Facts and Miraculous Evidence in Early Modern Europe," in *Questions of Evidence: Proof, Practice and Persuasion across the Disciplines*, ed. James Chandler, Arnold I. Davidson, and Harry Harootunian (Chicago, 1994), 243–74.

[25] Roland Barthes, *Camera Lucida: Reflections on Philosophy* (New York, 1981). *Punctum* is in fact very close to one of the three aspects of the second type of saturated phenomenon Marion delineates—the idol: "the picture as a spectacle that, due to excess of intuition, cannot be constituted but still can be looked at" (Marion, "The Saturated Phenomenon," 121). There is, however, no real "piercing" here, only contemplation.

The eye, it will be remembered, was insufficient proof of Jesus' resurrection for Thomas: he would not believe "Unless I see in his hands the print of the nails." But Thomas added that to believe he must also "place my finger in the mark of the nails, and place my hand in his side" (John 20: 24–29). "Have you believed because you have seen me?" Jesus asks Thomas. "Blessed are those who have not seen and yet believe." The point is, however, that even seeing was not enough for Thomas; he had to touch.

Of course, the early martyrs all persuade and convert through miracles, which are in fact visual (and frequently tactile) proof of the presence of God. The miracle in the early Christian texts is the revelation of presence, *parousia*. It is a time when the miracle is seen, to use Daston's terms, as having evidentiary autonomy. As Kenneth Woodward points out, Augustine was particularly influential "in defending the idea that miracles were signs of God's power and proof of the sanctity of those in whose name they were wrought."[26]

The erosion of the status of miracles correlates, as one might expect, with the advent of empiricism and rationalism in the seventeenth century. Until then, writes Daston, miracles were ideally "transparent; requiring no interpretation, and were as satisfying to the senses and to the imagination as to reason" (274). Once again, we confront division: "This dream of pure evidence," Daston concludes, "evaporated with the division of evidence into the internal evidence of things and the external evidence of testimony, which division structured the debate over the evidence *for* miracles."[27] This comes close to explaining what I mean in my claim that the early saint erases or denies otherness. Through miracles, the gift of the body, and what we might call a transubstantiative relation to the material realm, the saint appears to achieve a transparency that elides the polarity between external and internal. Alterity, or difference, cannot be *personally* acknowledged in genuine *caritas*. What this translates into is that after the saint has achieved the rupture from family to follow an apostle, for example,[28] the body and mind position themselves as indistinguishable

[26] Kenneth L. Woodward, *Making Saints: How the Catholic Church Determines Who Becomes a Saint, Who Doesn't, and Why* (New York, 1990), 62.

[27] See also Daston's *Classical Probability in the Enlightenment* (Princeton, N.J., 1988), chap.6ff.

[28] A topos that has been frequently noted. See, for example, Virginia Burrus, *Chastity as Autonomy: Women in the Stories of the Apocryphal Acts* (Lewiston / Queenston, 1987), 34–35ff. Burrus does a Proppian analysis of the apocryphal narratives.

in their surge toward God. Parousia of divinity radically transforms logos.

While such is the case, clearly, in the Hebrew scriptures as well, early Christianity adds a twist that seems to hold particular fascination for postmodernist malaise: the call for chastity. It is a call that engages the body in such a radical manner, given the historical-cultural context from which it springs and which places alterity in such an economy of denial, that it cannot avoid obsessing a secular discourse overwhelmed with issues of otherness.

In the first place, those who answer the call to chastity in the texts of early Christianity demonstrate a kind of certainty that in itself must attract our age (for want of a better term). The predicament of modern moral culture, writes Charles Taylor, stems in part from its multiple sources. "The fact that the directions are multiple," he adds, "contributes to our sense of uncertainty. This is part of the reason why almost everyone is tentative today, why virtually no one can have the rooted confidence in their outlook" (317). Gone, needless to say, is Augustine's conviction that indecision vanishes when the "one course" toward God is chosen. The early saint presents a certainty; an apodictic that, while it is not ours (and perhaps because it is not ours) haunts us. Peter Brown ends his brilliant study of sexual renunciation among the early Christians in just these terms: "To modern persons, whatever their beliefs," he writes, "the Early Christian themes of sexual renunciation, of continence, celibacy, and the virgin life have come to carry with them icy overtones. The very fact that modern Europe and America grew out of the Christian world that replaced the Roman Empire in the Middle Ages has ensured that, even today, these notions still crowd in upon us, as pale, forbidding presences."[29] The role of the historian, adds Brown, is to give these specters "their due measure of warm, red blood" and to return to them in so doing "a little of the human weight that they once carried in their own time." Then perhaps they will speak to us "more gently" in the strange tongue of a "long-lost Christianity." The reader of Brown's book will have to decide for him- or herself, however, whether those specters "will say anything of help or comfort for our own times." If the subtext of postmodernism's mosaics is a nostalgia for unity, it is also a frightening prospect.

---

[29] Peter Brown, *The Body and Society: Men, Women, and Sexual Renunciation in Early Christianity* (New York, 1988), 446–47.

In an era of uncertainty replete with multiple directions, to return to Taylor's terms, the single-minded and totalizing ecstasy of the early saint does indeed carry some "icy overtones." This is the case, I would argue, not only because of celibacy itself (which is, after all, only one of the several symptoms of the pious life in early Christianity) but because of the attraction, and anxiety, generated by an *engagement* (in the Sartrean sense) so encompassing, particularly from the perspective of the secular, that it dissolves the burdensome ubiquity of the very notion we labor relentlessly to undermine: subjectivity. The cult of the individual in the age of late capitalism may be at issue in every text from the Frankfurt School, to Foucault, Derrida, Benjamin, Certeau, and others. Nevertheless, individuality is so ingrained in our perspective on the world that we scarcely question, on what Andreas Huyssen calls an *experiential* level, Kierkegaard's remark that "subjectivity is the only truth."

Brown's conclusion holds another significant aspect: the Christian world, with its "forbidding presences," replaced the Roman Empire and became the foundation of modern Europe and America. Thus, to look back to the early saints is to contemplate our cultural ancestors and to try to glimpse something of ourselves in what seems utterly foreign. Like Freud's definition of the uncanny (taken from Schelling), the vision of the saint is as if something long familiar and yet repressed at the foundations of our own cultural constructs.

While such an approach presupposes a genealogical notion of human thought, we are perhaps too Darwinian to imagine things otherwise, despite our insistence to the contrary. As the scientist and theologian (admittedly vigorously nonsecular) Teilhard de Chardin puts it, evolution is no longer a hypothesis; it is the very condition of all thinking, the fundamental category that allows us to apprehend the real.[30] One need but think of Nietzsche, whose "fable" of Christianity becomes the crux of most human ills, to see the extent to which a wrong turn (on Nietzsche's account, at least) creates an evolutionary trajectory requiring centuries to correct, if it can be "corrected" at all. To "look back," in Maurice Blanchot's sense, at early saints is to undertake a perilous and simultaneously obsessive journey in which an attempt is made to recapture beings who, like Eurydice, no longer belong here but are nevertheless somehow a part of us. Certainly the plethora of recent books on the

---

30 Claude Cuenot, *Teilhard de Chardin* (Paris, 1962), 83 and *passim*.

subject of the early Christian notion of virginity attests to such an Orphic obsession.

In any case, to return to the "founders" of modern European and American culture, early Christianity, I will be arguing, also engages of necessity issues of nascent nationalism, patriotism, and community. Jesus' comment "My Kingdom is not of this world" is literalized by many early saints in the struggle between the pagan and Christian *polis.* "If spirit govern you," Saint Catherine had said to the pagan king, "you will be king." "Spirit" here has to be read as conversion to Christianity and "king" as the ruler of a different realm from the one he already possesses. The implication is that Catherine does not just mean he will be a king in the afterlife; she also suggests that he will rule in a different society: a Christian one, with a new sexual morality that makes chastity the highest bidding to be answered.

But things are not that simple, of course. As Peter Brown notes along with Foucault, who echoes him, even though we claim that the call to chastity was specifically Christian, destabilizing the ground of pagan culture and identity, it is at best difficult to draw a clear line between a Judeo-Christian sexual morality and antiquity. Foucault adds:

> As far as a reflection on sexual conduct is concerned, very complex developments unfolded from the Hellenistic era until that of Saint Augustin. Certain clear epochs are easily distinguishable: in the direction of stoico-cynical consciousness, and in the organization of monasticism. Many others are equally decipherable. On the other hand, the advent of Christianity, in general, as the imperious principle of another sexual morality, in massive rupture with those which preceded it, is barely perceptible. As P. Brown notes, with respect to Christianity in the texts of global Antiquity, the cartography of the parting of the waters is difficult to establish.[31]

It may be difficult, but we seem intent upon establishing boundaries of where, for example, Rome begins to ebb and Europe starts to appear. Such a massive change is a large part of the drama in the acts of the martyrs. Brown puts it succinctly: "We can chart the rise to prominence of the

[31] Michel Foucault, "Le Combat de la chasteté," in *Communications, sexualités occidentales* (Paris, 1982), 35: 24; my translation.

Christian church most faithfully by listening to the pagan reactions to the cult of the martyrs." By insisting on their new faith, they not only rocked, and ultimately destroyed, the old order; they also, by virtue of their very belief in transparency, paved the way for a Cartesian subject, the divide of which (body and mind) is founded on an a priori, historical conviction in unity despite the *appearance* of separation from the divine.

Division, in other words, is posited on a preliminary faith in a totality that defies the material realm, a faith that is no doubt unavoidable with the individualism the *cogito* posits. A critique of the Cartesian subject, founded as it is in contemporary texts on rejecting that sovereignty, seems with notable frequency to entail a paradoxical examination of what is perceived as the time of unity. Ironically enough, Augustine and other early Christian writers are obsessed with restoring unity to postlapsarian man. Postmodernism, caught in its own prelapsarian myth, echoes on secular grounds such an attempt at restoration. Here, too, may lie the motivation for the interest in the life of chastity in early Christianity.

Foucault's reading of chastity as a combat, for example, relies on the fourth-century writings of John Cassian, who disagreed with Augustine on the role of sexual desire in the nocturnal life of an otherwise chaste monk. In contrast to Augustine, who condemned all concupiscence, Cassian argued that nocturnal emissions were useful reminders to the hapless monk that the danger of egotism and anger were constant. Only when these passions were stilled, writes Brown, "would the monk come to sense a delicious freedom from sexual fantasy, associated with the state of total *purity of heart*" (421). It is this concept of total purity, which we can read as transparency, that fascinates Foucault in Cassian.

Fornication, writes Foucault, is for Cassian one of the eight possible vices. It is also the most difficult to combat. Foucault does a careful reading of the six stages a monk must get through to succeed in attaining chastity of body and mind. These six stages, Foucault writes, should be understood as a work of disassociation. First the body must distance itself from sexual desire, and then the mind is to follow. We are very far, writes Foucault, "from the idea of a separation as radical as possible between the mind and the body." It is this *lack* of separation that intrigues Foucault. Indeed, his summary of Cassian is uncannily like Althusser's perspective: "What is at issue here," says Foucault, "is a perpetual labor on the movement of thought" (20).

Cassian's last stage in the fight for chastity is attained by the saint, notes Foucault; it is grace. "That is why non-pollution is the mark of sanctity, of the highest chastity possible; a blessing to be hoped for, not acquired" (22). Grace entails a process of "subjectivization": the subject is erased in its abandonment to grace.[32] In this model, then, the state of grace will be attained only if (but not necessarily because), chastity of mind and body has been achieved. In the words of Woodward, "Just as the martyrs were made pure by their suffering and death, so, it was thought, were the ascetics purified by the rigor of their spiritual discipline"(61).[33]

Psychoanalysis, as Charles Elder (among others) has shown, with its articulation of an inaccessible and atemporal unconscious, has many affinities with notions of divinity.[34] It is no coincidence, in this sense, that many contemporary studies on early Christianity and on saints in general have recourse to psychoanalytic theory. The idea that the mystics and saints were capable of what I have been calling a "transparency," for example, can readily be translated into contemporary psychoanalytic terms: primary narcissism, that stage at which the self feels no boundaries and makes no distinction between itself and the other, or internal and external. Postmodern reflections on the ascetics betray a nostalgia for this totalizing stage as well. Indeed, primary narcissism is a prelapsarian time of its own: before the Fall from the mother or, in Lacan's terms, before the recognition of lack as constituting the subject. As Kristeva puts it, "the most intense revelation of God, which occurs in mysticism, is given only to a person who assumes himself as 'maternal.'" The monks who led lives of pure chastity, in other words, "played the part of the Father's virgin spouses." She continues: "Freedom with respect to the maternal territory then becomes the pedestal upon which the love of God is erected. As a consequence, mystics, those 'happy Schrebers' (Sollers) throw a bizarre

32 It has been noted of late that Foucault's history of Western sexuality relies too heavily on Plutarch. See, for example, Simon Goldhill's *Foucault's Virginity: Ancient Erotic Fiction and the History of Sexuality* (New York, 1995), 156–61ff.

33 The most celebrated example of the ascetic life was *The Life of Antony*, attributed to Athanasius (355 C.E.). Antony's combat for faith is described as a form of daily martyrdom.

34 See Charles Elder, *The Grammar of the Unconscious: The Conceptual Foundations of Psychoanalysis* (University Park, Pa., 1994).

light on the psychotic sore of modernity: it appears as the incapability of contemporary codes to tame the maternal, that is, primary narcissism."[35]

"Stabat Mater," from which this passage is taken, is a postmodern meditation on early asceticism; one of the many that conflate the discourses of psychoanalysis and mysticism. While Kristeva is specifically concerned with the cult of the Virgin Mary, she directly addresses in psychoanalytic terms the modern fascination with mystics. She does so through what she calls "maternality": "Christianity is doubtless the most refined symbolic construct in which femininity, to the extent that it transpires through it—and it does so incessantly—is focused on *Maternality*" (161). Thus, the "psychotic sore of modernity" is baffled by the early mystics who (psychotic as well but happy) are able, unlike our contemporaries, to "tame the maternal." Gender consciousness (or self-consciousness), another postlapsarian division of sorts, seems to disappear into the transparency achieved when one is the "Bride of Christ."

But if femininity "incessantly" transpires through Christianity, there is more than one catch. On the one hand, the Virgin Mary is as close to a goddess as Christianity has to offer: virginal and mother of a god, she is a model to all Christians, especially those of her sex, in her chastity and unquestioning piety. But major difficulties are present here. To begin with, Mary is not a woman in any of the ways in which the feminine is defined and indeed essentialized. She is, rather, a being divested of nearly all human female attributes: she becomes pregnant without intercourse; gives birth without pain; remains a virgin before, during, and after the birth of Jesus; is amenstrual; and does not die but is lifted into heaven. She is also born without sin, unlike the rest of humanity. As Marina Warner, whose notable book on Mary directly inspired Kristeva, notes, "The Virgin Mary is not the innate archetype of female nature, the dream incarnate; she is the instrument of a dynamic argument from the Catholic Church about the structure of society; presented as a God-given code."[36]

Warner ends her book with the conviction that the Virgin's days are over; she will not be viable in "the new circumstances of sexual equality" (339). She adds, "the reality her myth describes is over; the moral code she affirms has been exhausted." The moral code is the innate inferiority

35 "Stabat Mater," in *The Kristeva Reader*, ed. Toril Moi (New York, 1986).

36 Marina Warner, *Alone of All Her Sex: the Myth and the Cult of the Virgin Mary* (New York, 1983), 338.

of women, which Mary both reinforces and gives succor for. Warner's optimism is heartening, if not entirely convincing.

If the revelation of God, to return to Kristeva, allows monks to play the role of the young virgin girl, the Desert Fathers make clear that the chosen are ultimately male, even if they are born women. This is not contradiction in early Christianity. Gregory of Nyssa, for example, argues that the distinction between male and female is absent in God's nature; gender is not an issue in his ontology. Nevertheless, Gregory uses gendered attributes as symbols for the progression of the soul.[37] Consider as well (again) the Gospel of Thomas, where Jesus says, "Every woman who makes herself male will enter the Kingdom of Heaven." The full text, which has been much cited of late, concerns an argument between Jesus and the disciple Simon Peter about Mary's adherence to the group. Simon Peter begins the argument by saying, "Let Mary leave us, because women are not worthy of life." Jesus answers, "Behold, I myself shall lead her so as to make her male, that she too may become a living spirit like you males. For every woman who makes herself male will enter the kingdom of heaven" (114).

Fourth-century communities of Christian ascetics consisted of both genders, the argument being, as one critic has noted, that "if there is neither male nor female in Jesus Christ, then the symbiosis of male and female ascetics represents the highest form of ascetic perfection."[38] But what would such a symbiosis entail? Elizabeth Castelli has commented on the same text: "The double insistence attributed to Jesus in the Gospel of Thomas saying—that Mary should remain among the disciples at the same time as she must be made male—points to the paradoxical ideological conditions that helped to shape the lives of early Christian women. At once they are to have access to holiness, while they also can do so only through the manipulation of conventional gender categories."[39]

The Martyr Acts are full of stories of women dressing as men to fol-

---

[37] See Verna E. F. Harrison, "A Gender Reversal in Gregory of Nyssa's *First Homily on the Song of Songs*," paper presented at the Eleventh International Conference on Patristic Studies, Oxford, 19–24 August, 1991, *Studia Patristica* (1992): 35–38.

[38] Susanna Elm, *"Virgins of God": The Making of Asceticism in Late Antiquity* (Oxford, 1994), ix.

[39] Elizabeth A. Castelli, "'I Will Make Mary Male': Pieties of the Body and Gender Transformation of Christian Women in Late Antiquity," in *Body Guards: The Cultural Politics of Gender Ambiguity*, ed. Julia Epstein and Kristina Straub (New York, 1991), 33.

low an apostle, the most famous one being the story of Saint Paul and Thecla. Thecla hears Paul preach and is entranced. She subsequently refuses all sexual relations with her husband, cuts her hair, dresses like a man, and follows Paul throughout his travels. In The Acts of Andrew, the apostle insists that Maximilla leave the marriage bed to preserve her mind: "I beg you then, O wise man, that your noble mind continue steadfast; I beg you, O invisible mind, that you may be preserved yourself."

Voragine tells the story of Saint Margaret of Antioch (one of the three saints to appear before Joan of Arc), who on her wedding night cut her hair as well and disguised as the monk Brother Pelagius, lived in a monastery, and then became the head of a convent of virgins. She was accused of impregnating a nun and exiled to the desert without a trial. There she lived until she died. At her death, she wrote a letter saying that her body would be proof of her innocence and that the women attending to her body would "know" that she was a virgin. Thus, virginity, again, becomes proof of purity and virtue and the body itself evidence of piety. To the prefect who tries to save her from execution, Margaret retorts, "this torment of the flesh is the salvation of the soul" (vol. 1, 453).

There are many such stories, and, while it is true that early Christian men emulated women as well, it is clear in either case that gender categories neither dissolved into androgyny nor in any way were erased from early Christian society. Moreover, as these stories attest, a woman who wishes to lead the true life of chastity and to follow an apostle must do so as a man. The body of a woman, in other words, *shows* chastity through the anatomical proof of virginity. Saint Margaret leaves her body as proof; the same cannot be said of a male ascetic.

But the Gospel of Thomas also contains a passage in which, rather than the hierarchy of male over female, the Platonic idea of oneness, or union, is espoused. "When you make the two into one," says Jesus, "and when you make the inner like the outer and the outer like the inner, and the upper like the lower and when you make male and female into a single one, so that the male will not be male and female will not be female, when you make eyes replacing an eye, a hand replacing a hand, a foot replacing a foot, and an image replacing an image, then you will enter the kingdom" (22). Here gender distinction is to be obliterated in the perfection of unity. Thus, even this apocryphal Gospel, for example, problematizes gender in the context of faith, since there are two possible models: either the woman becomes a man to attain salvation, or woman and man dissolve into one in preparation for the genderless afterlife. Indeed, the famous passage from Galatians on this matter demonstrates in its varying translations the ambivalence of the gendered role of salvation. The *Oxford Annotated Bible* reads, "There is neither Jew nor Greek, there is neither slave nor free, there is neither male nor female; for you are all one in Jesus Christ" (3.28).[40] But the translation used by Mary Douglas reads, at the end of this citation, "for you are all one man in Christ Jesus."[41] The first translation can be used to argue for the unity model, the genderless oneness into which the soul enters with faith. The second version supports the notion that true salvation must come in the form of man.

Douglas cites the passage from Galatians to argue that virginity was important to "the primitive church of the Acts" because Christianity was "setting a standard of freedom and equality which was against the traditional Jewish custom." Virginity was a notion that substituted the Old Eve of the serpent, together with sex pollution, with a "Second Eve, a virgin source of redemption crushing evil underfoot" as a potent new symbol (187). We have seen, however, that the Virgin Mary, potent a new symbol as she was, could only be problematic as a feminine gender exemplum: precisely because she falls outside any notion of pollution, Mary helps very little in the image of the feminine or, indeed, of gender imaging in general. Pollution, in other words, as Douglas argued more than thirty-five years ago, not only structures our social codes but actually gives meaning to existence (Douglas's terms). If Mary were recognized as a goddess, her lack of human gender qualities would be less significant. As it is, however, she is precisely *not* a goddess by doctrine (although mother of a god) and so, the great cults devoted to her notwithstanding, confusing as a model for women.

Even when gender is to be elided into oneness, the specific characterizations of each sex remain clear in the here and now. As Castelli notes, the first-century Jewish philosopher Philo Judaeus catalogs them in his larger attempt to combine Platonism and Judaism. For Philo, spiritual progress "is indeed nothing else than the giving up of the female gender by changing into the male, since the female gender is material, passive, corporeal, and sense perceptible, while the male is active, rational, incorporeal, and

40 In general, I will be referring to *The New English Bible, with the Apocrypha* (Oxford, 1970).

41 *Purity and Danger* (London, 1966), 186.

more akin to mind and thought."[42] Except for the fact that this passage is meant to describe the progress of the soul, it could come straight out of Freud. Contemporary culture, I want to argue, is still laboring under the same gender stereotypes at the base of its social constructs, Warner's optimism notwithstanding. More to the point, however, is the fact that already for Philo (and he is hardly alone), the body is feminine and the mind masculine. "According to nature I am a woman, but not according to my thoughts," says Amma Sara, who led the pious life.[43] This cleavage, which will have its echoes in Descartes, demonstrates the extent to which gender is implicated *especially* in what regards the soul, which ostensibly transcends the male/female distinction in the face of divinity. "And then there are bodies, and they have sexes."

The greatest of early Christian female martyrs are virgins—Agnes, Agatha, and Cecelia, for example. There are notable examples of married women who are martyred, such as the mother mentioned in the second Book of Maccabees who witnesses the deaths of her seven sons before being martyred herself.[44] In his treatise comparing virginity and martyrdom however (1523), Erasmus argues that the mother, "with the martyrdome of so many sonnes vyrgyns" actually "restored" her virginity through the suffering of her sons and her own death. For Erasmus, martyrdom is a rose; virginity, a lily. When he asks himself which is the greater, he seems to lean toward virginity, because it is freely offered and thrives during life, whereas martyrdom is recognized only after death. Erasmus, who is writing some hundred years after the death of Joan of Arc, bases his argument on the writings of Prudentius, Tertullian, the Hebrew Bible, and the New Testament. A good deal of his thinking on the matter, however, is also drawn directly from the writings of the Church fathers: Jerome in particular but also Cyprian, Ambrose, and John Chrysostom. We will look at some of these writings more closely in the subsequent chapter. For now, however, I wish to stress that the mar-

---

42 Philo, *Quaestiones et Solutiones in Exodum*, I: 8; cited in Castelli, "'I Will Make Mary Male,'" 32.

43 *The Desert Christian: Sayings of the Desert Fathers: The Alphabetical Collection*, trans. Benedicta Ward (New York, 1980), 230.

44 The story is in 2 Maccabees, VI:18–31; VII:1–41. See also *Butler's Lives of Saints*, ed. Herbert Thurston, S.J., and Donald Attwater (New York, 1956), iii, 237–38. This story obviously does not recount the life of a Christian but is read by Christian interpreters with the same assumptions concerning "the crown" of Christian martyrdom.

tyred Christian woman and the feminine virgin who devotes her life to Christ achieve, according to the Church fathers, the holiest state to be attained by a woman. The combination of these two is even more glorious. In both cases, and especially in their combination, the specificity of femininity is erased in the sociocultural (and political) context. Neither male nor female, nor even androgynous, these are Brides of Christ for the Apocalypse, but without clearly gendered attribution in the meantime.

Indeed, despite the praise of the Church fathers, female virgins by their social unconventionality (their refusal to be wives and mothers or dutiful daughters) disrupt the social sphere. Their exalted state is double-edged. On the one hand, as Mary Beard has noted of vestal virgins in Rome, on an official, ceremonial (religious) level, their virginity gives them special status.[45] On the other hand, because they blur traditional gender roles, they are also seen as dangerous to the social code. Ambiguity, as Douglas notes, is always a menace to the social structure.

By the fourth century, writers such as John Chrysostom are already warning against the cohabitation of men and women among the ascetics. The company of women, he writes, is not fitting for the soldiers and athletes Christ wants men to be: "He [Christ] has not furnished us with spiritual weapons so that . . . we spend all day having our souls stamped with women's habits and speech."[46] Watching women "spin and weave" is not conducive to virile military prowess. Virgins may be glorious, but they had best be kept from temptation. Eve is never far away, even for a woman whose life is committed to emulating Mary.

Female virginity is, then, both the most sacred vocation for a Christian woman and the most fragile, even aberrational, state. We shall see that this double valence persists and that more than one thousand years after the great treatises on virginity, this twinned valence underlies the drama of Joan of Arc. Consequently, it is worth taking a closer look at the female virgin in early Christianity and to listen again to what Brown calls "the strange tongue of a long-lost Christianity."

Because so much has been written of late on this topic (which, as I ar-

---

[45] Mary Beard, "The Sexual Status of Vestal Virgins," in *Journal of Roman Studies* 70 (1980): 12–27.

[46] John Chrysostom, "Instruction and Refutation against Those Men Cohabiting with Virgins," in *Jerome, Chrysostom, and Friends: Essays and Translations*, ed. and trans. Elizabeth Clark (Lewiston, N.Y., 1979), 195–96.

gued earlier, is the result of the contemporary fascination with this period), I will examine a limited aspect of the notion of female virginity. My purpose will be to consider how the assumptions about female virginity, as articulated in the second through fourth centuries by Christian writers, continue to fashion the network of social codes in Joan of Arc's day and thus make the choice of virginity for her a necessity. For the phenomenon of female virginity, I will be arguing, is a site both of gynophobia and of the articulation of gender difference.

CHAPTER TWO

THE DISCOURSE OF VIRGINITY: A FLIGHT BEFORE LIGHT

"Ontogeny recapitulates phylogeny" must be applicable to mental life.

—Sigmund Freud

VIRGINITY IS PLACED by Greek medical tracts in the taxonomy of diseases.[1] The famously wandering womb, a pathology suggested by Plato, was only part of what was to become the etiology of hysteria, and this held true for centuries. What is striking in Plato's few passages about women and virginity is the extent to which breath and reason predominate as givens informing not only gender distinctions but the creation of humankind itself. Both the womb and penis are, in the *Cratylus*, like animals without reason. When the womb remains unfruitful, it causes "all

---

1 Although virginity is, in fact, a transgendered state, the body of a female virgin answers to a different demand for proof. Male virginity is generally less prized civilly and more difficult to inscribe anatomically (for example, intercrural and/or nocturnal emissions are in most cultures no obstacle to male "virginity"). It is the peculiarity of feminine virginity, its specificity, that will be examined here, in the context of European/pan-Mediterranean notions. On the prizing of female as over male virginity, see Jane Schneider, "Of Vigilance and Virgins," *Ethnology* 10 (1971): 1–24. Schneider argues that the pan-Mediterranean value given to female virginity stemmed from a political economic situation that was, in turn, the result of ineffective state control.

varieties of disease" by its wanderings—most important, closing up "the passages of the breath" and "obstructing respiration."[2] The condition creates the desire for procreation, which, once undertaken, eliminates the symptoms. This may be seen as another (somewhat more anatomical, heterosexual) version, grounded as it is in bodily function, of the "desperate yearning for the other" proposed in the *Symposium*. There, it will be recalled, the body striving for unity with its split-off, other half is really driven by the fact that with (particularly male) lovers, "both their souls are longing for a something else—a something to which they can neither of them put a name, and which they can only give an inkling of in cryptic sayings and prophetic riddles" (*Plato*, 192c). This "something else" is to do with "that original state of ours, when we were whole." Desire, as Lacan was to echo, is grounded in lack.

Although the works of Plato spend little time worrying about virgins, it follows from the description of love that an unmarried woman *(parthenos)*[3] who denies the drive to procreate, or to unite with the other, is occluding not only desire but breath as well, not to mention health. On the other hand, when Socrates speculates on Artemis's name in the *Cratylus*, he says that its etymology may have come from her healthy *(artemes)* state. She scorned intercourse, and since the healthy soul abstains from base pleasures, her name may also be tied to the word for virtue *(arete)*.[4] Indeed, virtue is linked with abstention. This apparent confusion and ambiguity concerning female sexuality are resolved when we remember that in Plato, the urgent need to procreate is positioned in the lowest, ignoble part of the soul, which is concerned only in fulfilling bodily desire (and Artemis, after all, is a divinity). Thus, the rejection of homosexual sex (in Plato's work the most powerful, and the loftiest in the *Symposium* in terms of the soul's yearnings) is a virtue, because all things that transcend the corporeal are good. It is Alcibiades, in the *Symposium* (217a–20), who delivers the excursus on Socrates' well-known ability to abstain from homosexual sex. The body, after all, is the source of evil in various

---

2 *Plato: The Collected Dialogues Including the Letters*, ed. Edith Hamilton and Huntington Cairns, (Princeton, N.J., 1961), 91c.

3 Hence the epithet Parthenos for Athena, virgin goddess of war.

4 The standard scholarship on the *Cratylus* does not take these etymologies very seriously. See, for example, William Keith Chambers Guthrie's *History of Greek Philosophy* (Cambridge, 1962).

writings of Plato (*Phaedo* 66, *Timaeus* 70e); it is the prison of the soul (*Phaedo* 80, 94; *Timaeus* 34c), and it is the tomb of the soul (*Cratylus* 400c; *Gorgias* 493a).

But abstention is mostly a virtue in men only.[5] In his version of the creation in the late *Timaeus,* Socrates proposes that men "who were cowards or led unrighteous lives" return in their next life as women. The gods created in us "the desire of sexual intercourse," a desire that weakens humankind, to prevent the race from dying out. But it is the basest of desires, as I have noted, and although women are capable of finding happiness in the consummation of love, they are barred by their limitations from the "sacred rage" that is philosophy.[6] Thus, abstention by a (mortal) woman remains at the level of bodily denial, creating "all varieties of diseases," beginning with blockage of breath. There is no reason, in Plato's work, for a woman to abstain from sex for reasons of virtue, since doing so would be a philosophical as well as moral stance. Female virginity, then, in Plato remains on the level of physiology, a technical term meaning "unmarried woman," *parthenos.* It does not engage notions of virtue, so that the term *abstention* in this case cannot be used. Artemis, after all, is not powerful because she is a virgin; she is a virgin because she is powerful and a goddess. Her body is in a different "register."

Nevertheless, the notion for men of transcending the body and its demands, of attaining the highest levels of sexless love through abstention, may be one of the most important sources for Christian asceticism. Sexually inactive women, however, relegated as they are in Plato to medical categories, remain so in the medical texts of the ancients, which regard secular female virginity as an unhealthy, even dangerous, condition eas-

---

5 Throughout this discussion it should be borne in mind that in antiquity, vestal virgins enjoyed a special status, one that has been debated at length. The general consensus is that the purity and virginity of these women formed the basis of their holiness. Plato, however, is talking about women "in general," in the most essentialist sense and of necessity, in his view, unconnected to divinity. The holiness of the vestal virgins is etymological here: they were, quite literally, set apart, anomalous. For a review of the debate, and a variance thereof, see Mary Beard, "The Sexual Status of Vestal Virgins," *Journal of Roman Studies* 70 (1980): 12–27.

6 It should be remembered that in the *Republic,* "capable" women are made guardians of the state and, furthermore, admitted to the same education as men. This statement comes on the heels, however, of a discussion on how even superior women are "far surpassed" by the other sex. *Republic* V: 455–56.

ily cured by marriage and childbearing. So Hippocrates counsels girls afflicted, in his view, by their virginity: "I recommend to young girls, experiencing such difficulties, to marry as soon as possible. Indeed, if they become pregnant, they are cured. In the opposite case, at the time of puberty or a bit after, they will be taken by this affliction, if not by another."[7] These young girls, Hippocrates explains, are prey to illness at the beginning of menses. Because the blood is blocked from flowing out through the vagina by the membrane (I do not say hymen since it is not clear that all ancient Greeks believed in it),[8] the blood pools around the heart and the diaphragm, causing pressure. Once flooded by the blood, the "heart becomes torpid, the torpor creates numbness, which leads to delirium" (467). The patient will experience hallucinations, night terrors, and anxiety. Many such girls have been found strangled by their own hands because women are "by nature less courageous and less firm."

Hippocrates (460–377 B.C.E.) classifies the illness of virgins under sacred maladies. The implication is that reason being obliterated, a type of madness or altered state prevails, aping the rhapsodic trances of certain ancient prophets or oracles. Holy, after all, means to be set apart, so that madness and religious fervor are explicitly linked. While such a connection is prevalent throughout Western thought, it should be noted that even in the case of an explicitly medical condition in girls, and even with the continual bow to Plato, there is an element of holiness / danger in the strange diseases of the virgin, even when she is clearly unrelated to the anomalous status of the vestal virgins. Unsurprisingly, then, we find in Hippocrates an emphasis on reason, here as the first sign of a return to health. But, as in Plato, we also discern obstructed breath as the first symptom of compromised blood flow. Girls will experience a desire

---

7 "Des Maladies des jeunes filles," in *Oeuvres complètes d'Hippocrate,* vol. 8, ed. E. Littré (Amsterdam, 1961), 469–71; my translation. The article is from the "Corpus Hippocraticum" and generally attributed to later authors.

8 See, for example, Giulia Sissa, *Le Corps virginal: La Virginité féminine en Grèce ancienne* (Paris, 1987). The English edition, to which I will be referring, is *Greek Virginity,* trans. Arthur Goldhammer (Cambridge, Mass., 1990). For a more complete discussion than I am giving here of the history of feminine virginity in several cultures, see my "Der Diskurs der Jungfräulichkeit oder von der Geschlechtlichkeit des Heiligen," in *Die Ungewisse Evidenz: Für eine Kulturgeschichte des Bewweises,* ed. Gary Smith and Matthias Kross, trans. Wolfert von Rahden (Berlin, 1998), 69–93.

to strangle themselves because of an "acute inflammation" beginning around the heart and spreading to the throat.

The Greco-Roman physician Galen (129–c. 199) will similarly see the uterus (which he insisted does not wander) as the cause of illness in women, primarily manifest by a complete lack of psychological control. The uterus itself, he argues, is affected by the moon and the imagination (hence all the subsequent treatises about how contemplating monsterlike images during pregnancy will result in the birth of a monster). In addition, although the medical Methodist Soranus (second century C.E.) was to argue against Hippocrates and claim that pregnancy was an unhealthy state, virginity a healthy one, and abstinence justified, his view was in the minority in the ancient medical field.[9] Perhaps because Soranus did not subscribe to Aristotle's view on women—the most positive note of which was that women could not be monsters, since God had created them, too—Soranus's ideas and his important gynecological tracts were largely ignored until the Renaissance, or about 1600.[10] By then a modified Galenism had replaced Aristotle's notions on the imperfection of women.[11] It should be noted, then, that in Joan of Arc's day, the views of Aristotle still prevailed in gynecological and medical circles.

---

9 According to Celsus (first century C.E.), there were three schools of Greek medicine: first, the Dogmatics (Hippocrates and Galen), who focused on anatomy, experimentation, and observation and who were rationalists, basing their views on medical theory; second, the Empiricists, skeptics who believed that nature has secrets that no amount of theory will divulge; finally, the Methodists, of which Soranus was the best known, who classified acute maladies and sacrificed theory for praxis when necessary.

10 Ian Maclean, *Renaissance Notions of Woman: A Study in the Fortunes of Scholasticism and Medical Science in European Intellectual Life* (Cambridge, 1980), 29.

11 In *De generatione animalium,* Aristotle argues that the male of the species is the "superior principle," having heat as a "motive force." This primal force acts in such a way, "whereby that which comes into being is male," which is in turn "better and more divine than the material whereby it is female" (732a: 5–10). In general, that which is hot in nature (male) is "more perfect" than the cold (female). Semen, for example, is hot and carries within it "the spiritus conveying the principles of the soul" (737: 7–9). A female is "a mutilated male," with colder blood that provides the material for new life, while the male "fashions it." Whereas the child's body is from the female, "it is the soul that is from the male, for the soul is the reality of a particular body" (738b: 20–28). But since nothing in nature is superfluous, woman is necessary for procreation and for nature's need to combine hot and cold, active and passive, form and matter, and so forth. *The Works of Aristotle,* 12 vols., ed. W. D. Ross (Oxford, 1908–1952); vol. 5, *De generatione animalium,* trans. Arthur Platt.

While it has been claimed that hysteria for the Greeks is somatic, clearly we are entangled in the texts of the ancients in a difference of registers. On the one hand, the blocked uterus (whether by youth or by fibroids in older women) poisons the patient with the pressure caused by blood having nowhere to go.[12] Such a hydraulic economy, I would suggest, is no different from that of Freud's notion of feminine "hysteria." For the ancients, too, the pleasure principle strives for a lack of pressure, the opening of canal locks that obstruct the flow—whether it be of unconscious drives, as in Freud, or of menstrual blood, as in Hippocrates. For both, hysteria or sacred malady is sexual in etiology and can be largely cured by a puncture to the hymen or membrane—that dam that holds back access to normal femininity. Such a view leaves the virgin in a state not only of medical abnormality but of clotted preexistence: always in potentia, hovering on the threshold (hymen) of complete womanhood.

On the other hand, this very anomalousness constitutes what Edward Leach calls a "third term," marking the place of danger and the sacred. The vestal virgin is then not so removed from her medical, "pathological" counterpart. She, too, is set apart, in her case by a social consensus of holiness. She, too, falls outside the social and gendered registers. The history of female virginity, which has been traced at length, reads like a metaphor of female subjectivity. As prewoman, the virgin paradoxically emblematizes how womanhood itself is figured: a subject that does not exist as such and is thus understood as a near monstrosity (the medical view) or as a point of extreme ambiguity and otherness (the vestal virgins). Virginity is much more significant than a social anomaly or sacred vocation sanctioned by the state. In its position as *both* of these, virginity is positioned as foreign to male subject agency, as the ghost of subjectivity. More significant, virginity is at once a reminder that woman herself is a subject always to come and that as perpetual *Nicht Ich* in Fichte's sense, she helps to define that impossible masculinist insistence in the West: *das Absolute Ich,* the sovereign subject. Indeed, as I will be arguing throughout this study, virginity is dangerous in that it posits the liminal, not only medically and socially but also with respect to the notion of subjectivity

---

12 In medieval gynecological texts as well. See Ron Barkai, *A History of Jewish Gynaecological Texts in the Middle Ages,* ed. David S. Katz (Leiden, 1998), 20: 44 and *passim.*

itself and the way it is consistently posited as agency from Plato through Freud and, as Derrida puts it, beyond.

The beyond, of course, is the point. For if what is loosely (and too comfortably) labeled "postmodernism" has, of late, been strangely haunted by the limits and myths of subjectivity (the self, the speaking subject, the other, alterity, and so on), the virgin may help us in her very incapacity to "fit." The virgin, seen in this light, serves as a constant reminder that human agency, and the subjectivity it has so loudly cherished and simultaneously questioned, is, has always been, at risk. And this even (and perhaps especially) in the very texts that propose to dismantle the sovereignty of the subject.

Thus, it should be of no surprise that Levinas begins his study of the subject as "an existent," whose solitude comes from its relationship with the existing over which it is master: "This mastery over existing is the power of beginning, of starting out from itself, starting out from itself neither to act nor to think, but to be."[13] But in its contemplation of death, Levinas writes, the subject senses its *virility* at stake: "death is *ungraspable,* [that] it marks the end of the subject's virility and heroism. . . . My mastery, my virility, my heroism as a subject can be neither virility nor heroism in relation to death" (72). Death is for Levinas an "eternal futurity," an ungraspable. It marks the end of the subject's virility and heroism because these cease to exist in the face of death; thus, what is "existent," the foundation of subjectivity, is endangered.

It is possible to see here, without, I think, cheapening Levinas's argument, how central masculinity as a concept must be to the very notion of subjectivity. The concept of Being itself, as Levinas shows, is inextricable from the hero (his example is Hamlet), for whom Being and heroism are locked in a pre-Hegelian battle of paralytic proportions. The feminine does not play a role in this battle because it is not inscribed in the parameters of the subject. But let us consider the virgin as part of the otherness of death—a feminine subjectivity that is an eternal futurity, an ungraspable that, like the moment of death, marks a point at which, as (masculine) subject, "we are no longer *able to be able* [*nous ne pouvons plus pouvoir*]

[13] Emmanuel Levinas, *Time and the Other and Additional Essays,* trans. Richard Cohen (Pittsburgh, 1987), 67.

(74). It is exactly thus, continues Levinas, "that the subject loses its very mastery as subject." Death

> indicates that we are in relation with something that is absolutely other, something bearing alterity not as a provisional determination we can assimilate through enjoyment, but as something whose very existence is made of alterity. My solitude is thus not confirmed by death but broken by it.

So, too, the hypostatization of female virginity, which breaks the solitude of the subject by its existence as alterity. Virginity as an unattributable femininity threatens the subject, breaks the solitude of virility, refuses the recourse of heroism. Indeed, Levinas is explicit on the importance of maintaining the alterity of otherness, which for him is, precisely, the feminine:

> What is the alterity that does not purely and simply enter into the opposition of two species of the same genus? I think the absolutely contrary contrary [*le contraire absolument contraire*], whose contrariety is in no way affected by the relationship that can be established between it and its correlative, the contrariety that permits its terms to remain absolutely other, is the *feminine.* (85)

The feminine as mystery is a near-cliché in contemporary theory. But the otherness of woman has been largely neutralized on the experiential, social, and political levels through oppression. This much is clear. The otherness that Levinas attributes to the feminine is, contrary to Simone de Beauvoir's cursory understanding of it,[14] an attempt to insist on an alterity that, unlike the move in Hegel, is not grasped by already containing its otherness within itself. I see this as a radical departure even from Freud, for example, whose unconscious is the "other" to conscious thought. Un-

[14] In *The Second Sex* (New York, 1989), Beauvoir attacks Levinas for sexism because he puts women in a position of otherness, which she reads as secondary. I would argue that Levinas, who explicitly rejects the platonic notion that every term contains a sameness "and through this sameness contains the Other," is quite on the contrary forcing a fleeting admission of unfathomable unknowability. Hence, his choice of death to illustrate the point.

knowable as the unconscious may mostly be in Freud, it is still, in Levinas's words on the platonic binaries, the reverse side of its own identity.

The contemporary texts that address virginity—from Freud to Nietzsche, for example, to Foucault, Simone Weil, and Kristeva—are fascinated with the phenomenon without necessarily knowing, or wishing to know, entirely for what reason.[15] The double-edged aspect of virginity in a woman, however (purity / sexuality; innocence / danger), is rarely overlooked. I am suggesting that it is female virginity, more specifically than the feminine, that explicitly forces a recognition of full otherness in Levinas's sense. This is the same reason for which the double-edged nature of virginity is probed. It is easier to treat and analyze the symptoms in the scandal of otherness than it is to come to terms with its ineluctable refusal to be comprehended.

Thus, Freud, in his 1917 article "The Taboo of Virginity," goes straight to the catachresis of valences, interpreting virginity as a taboo that (like the uncanny) also means its own opposite. Although his essay was intended to examine "primitive" cultures, Freud demonstrates how various tribal customs resonate in modern social codes. As Jean Laplanche points out, Freud happily generalizes in his comparative ethnography (from culture to culture and epoch to epoch) because he believes "with a near a priori certainty in the existence of certain universal psychic structures."[16] Freud repeats in this essay the thesis from *Totem and Taboo:* that the basis of taboo is an originary ambivalence. In certain tribes, he notes, defloration must occur before the wedding night, and by ritual—by the father, the priest, the chief, or another man in the tribe. The taboo here is that virginity cannot be touched, not even by the husband (often, for example, pointed objects achieve the defloration, thus avoiding direct contact). Freud makes clear that the profoundly ambivalent status of virginity makes it both totem and taboo, both sacredness and danger. So much is evident in the texts of Christianity—from its beginnings

---

[15] In Nietzsche's *Will to Power* (New York, 1967), for example, Christianity is aligned throughout with the weak, including (European, modern) women, and the priest to misguided asceticism: "The Christian priest is from the first a mortal enemy of sensuality: no greater antithesis can be imagined than the innocently awed and solemn attitude adopted by, for example, the most honorable women's cults of Athens in the presence of the symbols of sex" (94).

[16] Jean Laplanche, *Problématiques II: Castration Symbolisations* (Paris, 1983), 92. I am grateful to Jeffrey Mehlman for referring me to this article.

through the Middle Ages. But in modern European culture there is a retention of the privileged (as well as powerful and dangerous) aspect of virginity, in which virginity is a taboo as well—not because of its anatomical state but because its history and mystery seem continually to engage the sacred.

Nostalgia for the sacred in secular contemporary culture is one of the assumptions of this study, as I have already argued. But in his commentary on "The Taboo of Virginity," Laplanche argues that Freud's brief study demonstrates a distinction between "primitive" (Laplanche's willful use of the term is constant) and modern cultures: in both, there is a valorization of virginity, "but in the case of the taboo, it is a sacred valorization" (93). It is certainly the case that modern culture does not valorize female virginity on overtly "sacred" grounds. Nevertheless, it is also evident that there remains, even in postmodern culture, not only a fascination with the sacred, as we have seen, but a shift from obviously religious views on the sacred to more philosophical, or theoretical, formulations of mystery. The profound otherness of death or the feminine in Levinas, for example, demonstrates a kind of mysticism that, Levinas's personal convictions aside, cannot help but reveal the way in which otherness delimits the notion of human subjectivity and represents the mystery of any unknowable.[17] Virginity partakes of this otherness. Its anatomical obscurity combines with (or helps to create) its cultural taboo; its ungraspability (in Levinas's sense) fosters its place in the sacred / danger duality. In the economy of being, Levinas sees the feminine as always withdrawing from the light: "The feminine is not accomplished as a *being* [*étant*] in a transcendence toward light, but in modesty [*pudeur*]" (88).[18]

[17] Indeed, otherness is posited in the linguistic foundation of subjectivity as well. In a passage by Émile Benveniste, which I will have occasion to cite again later in this study, he states, "Language is possible only because each speaker sets himself up as a *subject* by referring to himself as *I* in his discourse. Because of this, *I* posits another person, the one who, being, as he is, completely exterior to 'me,' becomes my echo to whom I say *you* and who says *you* to me." *Critical Theory since 1965*, ed. Hazard Adams and Leroy Searle (Gainesville, Fla., 1986), 729.

[18] The French word *pudeur* is much stronger than the English *modesty*. The French word implies delicacy, discretion, a certain manner of behavior that engages extreme consideration for others so as not to offend or shock. *Pudeur* corresponds to two Latin words, *pudor* and *pudicitia*. The first means "shame," and the second means "modesty" (and is thus closest to the modern French meaning). Hence, *pudenda*, which is the gerundive from the

Or: "The transcendence of the feminine consists in withdrawing elsewhere . . . and I see no other possibility than to call it a mystery." Or again: "The feminine in existence is an event different from that of spatial transcendence or of expression that go toward the light. It is a flight before light. Hiding is the way of existing for the feminine, and this fact of hiding is precisely modesty" (86).

It is not hard to hear echoes of Nietzsche, who famously equates Woman with the position of "Truth," in the guise of modesty.[19] Yet far from Levinas's flight before light, in Nietzsche one can never get to the depths of woman; she is "not even shallow." Her otherness in Nietzsche is less than the (masculine) norm and therefore signals a (less successful) sameness that in turn contains a domesticated other. There is no attempt to posit woman as a radical other but, rather, as the traditional secondariness that informs the Western tradition. And yet the positions, different as they clearly are, both lean to the mystery of woman, to her obscurity, to Freud's notion of woman as the dark continent. Woman as obscurity is a trope that has been noted many times, but I am making a different point here: that the obscurity of woman is a metaphor informed by female anatomy. The very *insideness* of her sexual organs, for example, lend themselves to tropes of mystery, darkness, obscurity, and shrouding. This is the case in Levinas as well as in Nietzsche, Freud, Plato. Anatomically speaking, her organs will for centuries be understood as hidden: the testes and sperm, for Galen; the wandering womb starting, we think, with Plato; a penis turned inside out for Aristotle, and so on.

The anatomy that is hidden from the light withdraws from the gaze, and thus from reliable analysis. The wandering womb is like an uncon-

---

verb *pudet* (those things before which we should feel *pudor*). Pudenda are thus literally those things from which, or before which, one ought to be ashamed. The same holds true in Greek: *aidoia* are those things that should inspire *aidos* (shame). *Aidoia* can also mean genitalia. The etymology of pudenda, then, recapitulates the point I am making: that which is hidden in woman (the vagina) inspires fear, but what is visible of her genitalia is that before which one feels shame. The double bind for the feminine is thus clear in the history of the word *pudeur.* For more on *pudeur* and its implications, see *La Pudeur: Le Réserve et le trouble,* ed. Claude Habib (Paris, 1992). I am grateful to David Wray for help with this term.

19 *Unter Frauen,* "O Sie kennen die Wahrheit nicht! Ist sie nicht ein Attentat auf alle unsere *pudeurs?*" From *Twilight of the Idols,* "Maxims and Arrows," no. 16. Cited by Derrida in *Spurs: Nietzsche's Styles,* trans. Barbara Harlow (Chicago, 1978), 83. Again, the untranslatable *pudeur* is used by Nietzsche.

scious metaphor for the incapacity to scrutinize woman, to bring her parts to light (where would one look, in dissection, for a displaced womb?). How much more the mystery, then, when the woman is a virgin. With the membrane, at times called the *hymen*, itself difficult to discern and inconclusive as evidence, with the purity of woman a near contradiction in the Judeo-Christian tradition, and with female anatomy itself so difficult to illuminate (in all senses), virginity is as if a phantasm—a phantasm, however, that holds great weight in juridical, medical, and theological discourse. Virginity is, then, a point of enormous importance that, like woman herself, is constantly elusive.

Virginity in young girls is still a form of madness in Johann Lange's "Medicinalium epistolarum miscellanea" (1554). Lange separates the particular "hysteria" of virgins from other classes of hysterias. When he writes to a father concerned about his listless daughter, Lange proposes that her disease be characterized as "virgineus" since it is peculiar to young girls. It is also called, he adds, white fever or pallor, "since lovers become pale."[20] Lange's description is identical to that of Hippocrates (whom he cites), and his treatment is the same as well: "I instruct young girls afflicted with the disease to cohabit and copulate for if they conceive they recover. Indeed, if a young woman is not attacked by this disease in puberty she will be at a later date unless she marries. In spite of marriage very many are sterile . . . in the treatment of this disease of virgins I have never been deceived or my hopes frustrated. Wherefore, be of good courage, you shall give away your daughter, moreover, I shall be glad to be present at the nuptials" (ibid.). *Morbus virgineus,* as Lange calls it, causes a psychosomatic condition in young girls that presents as depression and madness. Like the view of Hippocrates, it is the specific result of the lack of sexual activity and procreation. Following that of many of the ancients, this medical discourse aligns the state of virginity with what goes against nature, for the body is denied its *natural* appetite. Madness necessarily ensues.[21]

---

[20] In fact, the condition was probably anachromatic anemia. J. Lange, "Medicinalium epistolarum miscellanes" (Basel, 1554), 74–77. Cited in Cecilia C. Mettler, *History of Medicine,* ed. Fred A. Mettler (Philadelphia, 1947), 366.

[21] Sterility in married women was often seen as God's refusal to bless the union; and this until recently. Pope Pius XII, for example, darkly reminds midwives in one of his addresses that "perfect married life" has as its main function "service for new life." "The Apostolate of the Midwife," in *Major Addresses of Pope Pius XII,* ed. Vincent Arthur

But the great eighteenth-century philosopher Buffon sees it otherwise. In a remarkable passage, Buffon notes that because men have always been jealous and have always made much of what they thought they could possess "exclusively and first," it is *they* who enter into a kind of "madness" [*folie*]. For Buffon, the male fantasy of female virginity has been transformed into a "reality" nourished by a kind of insane obsession. In fact, he writes, virginity is a moral virtue consisting of a purity of heart; it is not physically discernible. Men, however, have turned a young girl's virginity into a physical object and have "established opinions, conventions, ceremonies, superstitions, and even verdicts and sentences: the most illicit abuses, the most dishonorable customs have been authorized."[22] Virginity is a paradox: in can only be ascertained by being annihilated. Buffon is outraged by the practice of "determining" virginity in a young girl: "The most secret parts of nature have been submitted to examination by ignorant matrons, and exposed to the eyes of guilty doctors, without a thought for the fact that such indecency is an attack against virginity; that to seek to recognize it is to violate it; that every shameful situation, every indecent state which makes a girl blush internally is a real defloration" (ibid.). Not only does the transgression here in "establishing" virginity (a contradiction in terms for Buffon) lie in the necessary physical penetration that such scrutiny entails; more important, it consists in the ocular transgression of seeing what should be kept hidden: "The most secret parts of nature." Virginity itself, then, both anatomically and conceptually, "flees from the light," to return to Levinas. I repeat his words: Hiding is the way of existing for the feminine, and this fact of hiding is precisely modesty.

It is in this arc of reasoning, then, that I am proposing virginity as the metaphor of alterity for alterity; as the thought of death within the thought of death—that which is eradicated from thought as soon as it is encountered *in thought*. For if virginity withdraws from the light, there is a mimetic move by he who attempts to scrutinize it, to bring it forth as an "expression that goes toward the light." So profound a move is this that

---

Yzermans (St. Paul, Minn., 1961), 1: 162. So, too, in "modern" literature, in Goethe's *Elective Affinities* or in Tieck's "Der blonde Eckbert," (as in most fairy tales) the lack of children in a couple signals a problematic (for example, incestuous or otherwise unnatural) union. These are just two random examples among many.

22 *Oeuvres de Buffon*, ed. M. A. Richard (Paris, 1827), 419. All translations are mine.

the so-called madness of hysteria is displaced, as Buffon intuits, onto the woman, when it is in reality the male phantasm, his madness, that attempts to veil the abyss.

The vagina of the virgin is imagined as containing nature's secret both by Buffon (who decries such a violation) and by those who would examine it. That it can never be fully apprehended by the gaze ties such a "secret" to *aletheia*, a truth that cannot be apprehended directly. We are back, then, to the myth mapping out such a terrain: that of Eurydice, who can perhaps now be seen as this problematic figured. A sacredness that is unseen but irretrievably lost if revealed to the direct gaze of the eye, Eurydice literalizes that which withdraws, flees, from the light. Steeped as she is in the realm of death, and possible only by being apprehended with the averted gaze, the figure of Eurydice delineates how mystery is configured in the West and how that which cannot be looked at directly partakes of the religious. For Jean-Luc Marion, a phenomenon that is religious in the strict sense "would have to render visible what nevertheless could not be objectivized. The religious phenomenon thus amounts to an impossible phenomenon, or at least it marks the limit starting from which the phenomenon is in general no longer possible. Thus, the religious phenomenon poses the question of the general possibility of the phenomenon, more than of the possibility of religion" ("The Saturated Phenomenon," 103).

Female virginity, like death, is an impossible phenomenon. It is a Eurydice. Moreover, virginity gives anatomical resonance to the discourse of mystery. It provides the architecture for the metaphors of death in modern texts. "Death," writes Edmond Jabès, "like the sky, is below. At the bottom of the ladder. At the top, there are wings, the soul, life." He continues:

> To fall, to give in to gravity, means going through death. Gravity. Grave: a cave artificially filled in. No stone to perpetuate memory, but the constant gaping of a hole. It makes you contemplate the universe as through a telescope, the unbroken day and night of an insatiable infinite.[23]

The metaphor of a cave, of a gaping hole, is like that in Marion—an eidetic image of revelation that, paradoxically, refuses sight and illumination. Death reveals itself as ungraspable (Levinas) by the eye and mind,

23 *The Sin of the Book: Edmond Jabès*, ed. Eric Gould (Lincoln, Neb., 1985), 36–37.

as black hole (Jabès), as an impossible phenomenon (Marion). Death partakes of the religious in this mystery. Heidegger reads Hölderlin:

> For something that man measures himself by must after all impart itself, must appear. But if it appears, it is known. The god, however, is unknown, and he is the measure nonetheless. Not only this, but the god who remains, must by showing *himself* as the one he is, appear as the one who remains unknown. God's *manifestness*—not only he himself—is mysterious.

God is revealed to us as unknown through the sky's manifestness, writes Heidegger: "God's appearance through the sky consists in a disclosing that lets us see what conceals itself, but lets us see it not by seeking to wrest what is concealed out of its concealedness, but only by guarding the concealed in its self-concealment."[24]

The manifestness of God itself, then, discloses its mystery by guarding the concealed in its very self-concealment. Such a guarding works by displacement onto the sky (Heidegger reading Hölderlin) or through the contemplation of a "saturated phenomenon" (Marion). The guarding blocks both a visual (fleeing from the light) and a conceptual proof, or affirmation. The averted gaze is also the averted mind. In the contemplation of the religious (of death, of god), we might say that the mind has an Orphic mode: it is incapable of believing without seeing, of resisting transgression, and loses forever that which is sought when it seeks to apprehend directly through the gaze or through thought. So, too, as Buffon notes, virginity is annihilated as soon as one seeks to ascertain it. It is invisible. It partakes of the same economy of mystery.

On the first level, virginity conceals itself by virtue of its anatomical presentation. It literally escapes the light, frustrating all attempts to see it conclusively. The mystery (or darkness) of the vagina gives rise to metaphors of enigma: the cave, dark continent, grave (Novalis's narrow grave, for example, in *Hymns to the Night*), "mystery of nature," and so on.[25] These metaphors in turn combined with notions of woman in *essence* (and I use the term advisedly) in the West make the female virgin neither man (that is, un-

---

[24] Martin Heidegger, *Poetry, Language, Thought*, trans. Albert Hofstadter (New York, 1975), 222–23.

[25] I am quite aware that writers such as Irigaray and Sarah Kofman have discussed Plato's

touched by the Orphic vision), nor hermaphrodite, nor woman on any level except *in potentia*. The virgin, like the unimagined female subject, is perpetually on the horizon of being. The gaze averts itself before the possibility of the abyss, as Nietzsche noted. Virginity presents this danger of the abyss, and thus of the infinite loss of subjectivity, or death. As Levinas posits death in futurity, so virginity hypostasizes itself in eternal *potentia*, in a saturated way. And this first, as I have noted, *on the level of the body*.

It is the body of the virgin that promises proof of purity. Saint Margaret of Antioch, mentioned in the previous chapter, is confident that her body will attest to her innocence. In the letter she writes to the abbey and to the monks at the time of her death, she leaves her body behind as evidence: "I am a virgin, and I have proven by my actions that I have not lied with evil intent. . . . I am left with one thing to ask, and that is that the men who were unaware that I am a woman leave to the nuns the care of shrouding my body. Then the sight of my body delivered up to death will be the justification of my life, since the women will recognize as virgin she whom her detractors called an adulteress" [*sic*].[26] It is significant that this "proof" of virginity is to be established by women, who will ascertain immediately the extent to which Margaret's body matched, and indeed spoke, her purity. Her intimate body will serve as "the justification of [my] life." In the Christian context, then, there is an ethics of the body,

cave as an unconscious metaphor for the womb. I take these arguments as part of the cumulative context of tropes, which help to inform the specificity of virginity and its anatomical structure, the membrane or hymen hidden in the vagina.

26 *La Légende dorée de Jacques de Voragine*, ed. and trans. Abbot J.-B. M. Roze (Paris, 1902), 3: 174–75; my translation. Consider also the story alluded to by Salisbury concerning the blind monk who is cured upon kissing the body of Castissima. One should not be surprised that nuns here perform the tasks of midwives. Even saintly women did so. See, for example, *The Life of Melania*, which describes the pilgrim woman who pushes aside a surgeon attempting to deliver a woman of a dead child. The surgeon's chosen method was to cut the fetus out of the mother. Melania's far more humane solution, in which she was assisted by two virgins, was to tie her belt around the woman's belly, thus delivering the child and saving the mother. As Salisbury points out, the notion of female body parts is (unsurprisingly) strikingly different among women, include chaste women, from what the early Church fathers preached. For Melania, no bodily female part can be filthy since it is made by God (113). Only sin is an abomination. This story gets at the heart of a major rift in gender understanding between Christian men and women in the time of the martyrs. Women do not fear their own bodies. Joyce E. Salisbury, *Church Fathers, Independent Virgins* (London, 1991), 107.

which in turn necessitates women who fulfill the function of checking for virginity. By giving these women agency in this regard, the male gaze is as if once removed (albeit mimed) from its source, thus echoing what Freud saw as the danger of the conceptual chasm that is virginity, the direct contact with which is to be displaced.

The women who performed this task were midwives, whose dominance begins in the Roman period and continued well into the nineteenth century.[27] Midwives played a judicial as well as medical role in determining a young woman's sexual experience for the courts as well as for medical purposes. The Church backed this role in 1220, when Pope Gregory IX ordered that women in divorce proceedings had to submit to examination by a midwife. But already in 533 C.E., the *Corpus Jures Civilis* of Justinian the Great had codified centuries of Roman law and devoted large portions to midwives, with very little text on physicians. Thus, midwives enacted the secular confirmation of the body's ethics in a woman. When Saint Margaret says the women will "know" of her bodily purity, she is relying on a medical practice that is centuries old and that assumes that only midwives can ascertain the presence or absence of the hymen.

And yet the midwife's expert, legal probings and glances, so furiously denounced by Buffon, are linked with transgression and the trope of the averted gaze long before Buffon's tirade.[28] The Virgin Mary herself was

---

27 See, for example, the entry "Midwifery, obstetrics" in *Encyclopedia of Medical History*, ed. Roderick E. McGrew with Margaret P. McGrew (New York, 1985), 203–8. See also the modern edition of the fifteenth-century *Medieval Woman's Guide to Health*, ed. and trans. Beryl Rowland (Kent, Ohio, 1981). The importance of midwifery continues, of course, although its role now is almost exclusively limited, in the West, to pregnancy, labor, and birth. In the Catholic Church, midwives are given the additional role of moral mentors, armed by their medical knowledge, in the words of Pope Pius XII, to "draw strength to oppose irrational and immoral practices—whatever their source may be—with a calm, fearless, and unshakeable 'No.'" This no has mainly to do with abortion and contraception. See "The Apostolate of the Midwife," in Yzermans, ed., *Major Addresses of Pope Pius XII*, 1: 162.

28 Ambrose, for example, argued against a bishop who wanted to have a midwife check whether a virgin was still in fact intact. Ambrose believed that this would set a dangerous precedent, since it could lead to the regular checking of virgins (who might, among other things, be damaged by an incompetent midwife). More to the point, however, he argued that to "open" a virgin in such a way was an outrageous violation, of both her spiritual and physical integrity. Such an examination, he concluded, "prostitutes the other's modesty." Ambrose, "Letter 32," in *Saint Ambrose: Letters*, trans. Sister Mary Melchior Beyenke (New York, 1954), 157–71.

"checked" for virginity. Two apocryphal books of the Bible (James 19–20 and Ps. Matthew 13:3–5) tell of the midwife present at the birth of Jesus. In James, a "Hebrew midwife" rushes to tell a certain "Salome" of the miracle of virgin birth: "Salome, Salome, I have a new sight to tell you; a virgin has brought forth, a thing which her nature does not allow." Salome, however, has her doubts: "unless I put forward my finger and test her condition," she tells the midwife, " I will not believe that a virgin has brought forth."[29] In the James version, Mary has, significantly, given birth in a cave, which during the birth is covered in a "shining cloud" and then by a great light "so that our eyes could not bear it."[30] Once the child is born, the light dissipates, leading the midwife to cry, "My soul is magnified today, for my eyes have seen wonderful things." What the midwife has seen, to return to the terms of Levinas, is the revelation of the concealedness of God. The cave, acting as a literal metaphor of the miracle of *both* virginity and virgin birth, combined with the great cloud and blinding light, conspire to make all sight impossible. What the midwife has "seen," then, which convinces her of the miracle, is that the birth has in fact been unseeable.

Salome, however, is not so easily swayed. She goes into the cave and says to Mary, "Make yourself ready—for there is no small contention concerning you." Salome then "put forward her finger to test her condition." Her transgressive hand is immediately withered, and she is con-

---

[29] Edgar Hennecke, *New Testament Apocrypha,* ed. Wilhelm Schneemelcher, trans. R. M. Wilson, vol. 1 (Philadelphia, 1963).

[30] Mircea Eliade's *Encyclopedia of Religion* notes that virgin birth, or parthenogenesis, exists in most of the major religions (Hinduism, Buddhism, Zoroastrianism), when such a concept is loosely described as "any miraculous conception and birth." These virgin births occur frequently in a cave (Dionysus), a myrrh tree (Adonis), a sacred grove (Buddha), or a manger / cave (Jesus)—almost as if virgin birth doubles the mystery of female reproduction, and its anatomy, by placing it in a setting that is like a metaphor of the vagina. See *The Encyclopedia of Religion,* ed. Mircea Eliade (New York, 1987), 15: 272–76. Similarly, Mary will be seen as a door that is closed to men but through which Jesus passes to reach the world. Ezechial 44 refers to the door that is closed and will not be opened. Here Mary is like Jerusalem and its gate for the Messiah. In contrast, the mortal woman's vagina is, in the words of Tertullian, "the gateway of the devil." The door metaphor remains, then, with differing valences. Eliade's *Encyclopedia* uses this common (and contradictory) trope as well: virgin birth, we read, "is the story of divinity entering the human experience by the only doorway available to it" (273). I merely note, without unpacking, this astonishing assertion.

vinced: "Woe for my wickedness and my unbelief; for I have tempted the living God; and behold my hand falls away from me, consumed by fire!" Thus, the "evidence" for Mary's virginity is not an intact hymen but the miracle of punishing disbelief. It is a displacement from a miraculous anatomical claim (Mary's virginity before, during, and after the birth of Jesus) to the wrath of a God who smites doubters.

The story could also be read, however, in the tradition of the averted gaze in the presence of divinity—a constant in Western traditions. After all, Thomas doubts and is allowed to see and to touch the wounds of Jesus. But Salome is seeking medical proof in a different register: that of faith. My point is that the trope of the averted glance concomitantly engages the notion of ocular transgression, of seeing what is meant to remain hidden or meant to remain in a separate register. When understood as an ethics of the body, as a bodily proof of faith, virginity as a concept becomes enmeshed in the register of religion and thus in that of ocular transgression. Probing is bad enough, as Buffon notes, but looking directly at the virgin's body for proof engages two taboos. The first is the mixture of medical register with that of faith, or of the religious: the midwife "sees" with the eyes of faith because she must avert her eyes; Salome looks with the eyes of reason. It is a conflict of registers to which we will return. A taboo, it should be remembered, is precisely the impurity or scandal that results from the forbidden combination of willfully segregated elements.

The second taboo is more difficult to address. It is the one that Buffon almost unconsciously respects (and even fears) when he speaks of violating the secrets of nature. Virginity for Buffon is a "purity of the heart" that no amount of probing can detect. Thus, peering into the vagina of a virgin is a transgression, but one whose economy is ocular: the gaze sees what is meant to remain hidden.[31] Such a transgression is not limited to virgins (although it is gendered feminine), for it seems also to have to do with seeing the origin—of nature or of the species. Seeing the source of life can animate the taboo, for it is perhaps too close to death or to the limits of subjectivity. In the case of virgins, Buffon argues that the taboo is constant. In the case of Eurydice, a young bride at her death, the feminine "mystery of nature" is combined with the attempt to hypostatize death,

[31] Such a notion is quite similar to Freud's idea of the "navel of the dream"—that part which is incomprehensible and to which the dreamer remains blind.

which is conceptually identical with viewing the subject's origin. "Birth and death," writes Bakhtin, "are the gaping jaws of the earth and the mother's open womb."[32]

To give another example: One could argue that, contrary to Freud's reading, Oedipus did not displace his punishment from the penis to the eyes. Rather, he punished the proper organs, for his eyes had seen the hidden parts, as it were, of his own origins. On one level, Jocasta is a sexual being; a mere woman. But on a deeper, literal, level, her vagina is Oedipus' very source, as it were—the locus and origins of his being. There is then (again) a mixture of registers: that which is in place as social (the incest taboo), and that which is more elusive and yet powerful: mystery (the taboo of looking directly at origins). So, too, Orpheus, in looking at Eurydice, mixes the registers of the living and the dead and, more to the point, *looks at* death with the eyes of the living. Thus, the futurity of death, in Levinas's terms, is as if annulled in Orpheus's glance. The result is that the transgression becomes the necessary scandal allowing a return to order.[33] Like the stories of Oedipus and the skeptic Salome, that of Orpheus shows the desire to overcome taboo and the punishment that follows: the registers are returned to their proper places, and purity is restored. Moreover, in all three stories, the place of transgression is written on the body of a woman. At play here as well, then, is the secondary economy in which woman resides—her anatomical as well as original inferiority—and the simultaneous Western trope of woman as the site of truth. In a sense, then, woman embodies a taboo, for her anatomical register and her more metaphysical one, both marked by hiding or fleeing from the light (of knowledge, of scrutiny), nevertheless put two contradictory concepts at odds: inferiority, even abomination, and truth, or *aletheia*.

And death. The semiology of feminine virginity is that it means both incompleteness in a feminine economy of secondariness and *aletheia*, or the possibility of the truth in an economy of mystery, which is what re-

32 Mikhail Bakhtin, *Rabelais and His World* (Cambridge, Mass., 1968), trans. Helene Iswolsky, 352.

33 I wish here clearly to separate myself from René Girard's view that a scapegoat is necessary in order for the social order to be restored. I am talking about a mixture of registers that becomes a transgression, in turn restoring the purity or segregation of incommensurate registers. There is no personalized scapegoat, in the Girardian sense, since the transgression itself becomes, paradoxically, an affirmation of the taboo.

lates virginity to death. As Michel Foucault puts it, "Unlike other interdictions, sexual interdictions are constantly connected with the obligation to tell the truth."[34] In its essence as mutually exclusive registers, then, virginity is by definition shrouded in the mystery of the hiddenness of truth, of the sacred; it is as well the interdiction of sexuality with the concomitant abomination of a perpetual *in potentia* (as woman, as subject). This is the insight of Freud's essay on the matter, although (as so often with him) it is never fully acknowledged even as it is being discovered. The mystery of Joan of Arc, as we shall see, is that she enacts the double-edged aspect of virginity—what Freud called the "primal ambivalence in determining the formation of taboo."[35]

Freud begins his essay on virginity with his usual disclaimer: "Few details of the sexual life of primitive peoples are so alien to our own feelings as their estimate of virginity, the state in a woman of being untouched" (193). A few pages later, however, he admits that the taboo of virginity "has not died out in our civilized existence. It is known to the popular mind and writers have on occasion made use of this material" (206). Like the "Uncanny" essay, Freud's study of virginity rests on the antithetical meaning of a primal notion. And like the earlier essay, this one, too, alternates between disclaiming any understanding of such a "primitive" notion as prizing virginity and finding numerous examples in modern literature that display that notion, present to this day "in the popular mind."

The work he had recently done on taboo informs Freud's definition of a virgin as "the state in a woman of being untouched [*Unberührheit*]." Nevertheless, in a significant passage he notes: "Wherever primitive man has set up a taboo he fears some danger and it cannot be disputed that a generalized dread of women is expressed in all these rules of avoidance" (198).

"Dread [*Scheu*] of women" translates, in Freud's essay, into metaphors of light and dark, thus returning us to the tropes mentioned earlier in this chapter. The general taboo of women, he writes, "throws no light

---

34 Michel Foucault, *Technologies of the Self: A Seminar with Michel Foucault*, ed. H. Putnam (Amherst, Mass., 1988), 16.

35 "The Taboo of Virginity," in *The Standard Edition of the Complete Psychological Works of Sigmund Freud*, 24 vols., ed. and trans. James Strachey (London, 1953–74), 11: 200.

[*wirft kein Licht*]" on rules concerning sex acts with a virgin. Many "take flight" from a first sexual experience, but by certain pathological cases, "light is thrown on the riddle of female frigidity" [*ein Licht auf das Rätsel der weiblichen Frigidität werfen*]. Additionally, "The general taboo of women throws no light on the particular rules concerning the first sexual act with a virgin." He admits, "[W]e have not got beyond the first two explanations, based on horror of blood and fear of first occurrences, and even these, we must point out, do not touch the core of the taboo in question" (199).

The taboo of virginity, then, like the core, remains in the dark, and the "riddle" of femininity, like woman, remains intact. Freud concludes that the defloration of a woman in preparation for the husband is to save the latter the hostility that the woman will visit upon him for violating her maidenhead. But what remains is the virgin as flight from the light and as a potential danger signaling the fearful possibility of "first occurrences"—a first occurrence that is conceptually linked to death, since it too annuls an eternal futurity. Hence, the virgin occupies that place that is untouchable.[36]

But for reasons I have attempted to put forward here, the virgin resists precisely the attempt to make death *thinkable*. And yet, writes Maurice Blanchot, "It is a trait of modern man to render death thinkable." He continues:

> [T]he decision to be without being is the same possibility of death. The three systems of thought [*pensées*] which try to attest to this decision and which, because of this, seem most helpful in illuminating the destiny of modern man (in spite of the movements which oppose them) are those of Hegel, Nietzsche, and Heidegger. All three strain to make death possible.[37]

---

[36] Such a first occurrence should not be confused with Derrida's notion of "one time only," which he links to such an event as circumcision and dating. Circumcision, a "one and only time," is an event that cannot be reversed. This is true as well in the case of deflowering (or an individual death). Jerome, for example, writes to Eustochium, "though God can do all things, he cannot raise up a virgin when she has fallen." But I am speaking here of a first occurrence as a site of origin: the direct confrontation with either inception or death. See Jacques Derrida, "Shibboleth," in *Midrash and Literature*, ed. Geoffrey H. Hartman and Sanford Budick (New Haven, Conn., 1986), 307–47.

[37] Maurice Blanchot, *L'Espace littéraire* (Paris, 1955), 115; my translation.

Perhaps, then, Levinas (his contemporaneity with Blanchot notwithstanding), in figuring death as an unimaginable futurity, is marking the limit between a "modernist" view of death as possible and a "postmodern" approach to death as that which annihilates being (even being as nonbeing, *non-être*) and thus remains an impossible futurity. Perhaps, again, this is one of the places where we can trace the shift, in postmodernist theory, from technology to mystery and from mind against body to mind *as* body (and, in the case of Levinas and Jabès, for example, from the Greeks to the Jews). Perhaps, finally, such a shift in the approach to death explains the fascination with female virginity as a mystery. For as an ethics of the body, virginity combines conceptualization (purity of the heart) with embodiment, the latter an aspect that is singularly missing from Western mysticism.

Moreover, the female virgin, in her status as near woman and as pure, stands in contradiction, as I have noted, to the cultural subtexts in the West of woman as lesser, as filth, and so on. Because, to reiterate an earlier point, the virgin is woman *in potentia,* she not only describes the lack of female subjectivity as a hypostatized possibility in the West; she also suggests the limits of subjectivity itself. Buffon writes of virginity in girls: "This variance of opinions on a fact which depends upon simple inspection proves that men have wanted to find in nature what was merely in their imaginations." The hymen, he continues, does not exist. Anatomy leaves us with "a total uncertainty concerning the existence of this membrane" (422). The hymen, still largely insisted on to this day as a proof of virginity, is for Buffon a mirage of male medical phantasy. "Nothing is more of an illusion," he writes, "than the prejudices of men on this matter, and nothing more uncertain than these so-called signs of the body's virginity" (426).[38]

Buffon had good reason to be impatient with his predecessors. In 1610, for example, a book on virginity appeared by Heinrich Kornmann, a German lawyer. His explanations of virginity are rife with magic and superstition. His "scientific" arguments rest on Pliny, Isidore of Seville, and Bartholomaeus Anglicus to maintain, among other things, that a scorpion injures a virgin far more than it does other women.[39] He refers to astrol-

---

[38] See Sissa's discussion of this passage from Buffon, with which she ends her own study of virginity *(Le Corps virginal)*.

[39] *De virginitate* (1610) in *Opera curiosa*, Frankfurt edition (1694, col. B 156.4 K843), 139–40, 274.

ogy and believes that sitting on a certain root will break the hymen. A tree will be damaged if a virgin plucks its first fruits, but the idea that a virgin must throw her nightgown into a fire after her first menstruation is mere "superstition" (137).

Kornmann's work is but one among many just before the Enlightenment that include magic, astrology, and the "Mysteries of Nature" to define virginity.[40] Buffon, of course, rejects all such notions and proceeds by what he views as a reasoned discourse and logical, provable conclusions. If the hymen cannot be ascertained physically, it does not exist.

But the rationalist Buffon is finally not so far away from his intellectual ancestors as it might seem. For him virginity is a construct impossible to ascertain but powerful and essential to claim, as well as profoundly mysterious. Such is the case in an astonishing array of cultural and religious contexts.[41] Thus, it is not only the virgin who holds the place of a certain ambiguity in the social and sacred semiology; female virginity itself is ambiguous as a concept, since it is alternatively a state of bodily or moral purity, or both. Just as the Mirror Stage in Lacan simultaneously inaugurates the *méconnaissance* of the split subject and the image of wholeness, virginity is alternatively used to mean wholeness and purity, on the one hand, and a scandal or aberration, on the other. It is either nature's holiest temple or something that damages nature (the tree whose fruit is plucked by a virgin dies).

Although the hymen is at best anatomically difficult to determine, it seems conceptually to be a constant that "helps" in delimiting gender; in

---

40 For a full discussion of the history of such works as Kornmann's, see Lynn Thorndike, *A History of Magic and Experimental Science*, vol. 7, *The Seventeenth Century* (New York, 1958).

41 For further reading on the Jewish aspects of virginity, see, for example, Barkai, *A History of Jewish Gynaecological Texts;* Alain Goldschläger, "Le Corps dans la Judéïté" (unpublished manuscript); Tikva Frymer-Kensky, "Virginity in the Bible," in *Gender and Law in the Hebrew Bible and the Ancient Near East*, ed. Victor H. Matthews, Bernard M. Levinson, and Tikva Frymer-Kensky (Sheffield, England, 1998); *Journal for the Study of the Old Testament*, Supplement Series 262 ; H. Eiberg-Schwartz, *The Savage in Judaism* (Bloomington, Ill., 1990), chap. 7ff.; David Biale, "From Intercourse to Discourse," paper given at the Center for Hermeneutical Studies (Berkeley, Calif., 1992); and Judith Romney Wagner, *Chattel or Person? The Status of Women in the Mishnah* (New York, 1988), 19ff. See also "Virgins, Virginity," in *Encyclopaedia Judaica*, ed. Cecil Roth and Geoffrey Wigoden (New York, 1971–82), 16: 160–62.

particular, it demarcates the difference inscribed in womanhood. Even more abstractly, the hymen serves to articulate not only gender distinction from a masculinist perspective but again a *Nicht-Ich* of incompleteness to the (male) notion of subjectivity itself. In the secular tradition, from Descartes to Husserl, writes Foucault, "knowledge of the self (the thinking subject) takes on an ever-increasing importance as the first step in the theory of knowledge."[42] This is the step from which modern texts seem to be backing away. The so-called postmodern dismantling of the subject is the logical corollary of an age that puts subjectivity into question without wishing to endanger the male subject. For the latter to continue, femininity must remain as a riddle, as obscure. My insistence on female virginity as a notion unseen, and yet minutely described, in the West is for the purpose of considering the averted gaze, which, like the fleeting thought of death, permits the illusion of the subject to persist unimpugned.

It is this heavily baggaged notion of virginity, then, that both empowered Joan of Arc and, ultimately, led to her condemnation and murder.

---

[42] Foucault, *Technologies of the Self*, 22.

CHAPTER THREE

PROFESSIONS OF VIRGINITY

What is it we combat in Christianity? That it wants to break the strong, that it wants to discourage their courage, exploit their bad hours and their occasional weariness, convert their proud assurance into unease and distress of conscience, that it knows how to poison and sicken the noble instincts until their strength their will to power turns backward, against itself—until the strong perish through orgies of self-contempt and self-abuse: that gruesome way of perishing of which Pascal provides the most famous example.

—Nietzsche, *The Will to Power*

Religion without morality is superstition.

—Kant

FOR SIMONE WEIL, reading is an activity that poses an ethical dilemma, one that engages the risk of "a wrong reading of justice." What love of justice, she asks, can guarantee against a bad reading? Joan of Arc is Weil's example: "Those who declaim about her today," she writes, "would nearly all have condemned her. Moreover, her judges did not condemn the saint, the virgin, and so forth, but the witch, the heretic, and so forth." Wrong readings for Weil stem from "public opinion, the passions." People read in the story of Joan of Arc what contemporary public opinion dictates. "But it has been uncertain."[1] Uncertain indeed. Although we know more about Joan of Arc than we do about most historical figures because of the trial transcripts, the events and dialogue recorded have opened as wide a field of interpreting justice as for a figure about whom we know much less (Vercingétorix, for example, or the historical Jesus).

---

1 Simone Weil, *Gravity and Grace,* trans. Emma Craufurd (London, 1992), 122.

As Benjamin suggests, blasting a specific life out of the era is for the purpose of having a revolutionary chance in the fight for the oppressed past. In this case, the oppressed past is not only that of Joan of Arc herself but also the way that courage and strength, to return to Nietzsche's words, have been particularly occluded in the figuring of female subjectivity in the West. Joan turned to virginity as a way of empowering her discourse and position; as a way of being *heard.*

Certainly, Joan did not know of the Christian tradition in any scholarly sense. To begin with, she was illiterate and never took catechism; what very little she knew about religion she learned from her mother, which was a few prayers. Not until the Renaissance, as Maclean points out, are lay women actually urged to *read* the Bible.[2] Johan Huizinga puts it bluntly: "in her faith Joan of Arc was in the full sense of the word a primitive."[3] Whatever the "full sense" of the word might be, "primitive" has largely left our vocabulary, despite the attempt by Douglas to preserve it.[4] What Huizinga means, however, is clear from the context of his essay: Joan was possessed of what he calls a *sancta simplicitas:* a simplicity so ignorant of "book learning" that she did not know the difference between the Church Militant and the Church Triumphant, for example, even though her interrogators assumed this distinction to determine her guilt at her trial. It is the way Christianity informs the culture in a broader sense in fifteenth-century France that makes the choice of virginity for Joan both natural and crucial to her task.

It is precisely because she cannot read, and cannot engage in the debates of scholasticism and doctrine, that we are able to get a sense of how embedded the Christian notion of virginity had become in the social and cultural Catholicism of Joan's century. The treatises on virginity, of course, were written over one thousand years earlier by the Church fa-

---

2 Ian Maclean, *Renaissance Notions of Women* (Cambridge, 1980), 20.

3 "Bernard Shaw's Saint," in *Men and Ideas: History, the Middle Ages, the Renaissance* (Cleveland, Ohio, 1965), 237.

4 For example: "Finally we should revive the question of whether the word 'primitive' should be abandoned. I hope not" (112). Or: "I suspect that our professional delicacy in avoiding the term 'primitive' is the product of secret convictions of superiority" (91). *Purity and Danger: An Analysis of Concepts of Pollution and Taboo* (London, 1970). For a critique of the term *primitive,* see Claude Lévi-Strauss, *Structural Anthropology: Volume II,* trans. Monique Layton (Chicago, 1983). Laplanche, as noted previously, makes comfortable use of the word.

thers (Gregory of Nyssa, Chrysostom, Ambrose, Jerome, and late Augustine)—of whom Joan had never heard but whose influence through manifestos on virginity were to dominate her life.[5] From the second to the fourth centuries, as we have already noted, the foundations of the virginity issue were laid, such that the decision to "choose" virginity could not have been altered, given Joan's need to convince.

The medical view of virginity as an aberration would seem to counter the early Church's call for chastity as the purest state to be attained by the pious. But in many ways, these two views join paths. The Church fathers, by insisting on virginity, insist as well on the sacrifice of the body to Christ. In other words, it is *because* virginity is an aberration, and even a lethal one, for the body that virginity is all the more holy and set apart in its particular Christian valence. Augustine, for whom virginity is essentially integrity of the flesh, even claims that a ruptured hymen is unimportant, because the body remains whole and sacred in the life of piety:

> The body is not holy just because its parts are intact, or because they have not undergone any handling. Those parts may suffer violent injury by accidents of various kinds, and sometimes doctors seeking to effect a cure may employ treatment with distressing visible effects. During a manual examination of a virgin a midwife destroyed her maidenhead, whether by malice, or clumsiness, or accident. I do not suppose that anyone would be stupid enough to imagine that the virgin lost anything of bodily chastity, even though the integrity of that part had been destroyed.[6]

---

5 On the specific subject of women and virginity with respect to Christianity, see, among others, Kate Cooper, *The Virgin and the Bride: Idealized Womanhood in Late Antiquity* (Cambridge, Mass., 1996) especially the chapter "An Angel in the House." See also Susanna Elm, *"Virgins of God": The Making of Asceticism in Late Antiquity* (Oxford, 1994); John Bugge, *Virginitas: An Essay in the History of a Medieval Ideal* (The Hague, 1975); Aline Rousselle, *Porneia: De la Maîtrise du corps à la privation sensorielle II–IV siècles de l'ère chrétienne* (Paris, 1983); Grace M. Jantzen, *Power, Gender and Christian Mysticism* (Cambridge, 1995); Peter Brown, *The Body and Society;* as well as his "The Notion of Virginity in the Early Church," in *Christian Spirituality: Origins to the Twelfth Century,* ed. Bernard McGinn, John Meyendorff, and Jean Leclercq (New York, 1985), 427–43; and Giulia Sissa, *Le Corps virginal: La Virginité féminine en Grèce ancienne* (Paris, 1987) (again, the English edition, to which I will be referring, is *Greek Virginity,* trans. Arthur Goldhammer [Cambridge, Mass., 1990]).

6 Augustine, *Concerning the City of God against the Pagans,* I: chap. 19, trans. Henry Bettenson (London, 1972), 29.

How, asks Sissa, who cites this passage, are we to interpret "integrity" that a clumsy hand can destroy? Clearly, for Augustine the hymen exists but is insufficient for establishing virginity or even for abolishing it. Integrity here must be read as the body of the pious equating holiness, despite what other less pious beings visit upon it. Doctors can produce "distressing *visible* effects," but they cannot destroy genuine virginity. There is no outrage here as expressed by Buffon that to establish virginity is to violate it. There are "accidents of various kinds," but they are, precisely, accidents, which change nothing in the purity of heart invisible to the sensorial eye. Yet the conclusion is the same: whether virginity is a mystery of nature to be respected, as in Buffon, or whether it is a holy state which the body does not always echo, as in Augustine, in both cases, virginity is invisible and partakes of mystery.

If virgins were frequently reminded, in the great treatises on virginity from the early Church, that physical integrity was not enough without other virtues, they were equally reassured that the virtuous need not fear physical imperfection or impairment; their virtue withstands, as does their virginity, any clumsy or evil hand. Once again, the hymen does not reign as evidence. More important, Aristotle's claim that the female of the species is an incomplete version of the male, and the supporting evidence in Genesis (1:26–27 and 2:22–23), are countermanded by the Christian idea of holy virginity.[7] Aquinas had elided Genesis and Aristotle to claim that woman is defective "only as regards nature in the individual." Since procreation is in the plan of God, "when he established nature, he brought into being not only the male but the female too."[8] Woman was thus the imperfect necessity of a perfect plan. But the earlier treatises on virginity, in arguing for a life of purity in body and mind for

---

7 Carol Delaney has argued that Aristotle's notion of monogenesis (that the embryo is contained *in toto* in the sperm), combined with monotheism, resulted in a rigid patriarchy that kept a tight control on women. While this is a fascinating hypothesis, it does not explain cultures in which there is no belief in monogenesis or in monotheism, and virginity is nonetheless prized (for example, India). See Delaney, "Seeds of Honor, Fields of Shame," in *Honor and Shame and the Unity of the Mediterranean*, ed. David Gilmore (Washington, D.C., 1987), special publication of the American Anthropological Association, no. 22.

8 *Summa Theologica*, trans. Timothy S. MacDermott (New York, 1991), first part, question 92; answer to objection 1, whether woman should have been made in the first production of things. Woman is defective "only as regards nature in the individual."

women, apparently and unexpectedly seem to circumvent the notion of woman as incomplete. They seem to propose that through a life of abstinence, fasting, and prayer, the (anomalous) possibility exists for woman to achieve a state of wholeness and perfection. As Gregory of Nyssa phrases it, Christian virginity will save a pious woman from nature, the very realm to which Aristotle, Genesis and Christian interpretations of "normal" womanhood relegate her: "the profession of virginity is an art and a science of divine life, teaching those who live in flesh to become like incorporeal nature."[9] Virginity goes against nature, and, given that nature is temptation, virginity is to be admired—especially in a woman who, in her ability to resist temptation, specifically transcends the parameters which traditionally delimit and define her sex. The paradox of Christian virginity for women is then twofold: it allows a transcendence of body even as it depends largely on a denial of bodily drives for its attainment (thus necessitating a constant vigilance on and obsession with the body), and it promises a purity and wholeness to woman in direct contradiction to her innately fallen and incomplete state.

As we have seen, however, this promised equality in the afterlife becomes the reward of eternal maleness as compensation for having endured life as a woman, even if a pious one. Unsurprisingly, then, female Christian virginity results in the defeminization of the pious woman in question. Jesus' remark in the apocryphal Gospel of Thomas is worth repeating here: "Every woman who makes herself male will enter the Kingdom of Heaven." This is in response, it will be recalled, to Simon Peter, who had said, "Let Mary go out from among us, because women are not worthy of the Life." Women, in other words, cannot live a life (Life) touched by spirit because of their sex. The solution is to reward female chastity with the gift of a male soul, which can then live the Life, or spirit.

Virgins made themselves "male" on Earth while they waited for heavenly confirmation. Fourth-century communities of Christian ascetics consisted of both genders, the argument being, as one scholar puts it, "if there is neither male nor female in Jesus Christ, then the symbiosis of male and female ascetics represents the highest form of ascetic perfec-

9 *Grégoire de Nysse, Traité de la virginité*, ed. Michel Aubineau (Paris, 1966), 333; my translation. The early Christian approach to the body is not, of course, monolithic. Paul, for example, as Daniel Boyarin has shown, does not reject the body. See Boyarin, *A Radical Jew: Paul and the Politics of Identity* (Berkeley, Calif., 1994), 59.

tion."[10] The contradiction is constant in fourth-century writings: there is neither male nor female in Jesus; it is all Spirit, which is, finally, male. While such a notion of "maleness" was to turn inward after the fourth century, so that only the soul of an ascetic woman could "become male," female virginity retains, in the Christian tradition, the idea of a masculine or at least genderless state (sexless, to reiterate, can be generally glossed as male). It is perhaps for this reason that Joan of Arc's cross-dressing caused little initial shock among her followers, although it was to be used later as a major reason for executing her.[11]

In present-day Catholic dictionaries (for example, *Sacramentum Mundi*), virginity is an eschatological ideal that is significantly explained as attainable "for all mankind equally, but not for all in the same way." Frequently, these dictionaries cite Jesus' remark (Matt. 22:30): "At the resurrection men and women do not marry; no, they are like the angels in heaven." In Revelations, those who follow Jesus are depicted as virgins who are, explicitly, "men who did not defile themselves with women, for they have kept themselves chaste" (14:4). Paul, who echoes this view, saw virginity as a way of avoiding women: "It is a good thing for a man to

---

10 Elm, *"Virgins of God,"* ix. See also Elizabeth A. Castelli, "'I Will Make Mary Male': Pieties of the Body and Gender Transformation of Christian Women in Late Antiquity," in *Body Guards: The Cultural Politics of Gender Ambiguity,* ed. Julia Epstein and Kristina Straub (New York, 1991).

11 The body of women, however, has a mixed status in the late medieval period. On the one hand, it is always inferior to maleness (which is consistently "reason"). On the other hand, as Caroline Walker Bynum has argued, women in the late medieval period are frequently very body identified. Fasting, as has been amply noted, can cause the diminishing (or disappearance) of certain feminine sexual attributes (such as menstruation). In this way, the transformation of female flesh can be "transfigured" into a mimesis of Christ's suffering on the cross. Such forms of hyperembodiment (stigmata and visions being other famous examples) can actually legitimize the texts of some female mystical writers. See Bynum, *Holy Feast and Holy Fast: The Religious Significance of Food to Medieval Women* (Berkeley, Calif., 1987). Although Bynum argues that this practice of faith through the female body is a move toward Christ's humanity, I would reiterate that female flesh is seen as successfully redeemed when it achieves a similarity to the body of Christ. While it may be true, as Bynum notes, that in the twelfth and thirteenth centuries women were more apt to "somatize religious experience and to write in intensely bodily metaphors," embodiment itself aims to achieve a departure from the sexed aspect of the feminine, or at least to attempt an approximation of the masculine body. *Mutatis mutandis:* we are back to making Mary male. See Bynum, *Fragmentation and Redemption: Essays on Gender and the Human Body in Medieval Religion* (New York, 1991), 194.

have nothing to do with a woman" (I Cor. 7:1). It is he who best articulates the divided mind: a married person will think first of pleasing his or her spouse; a Christian who has taken vows of chastity thinks only of pleasing God. Carnality gets in the way of contemplation. This theme, as it is first argued by Paul, will be assumed, and indeed reiterated, by all later Christian texts on the subject of virginity. Virginity is a virtue that allows women an equality "but not in the same way."

As has always been clear, the word *nature* (a term that is at best fluid and mostly prejudicial when applied to humans, especially women) is enlisted well before Aristotle to explain the innate inferiority of women.[12] The Church has collaborated vigorously in this agenda. An initially surprising passage in Horkheimer and Adorno, for example, automatically links the gendered notion of nature with the role of the Church. They begin by stating what seems to be the obvious:

> For millennia men dreamed of acquiring absolute mastery over nature, of converting the cosmos into one immense hunting-ground. It was to this that the idea of man was geared in a male-dominated society. This was the significance of reason, his proudest boast. Woman was weaker and smaller. Between her and man there was a difference she could not bridge— a difference imposed by nature, the most humiliating that can exist in a male-dominated society. Where the mastery of nature is the true goal, biological inferiority remains a glaring stigma, the weakness imprinted by nature as a key stimulus to aggression.[13]

---

[12] On the subject of women and nature, see Carolyn Merchant's *The Death of Nature: Women, Ecology and the Scientific Revolution* (San Francisco, 1989).

[13] Max Horkheimer and Theodor W. Adorno, *Dialectic of Enlightenment* (New York, 1998), 248. It should be added that Marx, too, sexualizes the relation of "man" to nature. In the "Economic and Philosophic Manuscripts of 1844" we read: "The direct, natural, and necessary relation of person to person is the *relation of man to woman*. In this *natural* relationship of the sexes man's relation to nature is immediately his relation to man, just as his relation to man is immediately his relation to nature—his own *natural* function. In this relationship, therefore, is *sensuously manifested*, reduced to an observable *fact*, the extent to which human essence has become nature to man, or to which nature has to him become the human essence of man." *The Marx-Engels Reader*, ed. Robert C. Tucker (New York, 1972), 83.

The relation of man to woman is for Marx "the most natural," but that relation quickly

The critique here is that physical weakness elicits misogyny and victimization. The authors do not question, however, how strongly cultural a construct the notion of "biological inferiority" might be, based as it is on a sweeping premise of feminine "weakness." Nor do they consider that virginity, which all the Church fathers figure as proof of biological and spiritual strength, might pose a rupture in this rhetoric of feminine weakness. The controls imposed on women in the late Middle Ages, both by the Church and by social codes, may in fact serve to mask the feared potency of "woman" rather than function, as they did officially, as a response to inferiority.

Significantly, Horkheimer and Adorno then move immediately to the Church:

> The Church, which throughout the ages has missed scarcely an opportunity of exerting its telling influence on popular institutions—whether in slavery, crusades, or plain pogroms—has sided, despite the Ave Maria, with Plato's assessment of woman. The image of the Mother of God stricken with sorrow was merely a sop to the last traces of the matriarchate. The Church set the seal of its authority on that very doctrine of female inferiority which that same image was intended to redeem.

They add that the witch trials "served at once to celebrate and to confirm the triumph of male society over prehistoric matriarchal and mimetic stages of development" (ibid.). Political powerlessness (as in the case of slaves and Jews) is here conflated with a weakness imposed by gender. The consequences of being a strong woman is, finally, a contradiction in terms, even in the mariology that the Church professes and simultaneously represses. Moreover, strength in a woman is in fact condemned a priori, since it is figured as going against "nature" and thus dangerous.[14] On the one hand, there is the Christian reverence for virginity—pre-

---

and bizarrely becomes that of man to man here. The linguistic "man" for human being elides the mastery of nature into the relation between the sexes but simultaneously turns the whole "natural" enterprise into the masculine.

[14] It is worth noting that Christine de Pizan in *Livre de la cité des dames* (1405) reverses the use of "nature." At the opening of the book, she chastises herself for having believed the male myth of woman, when she herself has personally and experientially met "natural woman" *(femme naturelle)* and should therefore have known better.

cisely *because,* as we have seen, it goes against nature and is therefore to be admired as a proof of fortitude against (given the female's traditional vulnerability in the face of temptation) nearly insurmountable instincts.[15] But the subtext, which counters this official view, is that what goes against nature can always turn monstrous, and what is weak needs constant surveillance to be protected from its own, "natural" inclinations and drives. Beneath the floral prose of the early treatises on virginity lies this conflict: the argument is to lull women into virginity and a life for Christ because they will be free from the burdens of motherhood, marriage, and life as chattel. At the same time, however, a simultaneously menacing tone reminds women that they must be closely supervised, controlled, and regulated by Church authority. Otherwise, as Joseph de Maistre points out, in a passage cited by Horkheimer and Adorno (who refer to him as "a true son of the Church if ever there was one"), infamy and chaos will reign:

> We have only to weaken in some degree the influence of divine Law in a Christian country by countenancing the freedom of women that stemmed from it, to see freedom, noble and moving though it be, degenerating soon enough into utter shamelessness. Women would become the baneful instruments of a general decline which would not be long in infecting the vital organs of the State.[16]

Weakness here applies to divine law if it is not vigilantly maintained. Far from being weak themselves here, "women" in a weakened system of law become the deadly virus which will quickly "infect the vital organs of the State." Such contamination must be contained by a vigorous preservation of the law. Women are mentioned in the same breath as slaves, Jews, and the infidel (not an uncommon catalog) by Horkheimer and Adorno as well as by Maistre. These are the subalterns who, one senses, can rise in

---

15 One example among many will suffice: "Since virginity," writes Gregory of Nyssa, "goes as it were against nature, it would be superfluous to take the trouble to write an encouraging and stimulating talk on marriage, putting at the forefront its most difficult defender—I mean voluptuousness." *Traité de la virginité,* 351.

16 *Eclaircissement sur les sacrifices,* in *Oeuvres* (Lyon, 1892), 5: 322; cited in *Dialectic of Enlightenment,* 248. It should be added that Maistre's conservative philosophy passionately upholds Church and monarchy and that one of his major works is a justification (if regretful one) of the Spanish Inquisition.

mutiny at any moment if left unfettered or unchecked. "Weakness," whether understood as mental, social, biological, or racial (to name a few), becomes the justification for strict hegemonic control. The laws—whether "divine" or civil—are as penitentiaries ensuring the bridling of such menacing, atavistic power. Similarly, military stratagems surround the potential enemies of order, whose deviant thoughts and nature pose a danger to the state. Germ warfare is the metaphor setting limits on what is paradoxically figured as the enemy's "weakness." Horkheimer and Adorno, whom I purposely juxtapose to Maistre's reactionary rhetoric, are not immune to such possible contamination themselves. With their reliance on weakness as a term for alterity, even when they decry the cruelty of the dominant culture in subjugating the vulnerable, their gesture toward Maistre's text (which they scornfully cite as an unenlightened example of misogyny) shows that they are finally not as far from his assumptions as they suppose. Perhaps Gregory of Nyssa was more pragmatic. It is the weak, he writes in his treatise on virginity, who benefit most from virginity: "That is why we believe that weaker people will profit in taking refuge in virginity as in a secure citadel, in avoiding stirring up temptations against themselves by descending into the fatal wheels grinding in this life, in attacking 'those who do combat against the law of our reason' [diabolical forces] by means of the flesh's passions, and in running the risk of worrying, not about the boundaries of a plot of land or the loss of material goods, but about the hope which comes before everything" (*Grégoire de Nysse,* 367). Here Nyssa unyokes weakness from gender, arguing that the best way of maintaining virginity for the weak is to avoid the world altogether. The high citadel, from which the temptations are kept far below, represses carnality through isolation. Thus, the "vital organs" to be preserved are those of the soul, not the state; the danger is human passion, not women. More realistic and generous, if more personally austere than Maistre, Nyssa situates weakness in all human beings.

Indeed, as Marina Warner notes succinctly, given that the Church's protestation of equality of the sexes before God have not been borne out historically, "among the stratagems its women members have used to overcome deep-seated prejudice have been virginity—the renunciation of sexual relations—and transvestitism—the renunciation of sexual identity."[17] This was a stratagem that Joan of Arc sensed and openly, vo-

[17] Marina Warner, *Joan of Arc: The Image of Female Heroism* (New York, 1981), 148.

cally used; it was also a renunciation that she was more than willing to perform. (And it was no doubt the reason that two of her voices eventually identified themselves as early Christian *virgin* martyrs). But such a renunciation requires first a proof of virginity. The difference between the witch and the virgin is easily and dangerously elided in this tradition, so that the demonstration of "purity" becomes critical. We are back to the body as evidence.

The Church fathers did believe in the maidenhead, that membrane that was not, as we have noted, universally accepted in ancient medicine. But it alone did not serve for them as sufficient proof of virginity. The membrane itself, or *panniculus* (scrap of clothing or rag in Latin), was probably officially incorporated into Western medicine through Arabic medical sources. Translations of Arabic texts, it has been recently argued, account for European medical descriptions of the hymen beginning in the eleventh century: "If we move to the medieval period, we find evidence that the hymen was incorporated into western anatomical understanding by way of Arabic medical sources. . . . The translations from the Arabs appear to be the source for medieval Latin understanding of the hymen."[18] This influence begins what was to become a marked change: the hymen becomes increasingly important, indeed crucial. By the thirteenth century in the West, in a writer like Albertus Magnus, the description of the womb of virgins closely follows the Arab texts. Lastique and Lemay claim that this becomes a pattern in medical texts. Thus, the medical "accident" described by Augustine becomes, by the late Middle Ages, far more serious. The hymen is medical evidence of virginity; its absence—whether by a clumsy hand, rape, or ardor—proof of the loss of maidenhead.[19] Even the author of *Hali Meidenhad,* a contemporary of Magnus, argues that the loss of virginity is irrevocable. His comments on the subject are rhapsodic:

> Maidenhood is that treasure that, if it be once lost, will never again be found. Maidenhood is the bloom that, if it be once fully cut off,

---

[18] "A Medieval Physician's Guide to Virginity," in ed. *Sex in the Middle Ages: A Book of Essays,* Joyce E. Salisbury (New York, 1991), 59–60. See also Salisbury's extensive bibliography, *Medieval Sexuality: A Research Guide* (New York, 1990). For an excellent overview of virginity in the middle ages, see Bugge, *Virginitas.*

[19] As recently as November 1998, a medical journal refers to the hymen only in terms of its "elasticity" in relation to maturation, but it adds, "Psychosocially, it is unethical and in-

> never again sprouteth up; but though it wither some time with various thoughts, it may grow green again nevertheless. Maidenhood is the star that, if it be once gone out of the east adown to the west, never again ariseth. Maidenhood is the one gift granted thee from heaven: if ever thou put it away once, never shalt thou recover such another; for maidenhood is queen of heaven, and the redemption of the world, by which we are saved. Tis a virtue above all virtues, and to Christ the most acceptable of all. . . . Hence it is a loss that is beyond recovery.[20]

Here then, one hundred years before Joan's birth, is a thirteenth-century version of Gregory of Nyssa. The horrors of marriage and childbirth are similarly adumbrated, and the glory of virginity is likened to the tower of Zion, the virgin Mary (queen of heaven), the star of the East, the flower of all flowers, and so on. The flower can be "wilted" by sinful thoughts, yet that can be rectified through repentance: it will grow green again.[21]

---

appropriate to place dilators of differing circumference into the vaginal orifices of peripubertal girls in order to determine the degree of hymenal stretch." This is essentially the same point made by Buffon, although couched in contemporary medical discourse. *Journal of Reproductive Medicine* 43, no. 11 (November 1998): 947. I am grateful to Dr. Dona M. Perry, a specialist in obstetrics and gynecology, for helping me understand current medical practices concerning virginity.

[20] *Hali Meidenhad*, ed. F. J. Furnivall, revised from Oswald Cockayne edition (London, 1922), 14–15.

[21] So, too, Erasmus was to hold in his own treatise on virginity, it will be recalled, one hundred years or so after Joan, that a Jewish woman martyred by the Greeks for her faith along with her seven sons was herself to be considered a virgin because of the purity of her faith and heart. She restored her virginity "with the martyrdome of so many sonnes vyrgyns." (The story, as noted previously, is in 2 Maccabees, 6:18–31 and 7:1–41, and is said to have occurred in about 135 B.C.E.). Erasmus suggests that virginity is in fact holier than martyrdom, because it is freely chosen during life, whereas martyrdom resides in death. Thus, virginity is a greater victory over the flesh. The mother is particularly to be commended, in the views of both Erasmus and the narrator of Maccabees 2, because before her own death, she witnessed that of seven sons and remained resolute, "her woman's thoughts fired by a manly spirit" (7:22). See Desiderius Erasmus, *The Comparison of a Virgin and a Martyr* (1523), trans. Thomas Paynell (facsimile of Berthelet ed. of 1537, Gainesville, Fla., 1970). It is worth noting again here that this story reads, in terms of rhetoric, content, and tone, almost identically to those of Voragine concerning Christian martyrs. The model of martyrdom narratives, in other words, is already well in place long before the advent of Christianity.

But the loss of the maidenhead by carnal knowledge is irremediable; the flower dies. The message is loud, menacing, and repetitive, and there is no room for "accident" or a "clumsy hand." The loss of virginity here is an echo of the Fall; its preservation, both bodily and spiritually, promises the eternal life.

It is in the Middle Ages, then, that the hymen becomes legal and medical evidence for virginity in a woman. Since divorce, for example, is possible at the time only by proving that the marriage is unconsummated, a recognized method of demonstrating that the woman had remained "intact" was seen as a necessity. The Church's rules governing marriage and divorce are systematized by the reigning authorities. And so by the high Middle Ages, as the early thirteenth-century text *Hali Meidenhad* makes clear, the medical and legal discourses on virginity join to a large extent with Church law.[22] The role of the midwife, it should be remembered, becomes crucial.[23]

Facts become evidence, as Lorraine Dasten has noted, when put in service of a claim. No more obvious a case in point is Joan of Arc, whose self-professed virginity inspired much of the controversy surrounding her. For the French, she was a heroine and a saint sent by God—the fulfillment of a legend promising that France would be lost by a woman (popularly held to be the Dauphin's evil mother, Isabeau of Bavaria) and saved by a virgin who would emerge from a *bois chesnu* (oak forest).[24]

---

22 From a more recent edition *Hali Meidhad,* ed. Bella Millett (London, 1982). The notion of the "bride of Christ" is central to the argument of this anonymous but highly influential work.

23 When Pope Gregory IX ordered that women seeking a divorce had to be examined by a midwife, several notable authorities began to question (again) the existence of the hymen. Some historians have interpreted this to mean that the power of the midwives in the ecclesiastical courts generated jealousy and hostility. Even in secular courts, midwives were called on to establish paternity, virginity (and thus divorce), and the fulfillment of marital duty. See Lawrence I. Conrad, Michael Neve, Vivian Nutton, Roy Porter, and Andrew Wear, *The Western Medical Tradition: 800 B.C. to A.D. 1800* (Cambridge, 1995), 169–237ff.

24 The prophesy was recounted by a lawyer, Jean Barbin, in 1456. He had heard it from a professor of theology who in turn had heard it from Marie d'Avignon, a visionary, at the time of Joan's first meeting with the dauphin, in 1429: "a virgin *(pucelle)* who would come after her [Marie d'Avignon] would carry the same armor [as in her visions] and would liberate the realm of France from its enemies." See Régine Pernoud and Marie-Véronique Clin, *Jeanne d'Arc* (Paris, 1986), 51. Christine de Pizan, Joan's contemporary, also makes

The French consider Joan's virginity to *be* her identity, and this quite literally: she chooses to call herself *la pucelle*. Pure and intact, her first loyalty is to God. The English and the Burgundians see Joan as a witch and a sorceress sent by the devil. She is a whore and a heretic, states that are traditionally connected in the Europe of the Inquisition. As James Brundage reminds us, in the time of Joan there was "a widespread belief . . . that loose sexual habits were the peculiar traits of heretics. . . . Buggery, sodomy, incest, adultery, and indiscriminate fornication were, according to informants, commonplace among the heretics."[25] In either case, it should be noted, Joan's "natural" femininity is depraved. Her virginity becomes crucial to her mission, its demonstrable proof essential to her claims. Moreover, it is an antidote to the "weakness" that would otherwise debar her from action.

VIRGINITY, OR *FAUTE DE MIEUX*

The famous trials of Joan are the Trial of Condemnation (1431) and the posthumous Trial of Rehabilitation (1456).[26] But there were several less-

reference (twice) to this prophesy in her poem to Joan, written the same year. And Joan herself relates, in the Trial of Condemnation, that when she came to see the king, "quelques-uns demandaient si en son pays n'était point un bois qu'on appelat le Bois Chesnu. Car il y avait prophéties qui disaient que du Bois Chesnu devait venir une pucelle qui devait faire merveilles." Joan adds, however, that she took no stock in these stories: "en cela n'a point ajouté foi." Georges Duby and Andrée Duby, *Le Procès de Jeanne d'Arc* (Paris, 1995), 52. All translations are mine. I am frequently, though not always, using this modern French translation despite the existence of English versions, because I find it to be a generally good one. It is not, however, complete, and so at times I turn to the English versions. The standard English translations are T. Douglas Murray, *Jeanne d'Arc, Maid of Orleans*, in original documents (New York, 1902); W. S. Scott, *The Trial of Joan of Arc: Being the Verbatim Report of the Proceedings from the Orleans Manuscript* (London, 1956); and W. Barrett, *The Trial of Jeanne d'Arc* (London, 1931). For the Trial of Rehabilitation, there is the great Johannic scholar Régine Pernoud's edition, *The Retrial of Joan of Arc: The Evidence at the Trial for Her Rehabilitation*, trans. J. M. Cohen (London, 1955). The great standard and most exhaustively scholarly work is Jules Quicherat, *Procès de la condamnation et de la réhabilitation de Jeanne d'Arc dite la Pucelle*, 5 vols. (Paris, 1841–1849).

25 James A. Brundage, *Law, Sex and Christian Society in Medieval Europe* (Chicago, 1987), 493.

26 For a full bibliography of documents on Joan of Arc until 1894, see *Le Livre d'or de Jeanne d'Arc*, ed. Pierre Lanery d'Arc (Paris, 1894). For bibliographical references until

known "trials," both legal and physical. An examination was conducted at Poitiers, before she was allowed to meet the king in 1429. This "Book of Poitiers," as it is called, has been lost (perhaps destroyed by theologians as incriminating evidence, although a rumor insists that it lies in a secret cabinet in the Vatican).[27] We know from the Trial of Rehabilitation, however, that the doctors of theology to the king who interrogated her at Poitiers proclaimed that she was no tool of Satan but possessed, rather, only of "good, humility, virginity, devotion, honesty, simplicity."[28] But the examination at Poitiers was of necessity, given her claim, medical as well as verbal. In 1429, shortly after her first arrival at the court of the Dauphin, she was checked for virginity by two matrons (Jeanne de Preuilly and Jeanne de Mortemer) in the entourage of the Queen of Sicily, mother of the queen. As one testimony at the Trial of Rehabilitation puts it, Joan was handed over to the queen and to "certain ladies with her, by whom the Maid was seen, visited and privately looked at and examined; and after examination made by the matrons, the lady stated to the King that she and the other ladies found most surely that this was indeed a true Maid."[29] Joan's confessor, Jean Pasquerel, similarly testified that she was examined by the queen's entourage: "I heard tell that Joan, when she came to the king, was examined by women to see what she was about: if she was a man or a woman, and if she was corrupted or virginal. She was found to be woman and virgin and *pucelle*."[30]

1990, see Nadia Margolis, *Joan of Arc in History, Literature and Film: A Select, Annotated Bibliography* (New York, 1990).

[27] See also Charles T. Wood's hypothesis that the Poitiers manuscript was destroyed by order of Charles VII, because it might have raised questions concerning the legitimacy of his presence on the throne. "Joan of Arc's Mission and the Lost Record of her Interrogation at Poitiers," in *Fresh Verdicts on Joan of Arc*, ed. Bonnie Wheeler and Charles T. Wood (New York, 1996).

[28] Pernoud and Clin, *Jeanne d'Arc*, 51–52.

[29] Testimony of Seguin de Seguin, a Dominican, at the Trial of Rehabilitation, cited by Murray, *Jeanne d'Arc*, 309.

[30] From the trial records: *Et audivit dici quod ipsa Johanna, dum venit versus regem, fuit visitata bina vice per mulieres quid erat de ea, et si esset vir vel mulier, et an esset corrupta vel virgo; et inventa fuit mulier, virgo tamen et puella* (Quicherat, *Procès*, 3:102). *Puella* here means maiden as well as young girl, which is translated into French as *pucelle*. There is no exact English equivalent of *pucelle*, which means not only virgin but also a young girl who is intact as well as innocent (a meaning identical to that of *puella* in this context). On this point, see Marina Warner, *Joan of Arc: The Image of Female Heroism* (New York, 1981), 22.

It is significant that the examiners wanted to ascertain Joan's sex, as if to reassure themselves that a woman could exist beneath the armor and the strikingly confident pronouncements of this strange figure. In any case, Régine Pernoud and Marie-Véronique Clin cite this testimony and note that "this examination for virginity has frequently been misunderstood" (52). Our era, they argue, seems overly vested in stories about sorcery and witchcraft than was the fifteenth century. The reality of the matter is much simpler, they claim:

> The virginity examination was above all a proof of sincerity. Indeed in her time, no one would doubt that a person wishing to dedicate herself to God alone had to demonstrate that received calling by remaining a virgin—thus, fully autonomous, totally available for service to God, in heart and body, without sharing. Joan was the first to be persuaded of this when she declared that she had given herself to God from the moment she had understood that it had been the voice of an angel which had revealed itself to her. (52–53)

There is never any allusion, they continue, to sorcery or diabolical considerations whatever in Joan's words. "Suspicions of that kind," they conclude, "spring only in the mind of the twentieth-century intellectual." The choice had solely to do with the pious vocation.

Pernoud and Clin, then, reinforce the argument made here: that virginity was a necessity for anyone who dedicated her life to God. Indeed, Joan herself makes this clear in her Trial of Condemnation, "Item, said that the first time she heard its voice [the angel], she vowed to give her virginity to God as long as it pleased Him. And she was thirteen years of age, or thereabouts."[31] One can go further: virginity was also necessary—or at least extremely useful—in the late Middle Ages, for a woman who took on a role of strength outside social expectations for her gender. That is, since a woman was not regarded as a subject, and thus was seen as possessing no agency, she could ape a position of power through the mystique traditionally granted to the status of virginity. With the "abomination" of her reproductive fluids suppressed (Joan was said to be amen-

[31] Duby and Duby, *Le Procès*, 91; my translation.

strual as well, as women who fast often are),[32] a pious female virgin has some ground, even if limited, on which to legitimize her discourse as a self-proclaimed ascetic. I want, however, to go further than the argument that Joan's religious vocation necessitated virginity, although there is no doubt, given its long and weighty tradition that we have considered at some length here, that it did. That is irrefutable.

A frequent ancillary claim, grounded in sociological terms, suggests that Joan tried to make herself less threatening to the men around her by renouncing her sexuality. This is a speculation to which there can be little response except intuitive, if cautious, agreement.[33] What Horkheimer and Adorno note with respect to the bourgeoisie of the industrial West can be applied to the vast clerical class in the time of Joan: it profited from "female chastity and propriety—the defense mechanisms left by matriarchal revolt." They continue, once again, by making reference to a notion of *nature* so multivalenced and powerful as to be victim and demon at the same time—precisely the properties vested in women in the mythic proportions Horkheimer and Adorno are attempting to explode: "Woman herself, on behalf of all exploited nature, gained admission to a male-dominated world, but only in broken form. . . . At the price of radical disengagement from action and of withdrawal into the charmed circle,

---

[32] See, on the subject of amenorrhea in ascetic women, Rudolph M. Bell, *Holy Anorexia* (Chicago, 1985), and Bynum, *Holy Feast and Holy Fast*. Bell notes that amenorrhea is one of the six present-day criteria for diagnosing anorexia nervosa. Several of the soldiers who fought at Joan's side testified at the Trial of Rehabilitation that as far as they could tell, she did not have monthly periods. On the other hand, young women began menstruating far later in the fifteenth century than they do today, so that the soldier's presuppositions, even if true, are inconclusive for establishing that Joan was anorexic.

[33] For example, W. S. Scott has noted that society in general pushes independent women toward celibacy. Joan, Scott argues, gave up her sexuality to be less threatening to the males who watched her beating them at their own game (war). Scott, *Jeanne d'Arc* (London, 1974). This argument convinces Anne Llewellyn Barstow, who adds, "An active sexuality in an active warrior-transvestite would have been too much for her fellow citizens. Joan had to sacrifice her sexuality in order to be accepted." See Barstow, *Joan of Arc: Heretic, Mystic, Shaman* (Lewiston, 1986), 113. Vern L. Bullough argues in a similar vein in "Transvestites of the Middle Ages," *American Journal of Sociology* 79, no. 6 (May 1974): 1390ff. Bynum argues, on the other hand, that late-medieval women who cross-dressed did so for reasons of expediency, not to "become male." See *Holy Feast*. This last argument is the one that Joan was to use in front of her ecclesial accusers.

nature receives homage from the lord of creation. Art, custom, and sublime love are masks in which nature reappears transformed into her own antithesis" (249).

The elision of woman and nature is once again significant, even if conscious. The metaphors here abound, until nature itself becomes as vague and easily masked, covered, veiled, transformed (all metaphors of the feminine to which we will return) as "woman" herself. The *un*willed result in this passage is that like "nature," woman is reinforced as being enigmatic and mysterious and therefore dangerous and deceptive. That is both the critique and the unintended consequence of the passage, as if the symptoms of a "male-dominated society" had contaminated the physician. This is not the place to critique at any greater length the contrary assumptions in the brilliant and well-intentioned "feminist" passage of Adorno and Horkheimer; I use them here to point to certain essentialist givens concerning "woman" and the extent to which "nature" is used as a collaborator in both what is described and in those who do the describing.

It is striking how, even in a perspicacious prose that assesses the problem, woman continues to gain admission into the male text "only in a broken form." How much higher the stakes, then, when an individual female life is judged for the purpose of determining whether or not she deserves to live, or whether she will be burned. "The auto-da-fé," write the two authors, "was the Church's heathen bonfire, a triumph of nature in the form of self-preserving reason, to celebrate the glory of the mastery of nature" (ibid.). The paradoxes are intended, but given the valence of the terms reiterated here, the "mastery of nature" is visited upon what is gendered female, just as surely as its triumph is the male purview of reason. It will be remembered that, as Horkheimer and Adorno had noted, one of the goals of a "male-dominated society" is "acquiring absolute mastery over nature." Furthermore, such mastery is "the significance of reason," which includes stigmatizing and humiliating "woman."[34] She inherits "the weakness imprinted by nature," that difference that she cannot bridge between her and man: "biological inferiority." Thus the auto-da-fé is the Church's celebration of the goal attained: the mastery of nature and the preservation of reason are achieved through the burning of what opposes reason and mastery—woman. Curiously enough, in this

[34] On the notion that Reason is male, see Genevieve Lloyd, *The Man of Reason: "Male" and "Female" in Western Philosophy* (Minneapolis, 1984).

passage, the "triumph of nature" is the same event that professes its mastery, its eradication of all that is anathema to the kingdom of reason—the fire.

Clearly, auto-da-fés were not limited to women; but in the logic of the text (a logic that Horkheimer and Adorno both viciously critique and strangely reinforce), as I have argued, it is the woman who must be burned. In their words, through the masks of art, custom and sublime love, nature "acquires the gift of speech." Furthermore, "out of her distortion emerges her essence. Behind male admiration of beauty, however, lurks always the ribald laughter, the withering scorn, the barbaric obscenity with which strength greets weakness in an attempt to deaden the fear that it has itself fallen prey to impotence, death, and nature" (ibid.). I would add that the fear is greater yet when, as in the case of Joan of Arc, male "strength" is confronted with power in a young, uneducated woman. All the more need to "deaden," as the two authors in question put it, the uncanny recognition of its own weakness. Is this the "essence" that emerges from their (nature/women) distortion? The burning of Joan was an attempt to deaden a great deal more than a young woman with pretensions of prophesy. It was also an attempt to eradicate the nascent possibility of agency in a woman, of a possible weakness in the dominant discourse, requiring constant vigilance and cleansing, lest it be uncovered.

If we agree that the notion of subjectivity is discernible in the West by the utterance of "I" and the agency that ensues, it is clear that a woman in the fifteenth century has no such power, no such agency. Her utterance of "I," in other words, is circumscribed by her status as property, chattel, and secondariness. She does not partake of the mythical economy of sovereign subjectivity. The fact that such a state also describes those of different racial and class origin is incontestable. The nonsubject position of woman, however, in the fifteenth-century culture of Catholic France compounds the difficulty for reasons we have already considered. She is secondary on theological as well as social, political, economic, and sexual grounds.

While it is true that a female ascetic of that period would, as the Church fathers had argued more than a thousand years before, be freed of the social expectations forced on her, it is also the case, as we have seen, that she would substitute for the patriarchal society she rejected, the equally authoritarian and rigid power of Church institutionalism and its male structures. But one of the remarkable, perhaps even unique, aspects of Joan's mysticism is that her revelations are specifically *political*. They necessitate, therefore, active presence in the polis, so that a cloistered life under the protection and authority of the Church would make no sense for her.[35] During her Trial of Condemnation, she is specifically asked whether she shared her revelations with anyone from the Church (her priest, for example). She answers, "No. Only to Robert de Baudricourt and to her king. She further said that she was not constrained by her voices to hide them. But she greatly feared revealing them, for fear that the Burgundians would prevent her journey, and she especially feared her father, that he would prevent the journey."[36] In her silence, she was directly guilty in the eyes of the Church: her duty was to confess her visions and voices so that the Church could ascertain their source. She was further deemed guilty of not honoring her parents, both by remaining silent on her mission and voices and by leaving home without telling them. But the fact is that Joan "confesses" her voices to the political figures who are central to her mission: Robert de Baudricourt, the captain of Vaucouleurs who first believed in her and gave her men-at-arms; and the king himself, still dauphin at the time, whose coronation, according to the voices, was to occur as soon as possible. The point, then, is that Joan's revelations have local politics as their message, so that she would logically turn to those who would advance the fulfillment of her divine commands, not to the Church that had declared itself sole judge of all things mystical. She chooses, then, the freedom from social expectations that virginity brings to women without the Church's authority that would regulate a life of such "freedom." Thus, she is already by definition a threat to the state and one of the "baneful instruments of a general decline."

The apocalyptic aspect of Joan's faith, then, is unacceptable to the Church Militant of the time: because it is a vision that interprets itself, because it has its own teleology, because it has nothing to do with Christian

---

35 This distinguishes Joan from other medieval women who spoke (and, unlike Joan, wrote) on religious as well as political issues. Most, if not all, of these women were under rule: Hildegard, Elisabeth of Schönau, Bridget of Sweden, Catherine of Siena. See, for example, Barbara Newman's *Sister of Wisdom: Saint Hildegard's Theology of the Feminine* (Berkeley, Calif., 1987).

36 Duby and Duby, *Le Procès*, 91.

eschatology or anti-Christ rhetoric but only with the direct transmission of a divine revelation for the purpose of prophesy.[37] Most of her prophesies concern French political events (Charles will be crowned, the English will be driven out of France, Orléans and Paris will be liberated, and so on). The hour of fulfillment in Joan's vision occurs in the here and now. Her kingdom, in other words, is of this world. The Church has no power to contain or control her; she must be excised. Her sentencing, read to her on the scaffold, is in part as follows:

> [W]e declare you to have incurred the sentence of excommunication, into which you had previously fallen, and that you have returned to your former faults. For this we declare you a heretic. With this sentence, by the tribunal of justice, by this writ, we announce that, like a rotten limb, we have rejected you and expelled you from the unity of the Church and have named you to the secular justice.[38]

The Church is cleansed of its rotten limb (the metaphor traditionally used by the Inquisition in describing heresy); the threat to its omnipotence and ideology, expunged; Joan's virginity, a proof of arrogance, not holiness. Virginity serves only to allow her to boast that she will gain automatic entry to heaven. In her relapse, she is "like the dog which habitually returns to its vomit," unable to control her addiction to evil. In metaphors of filth and disease, the Church describes the nineteen-year-old woman whose chastity, courage, and mysticism delineated a feminine power beyond its reach.

But it is with her visions that the Church seems particularly obsessed, and not only because they cannot endorse their content. The apocalyptic aspect of Joan's faith has to do with immediacy and spontaneity in divine messaging; in knowing the will of God. Her announcements that she cannot tell all, and indeed must conceal a good deal, makes her relation to God and, in turn, to the court itself, apophatic, if we consider that term to mean that divinity is hidden and must remain so, even as its *will* is re-

[37] Apocalypse falls under the larger category of prophesy, but I am not conflating them. Joan is a prophet in that she predicts and preaches. Her prophesies are apocalyptic in nature in that they claim to reveal the will of God.

[38] Duby and Duby, *Le Procès,* 177.

vealed. This combination of normally noncontiguous registers bears further consideration.

DERRIDA'S HYMEN

In his study of the apocalyptic, Jacques Derrida begins with the more usual definition of apocalyptic: revealing, unveiling, eschatological, teleological, the Last Judgement, "and so on." He continues, "Without even referring to the Zoroastrian type of apocalypses (there was more than one of them), we know that every apocalyptic eschatology is promised in the name of light, of seeing and vision, and of a light of light, a light brighter than all the lights it makes possible. John's apocalypse, which dominates all the Western apocalyptic, is lit by the light of El, of Elohim."[39] Should we forget that woman is imagined as fleeing from the light in the tradition we have been considering, the aspect of light in apocalyptic events should be a reminder of a certain gender danger here. It is as if Joan, by conveying the luminance of her visions, were substituting for her feminine position a phallogocentric light to inspire her, which works to ground her speech through the luminous agency of her voices. Lest we have any doubt about this gender danger, a further reading of Derrida's text makes it explicit: "There is a light," he writes, "and there are the lights, the lights of reason or of the *logos*, that are not, for all that, some other thing." Even granting that he is ventriloquizing Kant's *Aufklärung* and the need to demystify, he makes such demystification synonymous with the desire "to deconstruct the apocalyptic discourse itself and with it everything that speculates on vision, the imminence of the end, theophany, parousia, the Last Judgement, and so on" (82).

This deconstruction of the apocalyptic discourse will return us to the veil. Although Derrida is not sure that there is *one* great paradigm on which all the eschatological strategies would model themselves, it would

39 Jacques Derrida, "Of an Apocalyptic Tone Recently Adopted in Philosophy," trans. John Leavey Jr., in *Semeia: An Experimental Journal for Biblical Criticism*, vol. 23, *Derrida and Biblical Studies*, ed. Robert Detweiler (1982): 82. For an unusually helpful and knowledgeable study on Derrida and his relation to religion, including the essay on the apocalyptic, see John D. Caputo, *The Prayers and Tears of Jacques Derrida: Religion without Religion* (Bloomington, Ind., 1997), 88–101ff.

still be "a philosophical, onto-eschato-teleological" interpretation to say that "the apocalyptic strategy is fundamentally one, its diversity is only of ways of proceeding [*procède*], masks, appearances, or simulacra" (83). The ruse of apocalyptic moves, for Derrida, is hidden under "the desire for light, well hidden . . . under the avowed desire for revelation." Its agenda is to preserve itself, and if it reveals anything, it is itself and its transcendental structure: "The end approaches, but the apocalypse is long-lived" (89). Indeed, for Derrida, the "come" of the apocalypse erases the very (teleological) structure that it would announce. Eschatology is perhaps a tone, he writes, "or even the voice itself." The voice, then, is the desire for light and, at the same time (as I would interpret Derrida's interpretation), the imposition of futurity ("come") by eschatology for the purpose of preserving itself. The use of gendered metaphors is neither innocent, nor unconscious, nor (by any means) merely decorative. It is *deadly*, and we must look at it closely and at some length.

To begin with, by twinning the voice with the desire for light, the move of apocalyptic discourse is delimited as masculine, and this for reasons considered in the previous chapter. The voice, its breath (which we began to allude to with Plato, also discussed in the previous chapter), its teleological uncoverings, are phallogocentric. Revelation itself initially poses as the uncovering "of the secret and the *pudenda*" (64). As André Chouraqui, the recent French translator of the New Testament who figures prominently in this Derrida article, puts it, "Someone's ear is discovered in lifting up the hair or the veil that covers it in order to whisper a secret into it, a word as hidden as a person's genitals. YHWH can be the agent of this disclosure, this uncovering. The arm or glory of YHWH can also be disclosed in man's gaze or ear. So nowhere does the word apocalypse . . . have the sense it finally takes in French and other languages, of fearsome catastrophe. Thus the Apocalypse is essentially a contemplation *(hazon)* . . . or an inspiration *(neboua)* at the sight, the uncovering or disclosure of YHWH." Chouraqui relies heavily on the Hebrew word *gala* as meaning reveal to read apocalyptic—an interpretation to which we will return shortly. The word *gala*, Derrida tells us, "seems to say *apokalupsis*, disclosure, discovery, uncovering, unveiling, the veil lifted from, the truth revealed about the thing: first of all, if we can say this, men's or women's genitals, but also their eyes or ears" (64).

The uncovering of genitals, despite the bigendered intention here, points, as we have noted, to pudenda. Another meaning of this word is indeed men's or women's external genitalia, but the primary connotation is those of women. Derrida uses the second meaning, and his elision of the gender-specific first definition is as if a model for the rhetorical moves of his argument. Indeed, most of the examples he gives for such uncoverings are male: the story in Genesis (9:21) when Noah gets drunk and reveals his genitals to his three sons; the sexual prohibitions dictated to Moses by YHWH; the example of "the glans when the foreskin is removed in circumcision" for laying bare, or apocalyptic unveiling; the passage from Leviticus that, notwithstanding the portion on incest, begins with "the man who lies with his father's wife / has uncovered his father's genitals"; Freud's notion of castration that, given that women have already incurred this mutilation (Freud's word, of course), applies as a threat only to the male. Despite all of these examples, the apocalyptic, even in Kant's *Religion within the Limits of Reason Alone,* still remains "a matter of the veil and of castration." And what have we here, with these metaphors elicited by, in this case, Isis and Freud? Woman as veiled, as mystery and enigma hiding the truth; and woman as danger, whose castrating potential initiates the primal scene of maleness. We have visited these metaphors throughout this study, and if Derrida can be said (as always) to be aware of these valences, his text deepens and reinscribes them, as surely as the bloody script of the writing machine in Kafka's penal colony, onto the body of "woman."

In this Derrida essay, the hymenal metaphors abound, and do so willfully. At every turn, however, they are read as male or as needing to be expunged. For example, Isis is the goddess near whose veil "Kant and Hegel more than once busied themselves." Derrida himself, he writes, will "expose" himself (again, the male genitals in rhetorical guise) and take up the threads of the veil "with the treatment of castration taking Isis into account" (75). Reading Kant, Derrida notes that while the veil of Isis cannot be raised, at least, in Kant's words, "it can be made so thin [*so dünne*] that one can have a presentiment of the goddess under it [*unter ihm*]." This move becomes "apocalyptic unveiling," connected with the *Aufhebung.* The lineup, according to Derrida, is as follows for Kant: metaphor and literary mystagogy, on the one hand, and concept and true philosophy, on the other. For Kant, the "new mystico-Platonic language" consists in the abuse of analogies and verisimilitudes, thus an "emasculation" (or, as Derrida reads it, a castration). In choosing castration as a metaphor or simulacrum, Derrida returns to the problem: a fight of metaphysics that is "the castration of reason" in Kant, the phallus and "not the penis, or the clitoris" (76). Derrida cites Freud's "The Infantile Genital Organization": this stage "wherein there is only male reason, only a masculine or castrated organ or canon of reason . . . there is definitely a masculine but no feminine" (77). Or, as Freud puts it, there is only one libido, and it is male.

Derrida, of course, is merely *reading* through, interpreting, Kant's concern about mystagogues and the death of philosophy. Both sides in the philosophical debate (Kant and his adversaries), Kant will say, kneel before the veiled goddess, she who is "the law above the body," and Derrida adds:

> Even if you do not want to grant some *signifiance* or significance to the fact that what the concordat excludes is precisely the body of a veiled Isis, the universal principle of femininity, murderess of Osiris all of whose pieces she later recovers, except for the phallus. Even if you also think that is a personification too analogical or metaphorical, grant me at least that the truce proposed between the two declared defenders of a non-emasculated *logos* supposes some exclusion. It supposes some *inadmissible.* (79)

So the fight between the defenders of a virile *logos* makes a truce that excludes the veiled goddess. That truce, here in these pages at least, is not granted. For the inadmissible is grafted onto the feminine, hiding (as I shall argue later) a greater unknown: the impossible.

Although Derrida does not note this, the Hebrew word *gala,* which like Chouraqui he uses for apocalyptic, means to exile rather than to reveal. The root is the same: G-L-H, but the two meanings are differently vocalized. *Gila* means "revealed," while *gala* has to do with being exiled, going into exile. Thus, one might note that Derrida has exiled the primary meaning of exile in *gala* and appended *gila* to its usual connotation. That said, let us return to his point: Willfully exiled here, as Derrida forcefully notes, is the feminine. The veiled goddess, murderess in some versions of the myth, must be removed from the *ratio.* And yet I would argue that more is exiled in all of these metaphors and simulacra—the veil as principle of the feminine hiding the truth (Derrida cites his own work *Spurs,* with Nietzsche's umbrella opening, like a hymen); Isis before whom too many philosophers kneel; castration or emasculation of the *logos* that must be stopped; the phallus, pudenda (including the clitoris), foreskin, and circumcision. Even so, something is more subtly exiled, from Kant and "his adversaries," and from the rhetoric of Derrida as he reads (from a distance, always only interpreting) the eschatological tone in philosophy, Marxism, and psychoanalysis.

Derrida alludes to his own texts concerning the veil (of Isis but also of "the Woman"): *Spurs/Eperons,* as we have noted, but also "Economimesis," *Glas,* and *The Postcard from Socrates to Freud and Beyond.* He does not mention, however, the work of his that specifically addresses the hymen, "The Double Session" in *Dissemination.* This (exiled) text haunts the others (indeed the phantom, he tells us in this essay, is equally feminized, hiding as it does "behind its veil or cloth" [75]). The divinity of the figure Isis is also alluded to, as when Derrida cites Kant's line about his adversaries in philosophy who try "to approach so near the divine wisdom that one can perceive the *rustle* of its garment" (ibid.). If Derrida reminds us that Kant sees the mystagogues "bring into play the phantom and the veil," I would submit *mutatis mutandis:* the hymen haunts Derrida's own essay like the ghost of an aspect of woman that remains unspoken by all of philosophers mentioned here: a hollowed out place where female subjectivity is left a berth but not an essence—in other words, the vagina (where the hymen, after all, is located). Exiled from the metaphors of the text under consideration, the hymen is scrutinized in Derrida's "The Double Session." Because Derrida is reading Mallarmé in this text, the hymen is immediately related to the cleft in the page: "Yet neither (is it) a fold in the veil or in the pure text but rather in the lining which the hymen, of itself, was."[40]

But again, as he reads (and ventriloquizes) Mallarmé, the hymen itself twists and turns until it, too, loses its feminine specificity and becomes a metaphor: " between the outside and the inside, making the outside enter the inside and turning back the antre or the other upon its surface, the hymen is never pure or proper, has no life of its own, no proper name. Opened up by its anagram, it always seems torn, already, in the fold through which it affects itself and murders itself (ibid.).

Granted that the *antre* plays, among other things, with the notion of in-betweenness, which in turn echoes the secondary meaning of hymen, marriage or union ("the hymen must be determined through the *entre* and

---

[40] Jacques Derrida, *Dissemination,* trans. Barbara Johnson (Chicago, 1981), 229.

not the other way around," writes Derrida [220]), on what grounds, exactly, aside from textual *Mitleid*, must the hymen "be determined"? Let us take note: the metaphors (on *both* Derrida's and Mallarmé's parts) have neutralized, once again, the specificity and scandal of the hymen, and thus of the feminine. Always torn here, never pure and proper, this reading of the hymen exiles virginity. (And yet, as if in spite of himself, it is Mallarmé's strange figure of Hérodiade who will say, "J'aime l'horreur d'être vierge.") But there is more about this notion of hymen in Derrida's Mallarmé: "Along the undiscoverable line of this fold, the hymen never presents itself. It never *is*—in the present; it has no proper, literal meaning; it no longer originates in meaning as such, that is, as the meaning of being. The fold renders (itself) manifold but (is) not (one)" (229). Nor, as Lacan has argued, is woman "one." The hymen, by this account, never is because it does not participate in meaning and thus in being. But it is to be noted that this is because the hymen "never presents itself." If this text, too, succeeds in producing metaphors that are not feminine, although generated by "the hymen," if it succeeds in exiling virginity without even noticing it has done so, it also succeeds in accomplishing more overtly what the text on "an apocalyptic tone" does more covertly. What is attached to the hymen (the feminine, the veil, the goddess Isis, silence, hollows, the abyss, obscurity, enigma, mystery) does not partake of revelation ("it does not present itself"). The feminine is exiled from the apocalyptic as it is figured in masculinist, philosophical discourse. And this by Derrida *as well as* by those whom he merely "reads" and whose metaphors he merely highlights. Absent from the present, incapable of revelation, always between, what is the hymen, then? A notion abstracted from meaning—that is, not only to be exiled from the *logos* but to be interpreted as if it marked a place that was never there. Femininity becomes the ghost of its own veil, even when the female body provides the metaphors. Those taken from the male body, however, retain their presence (and thus their meaning).[41]

This is evident in the tradition of the Church fathers; it does not come *ex nihilo*. Ambrose, for example, in contemplating perfection and Paul's comments on the same (I Cor. 13:10), explains that Christ's wholeness re-

---

[41] See, for example, Derrida's comments on circumcision in "Shibboleth," *Midrash and Literature*, ed. Geoffrey H. Hartman and Sanford Budick (New Haven, Conn., 1986), 340–47ff.

turns after the crucifixion. Jesus is "perfect in all things," although perfection was initially "deferred": "He was circumcised first in accordance with the Law so as not to destroy the Law, and later through the Cross in order to fulfill the Law. That which is only partial has ended, because that which is perfect has come, for in Christ the Cross circumcised not one member but the useless pleasures of the whole body."[42] Note how the crucifixion here is presented as a polycircumcision, as if the "partial" were in excess only to demonstrate the subsequent perfection of wholeness. Following Paul, Ambrose celebrates partiality in this life, so as to underline perfection after the resurrection. Conversely, the hymen in women is mystified as perfection and its absence as full "womanhood." In both cases, however, female anatomy is relegated to the body. She is not, in other words, in this economy of partiality symbolized by circumcision; she is already partial, she will never be "whole," either anatomically or spiritually. Thus, there is an ancient tradition to privileging the metaphor of circumcision: it partakes of the Law and, through the reminder of "partiality," promises perfection. Metaphors of circumcision already participate in notions of imagined perfection and completeness.

Derrida, in his reading of Kant in "On an Apocalyptic Tone," notes that the discourse of woman becomes "the law above the body, above this body found here to be represented by a veiled goddess" (79). It is the voice of woman that is "speaking in us, the singular voice speaking to us in private, the voice that could be said in its language to be 'pathological' in opposition to the voice of reason." It is that (feminized) voice (the "we" here can only be masculine) that the logos must eradicate, says Derrida reading Kant, or must exile, *gala*. The other side of revelation from this perspective is repression, or exile. If Derrida is adept in his essay at pulling all the threads (with which he also busies himself) on the veil of "Isis," he is singularly quick, as we have seen, to elide them into protrusions, not hollows, and to choose the talismanic metaphors accordingly: phallus, penis, circumcisions, pudenda, clitoris (even) proliferate, and Nietzsche's umbrella remains largely closed.

And all of this within an economy of castration that, while the essay points to Freud's article on "The Infantile Genital Organization," that dream of symmetry with which we are now so familiar, represses the

[42] Ambrose, in *Saint Ambrose: Letters*, trans. Sister Mary Melchior Beyenke (New York, 1954), 252.

vagina (in the same move that chooses one definition of a word over an other). After all, one of the seminal texts on castration in Freud occurs in the description of a dream by the Wolfman, one explicating the primal scene:

> Then suddenly, in connection with a dream, the analysis plunged back into the prehistoric period, and led him to assert that during the copulation in the primal scene he had observed the penis disappear, that he had felt compassion for his father on that account, and had rejoiced at the reappearance of what he thought had been lost. So here was a fresh emotional impulse, starting once again from the primal scene. Moreover, the narcissistic origin of compassion (which is confirmed by the word itself [*Mitleid*]), is here quite unmistakably *revealed* [my emphasis].[43]

In "prehistory," the vagina devours the penis, which itself plunges into a prehistory. When it reappears (an apocalyptic event?), the narcissistic origin of compassion is "unmistakably revealed" as well. Here again, the revelation is of the penis, returned from its journey to an underworld of sorts, emerging from the terrifying vagina from which the gaze is blocked and turned away. (The other aspect of Isis, of course, is the Medusa, that personification of the *vagina dentata.*) It is the primal scene, I would argue, that finally haunts as well the essay by Derrida, because the "prehistorical" recognition it *reveals* is apocalyptic (a revelation) to the point of blinding by its clarity. The penis is as if a displacement of such a vision that blinds in a light not of the *logos.* The gaze turns away from the vagina and seeks solace in the return of the penis.[44]

---

43 "From the History of an Infantile Neurosis," 1918 [1914], *The Standard Edition of the Complete Psychological Works of Freud,* trans. and ed. James Strachey (London, 1955), 17: 88.

44 Freud, it will be remembered, performs a series of moves to evade or to masculinize (albeit only partially, and so by definition a priori unsuccessfully) female genitalia. The clitoris, he writes, "takes on the role of a penis entirely" in a girl's childhood. (It is not, however, "big and visible.") Moreover, the vagina for Freud depends on the clitoris to gain sexual sensitivity: "The process of a girl's becoming a woman depends very much on the clitoris passing on this sensitivity to the vaginal orifice in good time and completely. In cases of what is known as sexual anaesthesia in women the clitoris has obstinately retained its sensitivity." See "Introductory Lectures on Psycho-Analysis," Lecture XX, "The Sex-

The narcissism of compassion that Freud finds in the Wolfman's dream extends far beyond it: it is the narcissism, perhaps, that chooses to prophesy itself again and again as a masculine site of agency and subjectivity, rather than face the otherness of an abyss the eschatology of which can only be a cause of horror since there may, in fact, not be one. The fear that the *logos* is being "emasculated," then, may in itself hide the greater fear that the *logos* exists, as it were, in a vacuum of unknown proportions. It is death, it will be recalled, that Levinas links directly with the problem of virility in the subject. I return to the passage cited in the previous chapter: "My mastery, my virility, my heroism as a subject can be neither virility nor heroism in relation to death." "What the hymen undoes," writes Derrida in "The Double Session," what it outwits, under "the rubric of the present (whether temporal or eternal), is the assurance of mastery. The critical desire—which is also the philosophical desire—can only, as such, attempt to regain that lost mastery. That desire tends to read the hymen alternately according to this or that species of presence: the work of writing *against* time or the work of writing *effected* by time" (230). Here again is the critical desire (which is also philosophical, exactly as I have been arguing) "to regain that lost mastery." It is the dream of men for "millennia," write Horkheimer and Adorno, of "acquiring absolute mastery over nature." Removed from the present, barred from the future, divested of voice, the hymen is mastered. The anatomy of woman, the specificity of the vagina, are sublated into philosophical dreams of mastery to avoid what is feared to be the place of death.

---

ual Life of Human Beings," *Standard Edition,* 16: 318. Thus, for Freud, the clitoris is the analog for the penis, and it is the male "stand-in" that allows for full womanhood. If this quasi-masculine aspect of the woman does not pass on its "information" to the vagina, the latter remains anesthetized. The vagina achieves its sexual function, in other words, only after it has been educated by its male portion, the clitoris. One might call this theory the anatomical literalization of the vagina evasion I am tracing here. Earlier in the same lecture, Freud is careful to remind his audience ("Gentlemen") that for a large number of adults, "homosexual and heterosexual alike, the anus does really take over the role of the vagina in sexual intercourse" (316). Even the childbearing aspect of the vagina slides into penile economy in Freud since woman have babies as substitutions for a penis. The point I am making in citing these well-worn assertions of Freud's is that in all of the cases the vagina is understood as a (diminished) phallic analog or similarly, it is easily substitutable by non-gender-specific anatomical aspects. Thus cast, the vagina becomes conceptually invisible, like the Invisible Man of the movies, whose presence is deduced only because of the visible consequences of his hidden actions.

And this even if such a move would be denied, which is why we must spend some time on the matter now. Geoffrey Bennington, for example, defends Derrida and his relationship to "'feminism' (especially outside of France, no doubt)" as one that "has never been, and never could be, an entirely peaceful one."[45] Some, he adds, have found it "provocative or even shocking" that Derrida should exploit "terms like 'hymen' or 'invagination,'" in order to "nickname" structures such as binary oppositions (male / female; inside / outside; primary / secondary, and so forth). On the contrary, says Bennington, a word such as "hymen . . . says separation *and* the abolition of this separation, and says it in a way which can appear violent" (226). Deconstruction must perforce "run the risk of being interpreted badly," so that it can destabilize the very structures that the metaphors uphold and trouble the dominant discourse." He adds that "one must accept that 'feminine' words be grafted onto other contexts and that 'feminine' predicates be extended to broader structures" (226–27). (Perhaps one "must," in Derrida's thinking, accept such grafting, but one of the propositions of the present book is that one must, precisely, not). Bennington notes that if one is "upset about this" (!), one is presupposing "Derrida's mastery over textuality and the effects it produces, to have already endowed him with 'masculine privileges.'" On the contrary, argues Bennington, one must (again) intervene in this "classical economy" with a share of "unconsciousness and nonmastery."

What is the feminism "especially outside of France, no doubt," that is "upset about this"? One suspects a certain sociology of monolithicism. Moreover, running the risk of being interpreted "badly" for the higher purpose of destabilizing the dominant discourse brings us face to face with the problem to which I have been pointing.[46] Bennington writes, "[B]ut what prevents such an essentialization-nomination is precisely what means that the determination of sexual difference as opposition cannot be separated from the most fundamental oppositions of metaphys-

---

45 Geoffrey Bennington and Jacques Derrida, *Jacques Derrida,* trans. Geoffrey Bennington (Chicago, 1993), 225.

46 Bennington and Derrida, *Jacques Derrida,* 225. I spend time on Bennington because, as I note in my own text, his essay is underwritten (literally as well as figuratively) by Derrida's comments at the bottom of each page. The book is coauthored by the two, and Bennington's explanatory and justifying remarks are clearly endorsed (and presumably edited and authorized) by Derrida himself.

ics." He would have us believe (along with Derrida himself, whose autobiographical text runs beneath, supporting that of Bennington) that these fundamental oppositions "cannot fail to be shaken up by their deconstruction" (228). This shaking up, as they would have it, is *in itself* "already a feminist gesture." I agree, and indeed I am assuming in this study that sexual difference as opposition cannot be separated "from the most fundamental oppositions of metaphysics." But I do not see reappropriating (or *propriating*) such "nicknames" (a curious choice of words, as if this were a light-hearted undertaking) as "hymen" or "invagination" for fundamental structures in metaphysics as a way of "shaking up" or troubling the dominant discourse. Even when they are pushed to an extreme that suggests their limits, they are forced in such a context to collaborate in the "classical economy." Derrida wants, we are told, for the hymen to mean (I repeat Bennington's words) "separation *and* abolition" (one thinks of the window in Mallarmé's verse). But this move turns the hymen, once again, into an instance of masculinist musings (even if critical ones) on the prevalence and symmetrical insistence of binary structures. Such a move further averts the feminine specificity of the hymen and the vagina, which are assimilated into "broader structures." For example, Bennington would have us read the word "invagination" as "much more general" than its feminine referent, since it is used in embryology.[47] Finally, such a move suggested by the authors reasserts not only the binary structures that deconstruction does at times destabilize but neutralizes feminine-specific words such that they lose their position of a blind spot in the tradition. It is a blind spot that no amount of abstracting can "fold" away, into, or out of, something more approachable. If we are to begin to comprehend how the alterity of alterity is configured, it is not by familiarizing on masculinist grounds the terms that betray a place of *incomprehensibility* in the "classical economy." These terms *(hymen, vagina)* are only assimilable into the text of metaphysical fundamentalism when they

[47] Moreover, the use of the term *invaginate* itself turns a feminine anatomical term into a masculine one: the vagina is as if formed, in other words, by the intussusception (the given definition of invagination). Indeed, the meaning of intussusception is "the process of taking in food or other foreign matter and turning it into tissue." *Webster's Unabridged Deluxe Dictionary* (New York, 1979). *Invagination,* then, suggests from a lexical perspective the ideology of the metaphors used by Derrida: the penis creates the hymen. That was precisely Buffon's point, on a more abstract level, but he was complaining about it.

are abstracted beyond recognition, even when they are deployed for the purpose of shaking up such fundamentalism.

There is a far greater risk for deconstruction here than that of being interpreted badly. Deconstruction, in its use of feminized metaphors to show separation and abolition, and in then eliding them, grafting them onto "broader structures," runs the risk of its own "double chiasmatic invagination"—putting its head in the sand. Justifications such as textual uncontrollability or the interjection of "unconsciousness and nonmastery" for disturbing the classical economy—these justifications serve to shield the inability and refusal to recognize, without "translating," the opaque mystery of otherness. The mystery, which in the West has been displaced to the feminine, cannot be sublated, even by a discourse that professes to *reveal* it and does so by denying its responsibility for, and activism in, consciousness and mastery. We have already noted the logic of mastery: it does not disappear by being negated, any more than demonstrating a lack of control means in any way to lose it.

The point about the hymen and the vagina that Bennington's logic ignores is that they cannot be set in binary oppositions except by repression or by a masculinist symmetry that uses anatomy as metaphor of the existing economy (for example, the vagina is the mold for or inversion of the penis). It is this repression, hardly limited to deconstruction but perhaps more hidden there because of the protestations to the contrary, that marks a large portion of metaphysical fundamentalism in the West. As long as mystery is gendered feminine, "woman" will remain the convenient repository of the mysterious. Mystery itself, meanwhile, that otherness of otherness, will be paradoxically imagined as possible.

In other words, it is not so much "feminism" (inside or outside France) that is at issue as it is (or should be, I am arguing) the averted male gaze that *is* metaphysics, having fashioned itself as subject by hypostatizing a mysterious opposition, the feminine, even as it neutralizes that mystery by structuring, sublating, and deconstructing it. The feminine as it is thus configured by the averted gaze is meant to represent the place of fear and enigma; this much is clear. My point, however, is to try to look at what is being avoided there where "woman" has been placed to block it—not to reify, destabilize, or otherwise shake the dominant discourse, but to make it stop looking at itself in the mirror.

What is the vagina (again), after all, if not death from this perspective of castration and coverings—a veiled abyss, a flight from the light as we have called it, one that Kant's *Aufklärung* decries? Apocalyptic eschatology itself exiles such obscurity: "we know that every apocalyptic eschatology is promised in the name of light, of seeing and vision, and of a light of light, a light brighter than all the lights it makes possible" (82). If death for Levinas is an "eternal futurity," Derrida's essay ends with "come," that word that concludes John's Apocalypse and that Derrida wants to read as seduction and as the event "that cannot be thought": "'Come' appeared to me to appeal to the 'place' (but here the word *place* becomes too enigmatic), let us say to the place, the time, and to the advent of what in the apocalyptic in general no longer lets itself be contained simply in philosophy, metaphysics, onto-eschato-theology, and in all the readings they have proposed of the apocalyptic" (93). The notion of place is "too enigmatic." What better motif for the "problem" of the vagina that, like death, is the "event that cannot be thought"? As Nietzsche notes, he who looks into the abyss will be blinded—once again, by the dazzling light of obscurity. Hence, displacement becomes, in Derrida's terms (with different intent), analogy, simulacrum, mask. The *Aufhebung* of Isis is endless, and great care is taken (with metaphors, displacements, even confessions on the exclusion of women) to see that it is never lifted or thinned. But metaphors, as a recent scholar of human consciousness has noted, "Like children trying to describe nonsense objects, so in trying to understand a thing we are trying to find a metaphor for that thing. Not just any metaphor, but one with something more familiar and easy to our attention. Understanding a thing is to arrive at a metaphor for that thing by substituting something more familiar to us. And the feeling of familiarity is the feeling of understanding."[48] Not just any metaphor indeed, and above all philosophy as "the feeling of understanding," as the familiar, such that feminine tropes must be disjuncted from the cavernous unseeable to familiar protrusions. In Kant, Mallarmé, Freud, Derrida, Hegel—some of the canonized texts assumed in critical discourse today—we revisit vestiges of the old fear of the mystery of woman and her body.

The hymen, writes Mallarmé as if in prophesy of Freud, is "tainted with vice yet sacred." It inspires a fear that Joan of Arc, even with the authority of her voices from a Christian source, is unable to allay. Joan the

---

[48] Julian Jaynes, *The Origin of Consciousness in the Breakdown of the Bicameral Mind* (Boston, 1976), 52.

virgin, who is examined and whose hymen is confirmed as being intact, is a self-proclaimed prophet whose visions are negated, whose notion of the apocalyptic does not fit into the male economy of same. Her voice is heard, but because it is of suspicious origin, it is exiled—by the Church, through excommunication; by the state through execution; by "philosophy," through the annulment of her virginity as a viable factor. One thinks of Joan in Kant's reading of Isis, which Derrida cites:

> The veiled goddess before which we on both sides bend our knees is the moral law in us in its invulnerable majesty. We certainly perceive its voice, and we understand very clearly its commandments. But in hearing it we doubt whether it comes from man and whether it originates from the all-powerfulness of his very own reason, *or whether it emanates from some other being, whose nature is unknown to man and who speaks to him through his own proper reason.*[49]

Kant is struggling here with the notion of a divinity and backs off ("at bottom we would perhaps do better to exempt ourselves entirely from this research, for it is simply speculative"). Backing off seems to be the rhetorical ploy everywhere. I am proposing that Kant's "other being," with a nature unknown to man, is a woman, and the virgin in particular. Her voice is heard, her commandments understood, her prophesies all too clear. But one backs off: there is doubt, for when hearing the voice, it is not certain that it speaks to *man* "through his own proper reason." It is not the *logos;* it is not the Church's understanding of apocalyptic; it cannot, therefore, be recognized as prophesy, even while it is heard. The voice is already exiled; Joan's virginity is as if annulled without being entirely questioned. Derrida's reading of Mallarmé could serve as the icon for the Trial of Condemnation: "Nothing is more vicious than this suspense, this distance played at; nothing is more perverse than this rending penetration that leaves a virgin womb intact. But nothing is more marked by the sacred" ("The Double Session," 216).

Derrida's text on the apocalyptic sees a current of concealedness, like

---

49 "Of an Apocalyptic Tone," 79. The citation is from "Von einem neuerdings erhobenen vornehmen Ton in der Philosophie (1796)," 494–95, in *Schriften von 1790–1796 von Immanuel Kant,* ed. A. Buchenau, E. Cassirer, and B. Kellermann, 475–96 in vol. 6 of *Immanuel Kants Werke,* ed. Ernst Cassirer (Berlin, 1923); my emphasis.

an apophatic, running as the subtext in the economy of revelation. Prophesying and showing turn out also to mean hiding, masking, covering, and so on, as we have noted. But such a (deconstructed) elision neutralizes the scandal of a stance such as that of Joan (as virgin, and specifically as a female, Christian virgin in fifteenth-century France) and in itself veils the danger that her own ventriloquized insistence on agency suggests. Justifying her military actions by divine revelation and visions, she engages in an apocalyptic faith—one of her own fashioning—for evidence of her innocence. But concealing as she does both the nature and specific aspect of those visions, she is herself veiling the God she understands as veiled, both to her (the messengers are saints, thus at a minimum of one removed from originary divinity) and to the court. But it is her virginity that, in the context of her apocalyptic stance, poses the real, if unacknowledged, danger.

The Church rejects the ground she claims to stand on, the voices she insists she speaks for, and this peculiar apocalyptic nature of her vision. On the other hand, it equally rejects the concealedness (to return to Heidegger for a moment) of her discourse, professing to uncover her (in Derrida's terms) while simultaneously keeping securely veiled the power she may somehow unleash. We will return to this complexity of conflict; to this strange blend of apocalyptic and apophatic registers that Joan unwittingly performs; to this clash of registers that cannot, indeed must not, be sublated or deconstructed into an opposing synchronicity. Her scandal, I repeat, must not be smoothed over, as the metaphors would have us do.

The traditional Christian notion of divine revelation is to make clear the glory and presence of God, on the one hand, and the ephemeral, "probational" aspect of life on Earth, on the other. In a Christian apocalyptic model, the world is as if in excess, with the end at hand; the world is like a remainder born of the vast division necessitated by existing on the other side of the divine (one of the many aspects of Christianity that Nietzsche decried).[50] Joan's peculiar brand of apocalyptic faith as I am arguing it,

50 For the "traditional" and historical overview of Christian apocalyptic notions, see *The Encyclopedia of Apocalypticism*, ed. Bernard McGinn, vol. 2 (New York, 1998). See

however, does the reverse: her revelations insist on a refocusing of the gaze onto parochial and human, political events—not for the sake of assuring the triumph of Christianity in the world but for the restitution of what she views as a profound injustice in the political order and monarchy. Despite the monarchy's claims to divine right, such visions cannot be sanctioned by the Church and indeed are barely fathomed by it—and this quite apart from the Church's obvious bias for the other side in the political struggle in question. Perhaps for all of these reasons, as one critic has noted, Joan's Trial of Condemnation, which begins as a purely political inquiry, turns more and more to the theological in its obsessive questioning.[51] The ecclesiastical court will increasingly insist that Joan reject her revelations, since they have neither sanctioned them nor been consulted in assessing them. But for Joan, adherence to these revelations is tantamount to the salvation of her soul, so that the paradox is unresolvable: the

especially Bernard McGinn, "Apocalypticism and Church Reform: 1100–1500," 74–109. McGinn notes that medieval people lived in "a constant state of apocalyptic expectation," having to do with the triumph of Christianity over the infidel, the Last Judgment, the Anti-Christ, various doomsday scenarios, and so on. This is not the way, obviously, in which I am using the term, although part of Joan's problem was precisely that her jurors understood it thus; and from her perspective, the infidel was most certainly the English and the Burgundians. Joan has something like a synecdochal relation to the apocalyptic: she adheres to its form of divine revelation and prophesy, but not to its larger eschatological frame and Messianism. She was not, nor saw herself as, messianic. She was viewed by many, however, as such (the white horse of the Apocalypse and the sword were easily "recognized" when Joan rode into battle). For a discussion on how apocalyptic tendencies have invaded modern philosophy (as Kant put it), and also psychoanalysis and Marxism, see the essay by Jacques Derrida that I have been considering at such length. Derrida considers primarily the eschatological aspect of the apocalyptic, from John of Patmos, through Kant, Freud, and Blanchot, among others. For a more radical interpretation of both the apophatic and apocalyptic traditions, see David Tracy, *On Naming the Present: God, Hermeneutics and the Church* (New York, 1994). My own use of these terms is heavily influenced by his. On the other hand, as is no doubt clear, I am and will be using them in a near-metaphorical or philosophical, rather than theologically accurate, sense; that is, I want to indicate the direction of Joan's beliefs and to suggest the places in Christian, especially fifteenth-century Christian, discourse where they most intersect. For a view of contemporary notions of apocalyptic visions of varying (secular) sorts, see Catherine Keller, *Apocalypse Now and Then: A Feminist Guide to the End of the World* (Boston, 1996).

[51] See Père François Marie Lethel, "La Soumission à l'église militante: Un Aspect théologique de la condamnation de Jeanne d'Arc," in *Jeanne d'Arc: Une Epoque, un rayonnement: Colloque d'histoire médievale, Orléans, October 1979* (Paris, 1982), 181–89.

Church is adamant that Joan's salvation can come only if she obeys the ecclesiastical dictates; Joan is equally adamant in her conviction that those dictates would force her to betray her voices and thus damn her in the eyes of God. Again, to reveal is also to exile.

As Joan makes clear, she only revoked, or abjured, the voices once, "for fear of the fire." The court minutes continue, "And if she did revoke, it was contrary to the truth. Item, said that she prefers to do penance once, that is to die, than to suffer the affliction of prison any longer. And also said that she had never done anything against God or the faith, no matter what they had commanded her to revoke, and that she never understood what was contained in the article of abjuration. And that she never thought she had abjured anything."[52] Note that what counts for Joan is that she has never done anything "against God or the faith." This statement omits, of course, any recognition of the Church's authority over her. The historical context is critical. In 1415, some fifteen years before Joan's Trial of Condemnation, the Council of Constance issued the decree of *Haec Sancta*, which stated that the Church held its power directly from Christ. The Church thus defined itself as infallible and universal, demanding obedience from every person. The Church Militant is then configured as clerical, since its representatives mediate between God and man [*sic*] and are the sole interpreters of how that link is to be understood and performed.[53]

A work of the period is typical of this mentality. In 1417, Jean Gerson published *Tractatus de potestate ecclesiastica*, which essentially recapitulates the *Haec Sancta*.[54] The work was widely read and circulated, and it emphasized the omnipotence of the Church Militant. Such ecclesiastical totalitarianism amply demonstrates, in the words of one critic, theology degraded into ideology.[55] As the historian E. Delaruelle argues, "The fifteenth century remains one of 'clericalisms' in the strict sense of the term . . . lay people in this Church are of an inferior social category; their great

52 28 May; Duby and Duby, *Le Procès*, 173.

53 The Council of Basel will attempt to turn this into doctrine (twenty-third session, May 1439), but this will be almost immediately condemned by Pope Eugene IV (Bull *Moyses*, 4 September 1439).

54 Jean Gerson, *Oeuvres complètes*, ed. Mgr. Glorieux, in *L'Oeuvre ecclesiologique*, vol. 6 (Paris, 1960). For an analysis of the Council of Constance's Decree, see O. De La Brosse, *Le Pape et les Conciles* (Paris, 1965), 81–145.

55 Lethel, "La Soumission," 187.

virtue is obedience, which defines their faith."[56] Joan's understanding of faith, however, is not tied to a recognition of the supremacy of the Church Militant. Moreover, she cannot obey its demand that she revoke her voices. Thus, in the eyes of the Church, her faith is in serious jeopardy because she does not acknowledge the notion of *potestas ecclesiastica*. The article of condemnation that results is clear on this issue. I cite it in its entirety:

> Item: you have said that if the Church wanted you to do the opposite of the commandment you say you have from God, that you would do it for nothing on earth. And you [say that] you know that what is contained in your trial came from the commandment of God and that it would be impossible for you to do the opposite. On all these things mentioned above, you do not want to turn to the Church which is on earth, nor to a living man, but to God alone. And you say further that you do not give these answers from the mind, but from God's commandment, despite the fact that the article of faith which is that everyone must believe in the Catholic Church has been declared to you several times, and that every good Christian Catholic must submit all his acts to the Church, especially with regard to revelation and such things.

Her acts, her choice of virginity itself, were never submitted to the Church for approval. Her faith stands outside the Church, and is therefore essentially annulled. Her virginity itself is unacknowledged as participating in the holy state recognized by the Church fathers and by the ecclesiastic hegemony. Joan's virginity is unsanctioned because it is not bound by "divine law in a Christian country," in Maistre's terms. The conclusion of the "analysis" in the article of condemnation cited earlier can only be seen, given the history of the Church's self-definition at the time, as inevitable: "As to this article, the clerics say that you are schismatic, that you are wrong-thinking on the truth and authority of the Church, and that until now you have perniciously erred in the faith in God."[57] In condemning Joan, the Church Militant asserts and demon-

[56] E. Delaruelle, *L'Église au temps du Grand Schisme et de la Crise Conciliaire*, vol. 14 of *L'Histoire de l'Église de Fiche et Martin* (Paris, 1962), xiii.

[57] Duby and Duby, *Le Procès*, 160.

strates its power. We read the struggle throughout the trial, specifically in the sixty-first of the seventy original libels *(libelles)* against her: "interrogated as to whether she would submit to the Church Militant, answered that she wanted to show it reverence with all her might. But as to her actions, she turned to God, who had made her do them. Interrogated as to whether she would tell the Church Militant what she had done, answers, 'Send me the clerk next Saturday and I will answer you.'"[58] Joan never showed any resistance to the Church (she several times refers respectfully to the *gens d'Église*); she merely would not obey its primary demand that, as mentioned, she reject her voices. Here, as in many other places in the trial, she has recourse to delay, deferral: she frequently invokes Saturday, the day of confession, as the one where her voices might give her permission to reveal an answer. Her other tactic, as we shall see, is silence. For eschatology, to return for a last time to Derrida, may be a tone, "or even the voice itself." But eschatology is not within the parameters of Joan's apocalyptic discourse; for she is prophetic about her king and his kingdom, but not about the end of things, nor is she concerned with a Last Judgment.

As the hymen and the virginity it promises are exiled, as we have seen, from their feminine specificity and logic, so will Joan's voice, with her body, be put in exile, silenced from the logic of her own trial. It is that voice, then, which must be examined next.

---

[58] Ibid., 140. The seventy articles comprise a "requisition" drawn up by Jean d'Estivet, the "promoter," which were read to Joan on 27 and 28 March. She was to answer only "I believe it" or "I do not believe it."

CHAPTER FOUR

RESPONSIO MORTIFERA: THE VOICE OF THE MAID

Dum medium silentium fieret. For if you want God to speak to you, you must be silent.

—Johann Tauler, disciple of Meister Eckhart

Socrates: But now tell me, is there another sort of discourse, that is brother to the written speech, but of unquestioned legitimacy? Can we see how it originates, and how much better and more effective it is than the other?

Phaedrus: What sort of discourse have you now in mind, and what is its origin?

Socrates: The sort that goes together with knowledge, and is written in the soul of the learner, that can defend itself, and knows to whom it should speak and to whom it should say nothing.

Phaedrus: You mean no dead discourse, but the living speech, the original of which the written discourse may fairly be called a kind of image.

Socrates: Precisely.

THE TRIAL OF CONDEMNATION was transcribed by the notary Guillaume Manchon and two assistants.[1] The manuscript has numerous inaccuracies: most of the original French, jotted down by the scribe, had been thought lost, and much of the Latin translation is fragmented or inaccurate. Until the manuscript at Orléans was carefully studied by Doncoeur in the early 1950s, the best that could be done was to work from

[1] The Trial of Condemnation lasted five months: from 9 January to 30 May 1431. For Régine Pernoud, it was composed of three parts, beginning with the *procès d'office* (the magistrate's investigations preceding the trial in open court), from 9 January to 26 March. This was followed by the regular trial, which ended with Joan's recantation (or abjuration, the technical term) on 24 May. Finally, there was the Relapse trial, which lasted two days, 28 and 29 May. In chapter 5, I suggest a slightly different division of the trial. The full Latin text of both the Trials of Condemnation and of Rehabilitation with commentary were published by Jules Quicherat, *Procès de condamnation et de réhabilitation de Jeanne d'Arc, dite la Pucelle* (Paris, 1841–49). The edition I am using is a reprint from a copy in the collections of the New York Public Library, in five volumes (New York, 1965). See also Quicherat's introduction to the edition, *Aperçus nouveaux sur l'histoire de Jeanne d'Arc*

a combination of fragments of the Latin and French. Even the Orléans manuscript contains summaries. Nevertheless, these documents seem by their very production and context to be about as close to written history produced in situ as one can get. Foucault notes that until recently, a transcription was viewed as being in the "language of a voice reduced to

(Paris, 1850), so important as to have been published separately. Quicherat's is the most fully documented and annotated edition, and it needs to be referred to by anyone studying Joan. For a thorough discussion of the manuscripts and translators, see Régine Pernoud, *Joan of Arc by Herself and Her Witnesses* (Lanham, Md., 1994), 224–27. Pernoud, who has devoted her scholarly life to Johannic studies, also includes in this work an excellent series of bibliographies on various aspects of Joan's life and times.

Minutes were taken by Guillaume Manchon, notary of the trial, every day at the Trial of Condemnation in French, and they were translated into Latin four years after her death by Thomas de Courcelles (who had been one of her judges) and Manchon. Five copies were made of the record (three in Manchon's hand), of which the three remaining are in Paris. They are known as the Authentic Document and have relatively sporadic variations; Courcelles, for example, falsified some of the testimony and trial proceedings to justify the outcome. Pierre Champion (who updated Quicherat and translated the trial from the Courcelles in 1920) produced invaluable notes and commentaries, but the manuscript that is the basis of his work is flawed. Champion notes that it is clear that when the scribes could not find the Latin for certain colloquialisms, they reverted to the French. See Pierre Champion, *Le Procès de condamnation,* 2 vols. (Paris, 1920–21).

The original French minutes were thought to have been lost, except for fragments from the d'Urfé manuscript (a copy), which is to be found in the Bibliothèque Nationale in Paris. On this, see Quicherat, *Aperçus nouveaux;* the introduction to Scott's translation; and the multiple books on the subject by Pernoud. There is, however, the Orléans manuscript, at the Bibliothèque Municipale (MS 518), which reports, in French, the life of Joan and the two trials. It is known that it was drawn up for Louis XII and so must be from around 1500. Quicherat did not use the Orléans manuscript because he believed that, in Scott's words, "it merely supplied the *lacunae* in the d'Urfé manuscript by a translation of Courcelles" (18). Champion did the same. In 1952, Fr. Paul Doncoeur published the first of a five-volume work based on his study of the Orléans manuscript, *Documents et recherches relatifs à Jeanne la Pucelle* (Melun, 1952–61). Having compared the d'Urfé and Orléans manuscripts, he became certain that because as of 3 March both manuscripts reproduced the original French minutes, the Orléans manuscript was in fact a complete copy of the French. The Orléans manuscript now provides us, by comparison with the Latin translation, with a confirmation of the fact that the chief magistrate Cauchon ordered Courcelles to falsify the record in order to justify the trial. It should be added that among the many irregularities in Joan's trial, which were noted by the Trial of Rehabilitation, was the fact that she had no counsel at any time during the proceedings.

silence; its fragile, but possibly decipherable trace."[2] Now, he writes, history has shifted to work "within" a given document, and, no longer attempting to discover where lies the truth within it, history "is one way in which a society recognizes and develops a mass of documentation with which it is inextricably linked." The document, then, for Foucault, is no longer memory but rather a means of finding "unities, totalities, series, relations." But I will be combining parts of these two approaches to documents; my approach will engage the second, "new" shift primarily but also (without searching for "the truth" or privileging "memory") the recognition that there is, within these trial documents, a voice reduced to silence with a fragile, if ultimately undecipherable, cultural (as against individual) trace. There are, as we shall see, many layers of silence in the trial on Joan's voices.

Confrontation with the trial begins with the immense quantity of documents. These not only comprise but are actually produced by a "history" understood as an a priori move of interpretation. As Michel de Certeau notes, in history, "everything begins with the gesture of *setting aside,* of putting together, of transforming certain classified objects into 'documents.' This new cultural distribution is the first task. In reality it consists in *producing* such documents . . . simultaneously changing their locus and status. This gesture consists in 'isolating' a body—as in physics—and 'denaturing' things in order to turn them into parts which will fill the lacunae inside an a priori totality."[3]

Any scrutiny of the trial will perforce "denature" it. The trial is removed from us in countless ways: by five centuries of time elapsed; by the layers of language that muffle the original (out of the spoken, Middle French, it is transcribed into French, translated into Latin, and in the present case, rendered into English); by the fact that the voices we hear and read are long since dead, so that they echo like hauntings on the page; by the rendering of voice into text in the first place; by the very syntax and protocol of fifteenth-century juridical proceedings; by the indirect discourse that characterizes most of the recorded aspects of questions and

---

2 Michel Foucault, *The Archeology of Knowledge and the Discourse of Language,* trans. A. M. Sheridan Smith (New York, 1972), 6–7.

3 Michel de Certeau, *The Writing of History,* trans. Tom Conley (New York, 1988), 72–73.

responses; by the defamiliarizing late medieval French and vulgate Latin in which the trial is transcribed; by the gaps and ellipses in the minutes, including lost documents, incomplete ones, and previous trials that are referred to but that have since been lost; by a succession of editors who have altered, interpreted, translated, amended, and otherwise corrupted the "purity" of the original, whatever it may have been; by the Church's own censorship, additions, and suppression of certain parts of the trial; by the ravages of wars and time that have colluded in losing, damaging, hiding, and otherwise corrupting the text; by the ensuing Trial of Rehabilitation, with its hindsight and justifications; by the beatification and ultimate canonization, five hundred years later, of the figure who is the defendant and whose condemnation we can no longer read without a constant perspective of backformation, so that every small and great event is doubly reinterpreted in the light of subsequent events. One could go on and on. Nevertheless, despite all of these caveats, "denaturings," and limitations, there is a way in which, upon reading the trial, one is riveted by the sense of immediacy and reality. As Georges Bataille notes, in the opening to his study of another, contemporaneous trial of heresy, "Few human beings have left behind traces permitting them, after five centuries, to speak thus! To cry thus! Such scenes are not the work of an author. *They happened:* somehow we have the stenography of them."[4] Despite all of the elaborate theoretical, textual, historical and hermeneutical (to name a few) considerations that would warn us against taking the trial too literally, too easily (considerations that I will myself be invoking), this is an aspect that we must not become too sophisticated to remember: *it happened.* Somehow we have the stenography of its trace. It is then with this double vision—of caution and awe—that we now approach the trial.

The question we are increasingly addressing is, whose voice is it that we hear in the trial of Joan of Arc? Or more precisely, what is the "I," the putative subject, who speaks in her voice? In many ways, she is to be found, if at all, more in her silences than in her responses (which, to repeat, are generally recorded in indirect discourse, so that the syntax mirrors the otherness of the defendant) to the "a priori totality" grinding the machinery of the trial. When she does speak, the few direct quotations seem to be of a different order of discourse, ruptures of an alternative

---

4 Georges Bataille, *The Trial of Gilles de Rais,* trans. Richard Robinson (Los Angeles, 1991), 19.

register in the text. In Certeau's words, again, "a necessary outer text within the text."[5]

But there is serious ambivalence in citation, that apparent recording of the verbatim. For Certeau, citation upholds the danger of an uncanniness that alters the translator's or commentator's knowledge. For discourse, citation is the menace and suspense of a lapsus. Citation is as if an otherness in the text. In the case of Joan, it constitutes the shock of alterity in the discourse of the trial, which itself performs the hegemony of the Church in fifteenth-century France.

If in the documents of the trial Joan's voice is at odds with the dominant discourse, it is for two fundamental reasons: the pervasive ideology of the Church of the Inquisition (which *is* that discourse) and the gender of the accused. We have already begun to look at the Church, but it bears further scrutiny.

The legal aspects of Joan's trial follow the decree made by Innocent III at the Fourth Lateran Council of 1215.[6] In place of the Roman protocol of *accusatio,* which required an accusing party to take on the responsibility of proof, there is that of *inquisitio.* Under this new system, an ecclesiastical judge would inquire into the basis of a collective belief, *fama.* In the words of Kelly, *fama,* or "fame," allows the ecclesiastical judge to summon the suspect and "*inquire,* that is, 'make inquisition,' as to whether the fame was true. The pope considered the fame, or public outcry, to be the equivalent of the accuser in the older system; this is how he forestalled the objection that the judge was acting as both accuser and judge" (995). With the burden now shifted from the accuser to the accused, questioning becomes fundamental in legal procedure. Adding to the clear unfairness

5 Thus, Certeau will argue, for example, that the role of quoted language is to accredit discourse. With its referential function, he adds, quoted language "introduces into the text an effect of reality; and through its crumbling, it discreetly refers to a locus of authority." This "split structure of discourse" functions like a machinery "that extracts from this citation a versimilitude of narrative and a validation of knowledge. It produces a sense of reliability" (*The Writing of History,* 94). It is not possible, then, to be too cautious in approaching a text such as that of Joan's trial.

6 I am basing most of the historical considerations on the work of H. Ansgar Kelly, to whose article I refer the reader for further details. See "The Right to Remain Silent: Before and after Joan of Arc," *Speculum* 68, no. 4 (October 1993): 992–1026. See also Karen Sullivan, *The Interrogation of Joan of Arc* (Minneapolis, 1999), which reads the trial as a clash between lay and clerical cultures.

of such a system, in 1298 Boniface VIII decided that in normal cases under the new system, the judge had to show the defendant a document specifying the charges. In heresy cases, however, a summary was allowed.[7] Joan's Trial of Condemnation, then, began with an exhaustive interrogation, the culmination of which was a list of formal charges. The University of Paris (completely under English rule at the time) drew up twelve articles against her shortly before her execution. Two months earlier, also after the interrogation was largely completed, the court had produced a "Text of Libel," as previously mentioned, with seventy articles against her. These were read to her, and she was to answer with what amounted to a yes or no. The subject accused of heresy, then, is already outside normal law and a priori in a state of assumed culpability.

Consider, for example, the analysis by the University of Paris of Article I of the final twelve drawn up for condemnation. The university's responses were read to Joan on 23 May:

> [. . .] You, Jeanne, have said that from the age of thirteen, you had revelations and apparitions of angels, of Saint Catherine and Saint Margaret, and that you saw them quite often with your corporeal eyes, and that they spoke to you. As to this first point, the clergy of the University of Paris have considered the manner of the aforesaid revelations and apparitions, the ends and substance of the things revealed, and the quality of the person. *All things considered which are to be considered* [*et, omnibus consideratis quae consideranda erant*], they have said and declared: that all things said about them are lies, deceptions, things of seduction and pernicious; and that such revelations are superstitious, arising from evil and diabolical spirits.[8]

The court considers "all things which are to be considered," thus pre-establishing the parameters and, in effect, the answers to the equally pre-

---

7 At one point in the trial, Joan asks to see the written account of the charges against her and is denied. This denial itself is legal proof, as if any were needed, that the trial was one of heresy. It should be added here that, since Joan was illiterate, her request to see the written charges is more the desire for ocular proof that the document exists—a test of the court's good faith—than it is a wish to know the charges in their specificity.

8 Georges Duby and Andrée Duby, *Le Procès de Jeanne d'Arc* (Paris, 1995), 155; my emphasis. For the full Latin text, see Quicherat, *Procès*, 1: 431.

determined questions. This self-confirming logic of tautological *demonstratio,* then, one that is a cliché in trials of heresy, functions to keep the dialogue of interrogation inside its own map. No answer by the defendant can fall outside the boundaries of knowledge that the court imposes and alone possesses. Neither a yes nor a no response, then, can extract the defendant from the architecture of the court's logic. Language becomes phatic; and every "answer" by the defendant, an occasion to demonstrate the court's hold on the truth—its ideological totalitarianism, to return to an earlier phrase. The options for the witness in such a linguistic panopticon become perjury or condemnation; silence is seen as disobedience. "All things considered which are to be considered" states, and amply so, the full thrust of the court proceedings. The trial itself becomes the declaration of the Church Militant's omnipotence. The defendant's discourse is at best superfluous, when she recites Church dogma; at worst evidence of anathema, when she deviates.

It comes as no surprise, then, that Joan strongly resists when she is asked repeatedly to swear to the oath of truth. The oath was, of course, customary, but taking it more than once was not. The initial oath was a difficult moment in itself: Joan finally swears on the Bible to tell the truth "concerning matters of faith." She adds a condition, however: "But as to the revelations already mentioned, she would tell them to no one."[9] When she is asked to swear again, on the following day, she refuses, directly challenging Cauchon, Bishop of Beauvais, who was chief magistrate. John de Montigny, doctor of canon law at the University of Paris at the time of the trial, notes that this was in violation of juridical procedure. Kelly summarizes Montigny's view: "[F]irst, because she was compelled by oath to respond to all subjects of inquiry, even the most occult *(ad omnia inquisita, etiam quecunque et quantumcunque occulta),* and she was compelled to respond generally and absolutely to all the things that were to be asked of her, whereas she should have been forced to reply by oath only concerning those points on which she had been defamed or found suspect in the faith; and second, she was forced to swear repeatedly, whereas, according to the law, the oath to tell the truth should be given only once."[10]

---

9 Duby and Duby, *Le Procès,* 29.

10 Kelly, "The Right to Remain Silent," 1022. Kelly notes that John Lohier, a respected canonist, told Cauchon on 17 March that he objected to the entire proceedings because "there had to be a preliminary process on infamy before there could be a formal process on

But an oath of truth is extracted several times when two truths are in combat, as was the case in Joan's trial. Over and over again, Joan says that she has already sworn and that in any case, her voices forbid her to do so again. "I have sworn enough," she says, "Pass on [*Passez outre*]." The private relationship she claims with God informs her refusal of a blanket oath in a court of law, even an ecclesiastical one. Indeed, two Church scholars at the time of the trial complained that Cauchon had no more right than the Church itself to question Joan on "occult matters" (that is, on matters that were private or secret in nature).

The *Oxford Latin Dictionary* gives seven definitions for the adjective *occultus-a-um*. All of these have to do with what is hidden, concealed, secret, inaccessible. The first definition links the word with secrets of nature: "(of the workings or forces of nature), invisible, secret." We are strangely back to Buffon, who equated the secrets of nature with that which should remain inviolable, hidden. If we hear echoes of Freud's uncanny in the Latin notion of *occultus*, it is perhaps because in the trial of Joan, too, that which is familiar remains secret—but in this case, the secret is withheld from the court, not from the conscious mind. It is not coincidental that Certeau's analysis of citation in discourse alludes to the uncanny as well. The full quotation reads as follows: "Something different returns in this discourse, however, along with the citation of the other; it remains ambivalent; it upholds the danger of an uncanniness which alters the translator's or commentator's knowledge" (94). The "occult" in this case, then, should be read as the fifteenth-century notion of what we would call privacy: that which has the *right* to remain secret for the individual. In the fifteenth-century context, this is a right because it is based on the individual's relation to God.[11]

The distinction between transgressions understood as *private* (between the individual and God) and those of *public* domain accountable under the rule of the ecclesiastical court, stem from the establishment of the *inquisitio* by Innocent III. It is a distinction that Joan refuses to recog-

the faith." He speculates that this is why Cauchon had the seventy articles against Joan hurriedly drawn up in mid-trial, on 18 March (1018).

11 As Kelly notes, at the time of the Fourth Lateran Council, there was to have been a "bill of rights" (never uniformly enforced), part of which stated that "the Church does not judge secret matters" [*Ecclesia de occultis non judicat*]." "The Right to Remain Silent," 995.

nize, and it is perhaps in this sense that she can be seen as an early modern. To explain what I mean by this, we have to keep in mind the medieval Christian notion of the individual, quite a different concept from what we call today subjectivity.

Louis Dupré notes that the Christian doctrine of individual salvation detached the person from the cosmic because each individual was seen as responsible to God: "Each person stood in a direct relation to God rather than to the cosmos. This intimate relation to a divine archetype of which each individual was a unique image constituted the very essence of personhood." But this did not mean that the person (a term that I use in this, its earlier, sense) was autonomous, notes Dupré: "This exalting of the individual self, however, did not transform the person into an atomic entity. The Church constituted a new community on which the individual depended as much for the attainment of his destiny as he had previously depended on the state, albeit in a different manner."[12]

Louis Dumont echoes Dupré, noting that whereas the modern notion of the subject sees itself as self-sufficient through the state (as had his or her privileged predecessors in the Roman *polis*), in Christian medieval thought, "the Christian is an 'individual-in-relation-to-God.'"[13] This means, according to Dumont, that on the one hand, "man is in essence an outwordly individual" (96), a move that Dumont, following Troeltsch, already sees in the new schools of the Hellenistic period. Dumont continues, "There is, Troeltsch says, 'absolute individualism and absolute universalism' in relation to God. The individual soul receives eternal value from its filial relationship to God, in which relationship is also grounded human fellowship" (98). But this validation of the individual comes with a tension: "The infinite worth of the individual is at the same time the disparagement, the negation in terms of value, of the world as it is: a dualism is posited, a tension is established that is constitutive of Christianity and will endure throughout history." As Dumont puts it, and as Nietzsche was scornfully to vent, the individual in this context is founded upon a devaluation of the world. Dumont suggests a "passable formula" for Chris-

---

[12] Louis Dupré, *Passage to Modernity: An Essay in the Hermeneutics of Nature and Culture* (New Haven, Conn., 1993), 95.

[13] Louis Dumont, "A Modified View of Our Origins: The Christian Beginnings of Modern Individualism," in *The Category of the Person: Anthropology, Philosophy, History*, ed. Michael Carrithers, Steven Collins, and Steven Lukes (Cambridge, 1985), 98.

tianity: "the union of outworldly individuals in a community that treads on earth but has its heart in heaven" (99). The result, of course, is a series of binary oppositions ("between this world and the beyond, body and soul, state and church, the old and the new dispensations—which are the basic framework used by the early Fathers and which Caspary calls the 'Pauline pairs'"). When Jesus teaches to "render unto Caesar the things that are Caesar's, but unto God the things that are God's," continues Dumont, "The symmetry is only apparent, as it is for the sake of God that we must comply with the legitimate claims of Caesar. . . . The worldly order is relativized, as subordinated to absolute values. There is an ordered dichotomy: outwordly individualism encompasses recognition of and obedience to the powers of this world" (100). On the worldly level, however, a man is not individuated but a "member of the commonwealth, a part of the social body." *Lebenswelt,* in other words, belongs to the Church in Joan's century.

The difficulty for Joan is that she blurs the distinction between "Caesar" and God. That is, she sees Charles VII as king by divine right and understands this as an extension of her god's hierarchy. On the other hand, she recognizes no role for herself in the commonwealth or social body, in the sense that she imagines herself to have only the fulfillment of her divine mission as her purpose (at least, in the portion of her life that we know). The power of the Church, or the Church Militant, is not a presence in the hegemony she recognizes. Fighting for Caesar through God, she refuses to adhere to the Church's demands because she sees them as countermanding her mission. In answering only to God, she is, in the eyes of the Church, refusing the Church Militant and recognizing only the Church Triumphant. Indeed, this was to be one of the final twelve charges leveled against her. For the Church probed Joan's thoughts again and again, to establish their "purity," just as surely as a midwife probes a woman to establish her virginity. Speculum into the *occulta,* the Church is unsuccessful in its violation and abandons its efforts with a blanket condemnation, motivated by the charge of disobedience.

It needs to be reiterated here that Joan does not comprehend the Church Militant or its distinction from the Church Triumphant, except to the extent that the former threatens her mission and, more and more clearly, her life. In other words, by insisting on a private relationship with God *and* with her king, and by retaining as *occulta* her thoughts on these, she is presenting herself to the Church as self-sufficient by way of the monarchy as well as by God. The "holism" (Dumont's term) of her society is of no real import to her. She stands outside it in almost every way: in her departure from her parents' house and her village, in her refusal to marry, in her rejection of Church authority (she does not confess about her voices, and she enters no ecclesiastical order), in her silence, in her attire, and so on. As such, Joan is a strange mixture of early medieval views (before the Church's self-declared omnipotence) and modernism, because she claims as private a relation to God and individuates herself through the state, "France."

In the fifteenth century, the French feudal domains are torn by war and civil quarreling; the king is weakened by powerful lords and, in the case of Charles VII, questions of lineage; the regions have different *patois,* spoken by most of the populations, as different one from the other as modern French is from Spanish[14]—French is the language of the court. It is the Church that serves to unite the populace and serves as the state. There is, in fact, no France as we conceptualize it today, except (to an extent) in Joan's insistent ideal. A subsequent chapter will treat this issue at some length. For now, however, it is enough to note that the Church sees Joan as a heretic for reasons having to do with her *modern* view of the state as a centralized, autonomous (although blessed by God) entity and her modern view of herself as a self-sufficient individual within that state. Let us not forget that Joan's campaign had the effect of strengthening the monarchy at the expense of feudal lords, thus paving the way for the modern state. Her private relation to God, which she insists she has the right to keep so, is equally anachronistic: it is as if left over from an earlier Christianity, before the Church's seizure of *Lebenswelt.* This the Church sees clearly, brutally stating it in the last article of condemnation:

> Item: you say that if the Church wanted you to do the opposite of the commandment you say comes from God, that you would obey it for nothing in the world. . . . Given all things said on this, you do

[14] These *patois* varied enormously even within the two large dialects that divided France throughout the Middle Ages, *langue d'oc* and *langue d'oil.* Middle French appears at the start of the fourteenth century, which is the language we read in parts of the trial manuscripts. But the regional *patois* persisted until well into the present era, and in some areas they continue to be spoken, with French as the "official" language.

> not want to submit to the judgement of the Church which is on earth, nor to any living man, but to God alone. And you say that you do not give these answers from your mind [*ex capite tuo*], but by God's commandment, even though the article of faith is that each person must believe in the Catholic Church, as has been often declared to you, and that every good Christian Catholic must submit all acts to the Church, especially with regard to revelations and such things.[15]

She is thus declared schismatic, "badly responding to the truth and authority of the Church." She responds, at one point however, with the terse declaration that she does not accept their judgement. To Cauchon, she says in a rare show of anger, "You say that you are my judge. I do not know if you are. But be careful not to judge badly. You would put yourself in great danger. And I am warning you so that, if Our Lord punishes you for it, I will have done my duty in warning you."[16]

The clash of power registers could not be more overt. We are confronted here with two different notions of knowledge, two different hegemonies, two different understandings of the individual, two different concepts of the private. Her voices tell her to take everything in stride, not to avoid her martyrdom. "You will finally come to the kingdom of Paradise," they reassure her. She acknowledges, then, two kingdoms, the first existing by virtue of the second: that of her king and that of heaven. The Church is completely absent from this schema. This increasingly becomes the Church's obsession in the trial—more, finally, than the fact that Joan is a political danger. She remains stolid in refusing to bow to the Church's power, even at the expense of her life. It is not just that she does not want to; she actually does not understand it. When Cauchon asks her whether her voices come from God, Joan's priorities are clear: "And I think that I am not telling you fully what I know; and I am more afraid of saying something which will displease them [the voices], than I am afraid of answering you."[17]

---

15 Duby and Duby, *Le Procès,* 160. For the Latin, see Quicherat, *Procès,* 1:436. This comprises the twelfth of the twelve articles against Joan in her condemnation.

16 Duby and Duby, *Le Procès,* 103.

17 Ibid., 46–74.

BATAILLE'S TAKE ON HERESY

One way of grasping the extent to which Joan's behavior is unusual, not to say courageous, is to compare her heresy trial with that of her contemporary, Gilles de Rais. Rais is of particular interest here because he actually fought alongside Joan many times, including at the successful lifting of Orléans's siege. He was with Joan during the unsuccessful attempt to take Paris, where Joan was wounded in the thigh by an arrow. She thought that she was near death, and, Bataille maintains, it was for Gilles de Rais that she asked.[18] One of the richest and most powerful lords of France, he, too, was tried and found guilty of heresy just ten years after Joan. As Georges Bataille points out in his remarkable study of the trial, "Abbot Bossard wrote that the trial of Gilles de Rais was 'in all things the polar opposite of Joan of Arc's.' But he adds that 'together they compose the two most celebrated trials of the Middle Ages and perhaps also of modern times.'"[19] Abbot Bossard's thorough study on Rais is now obsolete, as

---

[18] Bataille, *The Trial of Gilles de Rais,* 73. But this anecdote is not clear. The chronicler of the period whom Quicherat, as Bataille comments, considers "the most reliable" is Perceval de Cagny. Cagny writes that Gilles de Rais was one of those with Joan when she was wounded outside Paris but that it was the Duke of Alençon whom she asked for ("mon beau Duc," as she called him) (Quicherat, *Procès,* 4: 27) The chronicler Jean Chartier (brother to the poet Alain), also of the fifteenth century, relates it differently: Rais was already with Joan when she was wounded, and Alençon was sent for by him and the other nobles in the battle to convince her to retreat, which she was fiercely refusing to do (Quicherat, *Procès,* 4: 87). Another chronicle of the fifteenth century relates the events in the same way as Chartier (Quicherat, *Procès,* 4: 197–99). Bataille has read his Quicherat too quickly here, I think. A small but significant detail provides another similarity between Rais and Joan: both were given special permission by the king to bear the royal emblem, the fleur-de-lis, on their arms. This was a great and rare honor and adds the twist of Joan and Rais in battle: the two were fighting with the same (though differently decorated) royal emblem.

[19] Bataille, *The Trial of Gilles de Rais,* 5. See Abbé Eugene Bossard, *Gilles de Rais: Maréchal de France, dit Barbe-Bleue* (Paris, 1886). For further reading on Rais, see, among others, Jean Benedetti, *Gilles de Rais* (New York, 1972); René Girard, *La Violence et le sacré* (Paris, 1972) and *La Route antique des hommes pervers* (Paris, 1985); Lodovico Hernandez, *Le Procès inquisitorial de Gilles de Rais, Maréchal de France avec un essai de réhabilitation,* which is a verbatim translation of the ecclesiastic trial and a copy of the civil trial (Paris, 1922); the novel by Joris-Karl Huysmans, *Là-bas* (Paris, 1978); the more recent novel by Michel Tournier, *Gilles et Jeanne* (Paris, 1983), which specifically addresses the

Bataille notes, adding "this is not the case with the trial documents: this is not the case with these most terrible documents." Bataille's study pieces together and presents these documents, giving us the minutes of another heresy trial with which to compare Joan's, fifteen years before her posthumous Trial of Rehabilitation.

Gilles de Rais, frequently confused with Bluebeard, was condemned in 1440 by the Inquisition for sexually molesting and murdering nearly one hundred fifty young children (mainly boys). He was equally found guilty of trying to consort with the Devil and for violating the Church by entering a chapel with a noisy band of armed men, threatening and imprisoning the priest. He was hanged and burned on 26 October 1440. It is hard to imagine how this trial could be anything but the "polar opposite" of Joan's. In terms of willed evil, Rais is outstanding in his excesses, forming a good deal of Bataille's fascination with the case. Rais was indeed excessive in everything: in his eating, drinking, fornication, killing, gratuitous violence, wanton destruction, outrageous spending of a massive fortune to the point of bankruptcy, and Devil worshiping, to name the most obvious. Joan, who is a modest farm girl, a virgin who fasts and does penance, who prays and confesses constantly, who carries a banner in battle to prevent her from killing, who ejects the prostitutes from the army, who will not tolerate blasphemy in her presence, and who confers with saints—how much more diametrically opposed can she possibly be to the Lord Rais?

Both are tried and executed for heresy by the Inquisition (both are described by the court as "a dog returning to its vomit"), and both are excommunicated, although they seem to be contemporaneous examples of opposite ends of the spectrum: pure goodness and evil incarnate. And yet Rais was hanged before compassionate onlookers, then burned and lovingly pulled from the flames before the fire could "expose his entrails," given a church funeral, and buried in holy ground beside others of noble lineage. Joan, on the other hand, was given the crueler death of burning until she died. The flames were then extinguished so that the crowd could view her naked body and ascertain that "she was a woman." Her body was burned again until nothing was left but ashes, which were then thrown into the river. One is initially at a loss to understand how this could have happened.

---

possible friendship between Joan and Rais; and Wyndham Lewis, *The Soul of Marshal Gilles de Raiz* (London, 1952).

The most immediate answer to this question is, of course, class. Rais came from one of the noblest families of France. Far richer than the king, he possessed not only numerous châteaux but a fortune that today would be that of a billionaire. His grandfather, who raised him, was a powerful and corrupt influence at court. Rais himself was to be Marshal of France until his political luck turned, and one of the leaders of the army until his debts ruined him. The children he kidnapped for sexual crimes and murder were procured for him by his servants and accomplices, so that he could always claim he knew nothing about it. Moreover, these were the children of his vassals, who were afraid to complain, or children he stole while traveling through a region, leaving no trace. He frequently changed venues, traveling to other of his domains when too many grumblings began to be heard. His victims were poor children, then, who were often promised a life of ease as a page and whose uneasy parents were persuaded to relinquish their child through assurances that good food and a better life would be his or hers at the castle.[20] In other words, Rais was able to accomplish his vast crimes because of his rank and wealth. Interestingly enough, when his money began to run out, he gave himself importance by reminding everyone that he had fought at Joan's side.[21] He enjoyed, for example, participating in the parade for Joan in Orléans, every 8 May. In 1435, we know that he not only took part in the parade but financed extravagant pageants, theater, mystery plays, musical events, and comedies, indulging in what Bataille calls "scandalous expenditure."

Class accounts for most of the difference: there was certain terror in approaching someone of so powerful a family, even of collecting his enormous debts. Moreover, the Church, realistic as it was, trod softly when it came to feudal lords even if turned brigand. Rais, like Joan, is angry with his judges for arresting him. But whereas Joan warns her judges that a higher, divine authority will mete out its own judgment,

20 For this and all other biographical references to the life of Gilles de Rais, I am basing my comments on Bataille's detailed chronology.

21 Rais's crimes began in 1432, the year his grandfather died and one year after Joan was murdered. Bataille makes a clear connection between the crimes and the first of these events, which is the usual interpretation. But is there perhaps also a connection with the second? I suspect there may have been. Tournier has the same suspicion. In his novel *Gilles et Jeanne,* he suggests that it was Joan's death that motivated Gilles's crimes. In despair at the cruelty and execution to which she was subjected, Tournier's Rais decides that he, too, will be the victim of the Church and be burned at the stake.

Rais is scornful because the judges are, from his point of view, socially inferior to him. The court minutes show a contemptuous Rais who does not believe that his judges are more powerful than he is and who shows no interest in the forty-nine articles drawn up against him:

> Gilles said and responded proudly and haughtily that he did not intend to respond to these same positions and articles, stating clearly that the said Lords Bishop and Vicar of the Inquisitor had never been nor were his judges and that he would appeal. Moreover, now speaking irreverently and rudely, the said Gilles, the accused, declared that the said Lords Bishop of Nantes and Friar Jean Blouyn, Vicar of the Inquisitor, and all the other ecclesiastics, were simoniacs and ribalds; that he would much prefer to be hanged by a rope around his neck than to respond to such ecclesiastics and judges, and that he could not tolerate appearing before them.[22]

Note that much of this resembles Joan's statements. She, too, is not convinced that her judges are in fact in a position to judge her, and she, too, says at one point that she would rather die than acquiesce to their demands. Moreover, Rais also refuses to take the oath, "in spite of four demands and the threat of lawful excommunication" (124). The similarities, of course, stop there. Joan is obeying her divine voices and the hierarchy from which she understands them to originate. Rais is responding to his version of the *droits de seigneur:* no one has ever outranked or outspent him. His power structure is that of feudal lords; hers, that of an outwordly power. But because Rais will ultimately recognize the Church's authority (particularly after they threaten to torture him) and beg for forgiveness in a torrent of hysterical sobbing and endless hand-wringing verbiage, he will be reintegrated into the Church. Joan, who also "confesses" at one point (the abjuration), will recant and say that she abjured only out of "fear of the fire." She remains anathema until her trial twenty-five years later.

Even in his remorse, Rais is excessive, and that is the point. He confesses everything, *especially* what is *occulta*. In fact, he goes so far as to insist that his confession be published:

---

22 Bataille, "Records of the Hearings," in *The Trial of Gilles de Rais*, 160.

> [S]o that the secret confession would be committed the best way possible to the memory of men, it pleased the same Gilles, the accused, not to diminish but rather to fortify and reinforce it; and he asked that the aforesaid confession be published in the vernacular language for any and all of the people present, the better part of whom did not know Latin, and that the publication and confession of perpetrated offenses be set forth for his shame, in order for him to attain more easily the forgiveness of his sins and God's grace in absolving them.[23]

The "secret confession," then, is put out into the open, even published so that the maximum of people can remember his crimes. It is then followed by a new confession—a reestablishment of the *occulta* permitted to remain "private" because it is open to the all-seeing eyes of the Church. For unlike Joan, Rais gives himself over completely to the Church Militant: "[H]e exhorted the people there, and principally the ecclesiastics, there in considerably large numbers, to always venerate our Holy Mother Church, and to honor her greatly and never to separate from her, adding expressly that if he himself, the accused, had not directed his heart and his affection toward that same Church, he never would have escaped the devil's malice and intentions."[24]

Gilles de Rais knows how power works; he partakes of its domination through the privilege of rank. He follows his confession with a self-righteous speech about how parents should look after their children better so as to avoid producing monsters such as himself, and he blames his life of crime on laziness, gluttony, "and the frequent consumption of mulled wine." As a result of his public remorse, the Church immediately moves to reintegrate him after his excommunication, and Rais in turn immediately asks "with sighs and moans" to be confessed. This request is granted, and the religious trial ends. Once the Church has established that he will be hanged, burned, and fined for his crimes, he makes two more requests. He asks that his two accomplices be executed after him, so that they will see that he will not ultimately avoid his punishment. This wish is granted, and it is also decided (as a result of his previous entreaties) that

23 Bataille, *The Trial of Gilles de Rais,* 189–90.

24 Bataille, *The Trial of Gilles de Rais,* 197.

his body will be "rescued in time from the flames" (that is, before the entrails are exposed) and will be buried in a church of his choice. He then asks the bishop to arrange "a general procession in order to ask God to maintain in him and his said servants the firm hope of salvation."[25] This request also is granted. An immense procession accompanies him compassionately to witness his execution. Bataille describes the scene, worthy of a state funeral:

> The church songs that he always loved to distraction lent to his death the resplendence that he could never get enough of in his lifetime. It seems that as soon as possible, "women of noble lineage" took care to pull out of the flames the dead man who, from the end of a rope, had appeared for one instant engulfed in the flame's bewildering splendor.
>
> Then they placed him in a coffin, and solemnly the body was carried to its last resting place in the church, where the peaceful solemnity of the funeral service awaited him.[26]

Thus, the grandeur and resplendence of the funeral matched Rais's life and taste. As if in mimetic compassion, the secular and ecclesiastical courts, as well as the huge crowd, had been taken in by Rais's economy of excess. Just as surely and openly, Bataille himself is fascinated with the hyperbole of scandal that marks Rais's life, with this monster who can never get enough and whom the Church blesses even as it executes him.

It never occurs to Rais that he will not go to Paradise. In fact, he takes leave of this Earth telling his accomplices not to cry for him, since they will all meet again in heaven. Bataille has a theory about all of this. Violence, he argues, may be necessary to Christianity to allow for the forgiveness that is at its very foundation. In the words of Bataille, "Perhaps Christianity is even fundamentally the pressing demand for crime, the demand for the horror that in a sense it needs in order to forgive. It is in this vein that I believe we must take Saint Augustine's exclamation 'Felix culpa! Oh happy fault!' which blossoms into meaning in the face of inexpiable crime. Christianity implies a human nature which harbors this hallucinatory extremity; which it alone has allowed to flourish. Likewise,

[25] Bataille, *The Trial of Gilles de Rais*, 131–32.

[26] Bataille, *The Trial of Gilles de Rais*, 62.

without the extreme violence we are provided with in the crimes of one Gilles de Rais, could we understand Christianity?" (12). Bataille concludes that Christianity may above all be bound "to an archaic human nature," one unrestrainedly open to violence. Christianity, he speculates, "would not want a world from which violence was excluded. It makes *allowances* for violence; what it seeks is the strength of the soul without which violence could not be endured" (13). Indeed, it does not seem to Bataille that Christianity "above all requires the rule of reason." Hence, having expiated, Rais is sure that he will go to heaven, and the Church has achieved, with his trial, a successful catharsis. Clearly, there was no such catharsis in the trial of Joan.

It should be noted at this point, however, that Bataille himself blurs the distinction between the Church Militant and Triumphant. After all, it is the Church Militant that, while awaiting the Last Judgment, both metes out punishment to the sinners and grants forgiveness to the repentant. And it is of course the Church Militant that, changing like everything else over historical periods, views its role as more or less omnipotent, depending on the era. We have seen, for example, how the Church of Joan's day is particularly intent on asserting its hegemony. But it is certainly true as well that a religion grounded in forgiveness will *need* sin. And that such a position puts the *logos* of Plato, for example, in a somewhat curious dimension.

If we follow Bataille's argument, we might say that the Christian Church, especially under the Inquisition, needs unreasonable behavior to assert its power to forgive and, therefore, its very essence as a faith. Bataille notes: "Gilles de Rais' contradictions ultimately summarize the Christian situation, and we should not be astonished at the comedy of being devoted to the Devil, wanting to cut the throats of as many children as he could, yet expecting the salvation of his eternal soul. . . . Whatever the case, we are at the antipodes of reason" (12). Another way of saying this is that Christianity demands excess and that the moderation imagined for the logos is put to the side—excess so that the sinner can be forgiven but also an excess of love so that the soul can move beyond the worldly and the body to contemplate the God beyond rationality. Joan and Rais in this sense emblemize the same economy once arrested: transgression and a torrent of words of remorse in him, an excess of hiddenness and apophatic silence in her. Whether it be heinous crime and violent expiation, or the scandal of communicating with divine beings and refusing to divulge that communion, the excess is in both.

David Tracy has noted that such excess is precisely what postmodern theology struggles with, rooted as it is in "that early and partial harbinger of modern rational theology, Thomas Aquinas." He continues, "[F]or the God who is Love is beyond being and transcendentality, beyond rationality and relationality. God is Love—excess, gift, the Good. That is a thought that modern theology cannot think without yielding its *logos* to *theos* in ways it does not seem to know how to do."[27] But Bataille adds to this equation, by arguing that the excess of extreme evil and violence also fall within the economy of Christianity—indeed, for him, are *mandated* by it. Perhaps this mood that we loosely call "postmodernist" is echoing, in its theological version, the nostalgia we noted in the first chapter of this study: the time before the great Cartesian divide, when body and mind are imagined as one and, perhaps more important at this point, when excess is mapped into the architecture of Church thought. Tracy notes that in postmodern theology, "the modern *logos* in modern theology can no longer control God. . . . These postmodern namings of a Godhead beyond God disclose modern theology's inability to envisage God beyond its own *logos*" (45).

I would combine these views and suggest that until modernism (which, for the sake of a boundary, we will say begins with the response to the seventeenth century), excess is assumed and even required in European Christianity (Bataille). The logos exists to be reinstated *by* excess. Medieval hagiography is one such telling of that story: from the excess, in most cases, of disbelief or of a life of debauchery and opulence, for example, the saint moves to the extreme of self-mortification and an asceticism grounded in deprivation.

Thus, the Devil worshiper Rais is reintegrated. But the young girl whose discourse is in excess when she talks to saints and angels, and whose *occulta* remains excessively secret, must be ejected because the logos cannot itself be reintegrated by way of her near-aphoristic, cryptic narrative. Yet, as Bataille notes elsewhere, the mystical and the erotic are both transgressions that use similar images and yet ignore each other. Indeed, as he points out, both pose threats to the Church. As one critic puts it, for Bataille both eroticism and mysticism "are institutional deviants defying the conventions of acceptability, which condone sexuality in the

[27] Tracy, *On Naming the Present: Reflections on God, Hermeneutics, and Church* (Maryknoll, N.Y., 1994), 44.

name of reproduction and access to divinity by way of dogma. Although mysticism must be regarded as the epitome of values fostered by Christianity, it poses a tacit challenge to the authority of traditional theology."[28] But Bataille sees evil as "when reason thinks according to passions, and not itself"; and good as "the deliverance of reason, of light, and the reestablishment of an order where knowledge dominates ignorance."[29] From this perspective, then, we may follow Bataille and see Rais as reason gone astray, something that the Church can comfortably correct and chastise. The highly logical responses of Joan, however, leave the Church no room to rectify, since she is arguing for a logos that is not theirs but in its clarity refutes dogma and a preestablished notion of order.

Bataille's fascination with Rais, Althusser's obsession with a return to the excessive reality of embodiment—these are moments of a different age, one that wants to, but cannot imagine, a beyond the logos (Tracy). Such an incapacity is not there in the life of Rais, or of Joan, or of the Church that condemned them. Even the measured rationality of an Aquinas could not countermand the belief in a pervasive, ubiquitous transcendent.

But at the end of the Middle Ages, the Church also posits itself as seeing the other as menacing. The other becomes of necessity that which cannot be assimilated and therefore that helps to define community. Seen in this perspective, then, we might say that Joan infuriates the court by having nothing *religious* to atone for. Her crimes are of war and politics, but they can find very little to condemn in her that is obviously sinful. So the inquisition in her trial concentrates on technical points: she cross-dresses (they use a passage from Hebrew Scripture to condemn that); she left her parents' house without their permission (in violation of the sixth commandment); she jumped from a high tower to escape the English, which smacks of suicide, and she declared that God had forgiven her this, which is arrogance; she hates the English, which is in violation of the commandment that says to love your neighbor. The other six articles are

[28] Michele H. Richman, *Reading Georges Bataille: Beyond the Gift* (Baltimore, Md., 1982), 107.

[29] Richman, *Reading Georges Bataille,* 101. Bataille is citing Simone Pétrement here, who is better known perhaps for her study of (and friendship with) Simone Weil. The influence of Weil is throughout Bataille's discussion of attention, awakening, the sacred, and so on, and needs further scrutiny.

all about her visions: how she errs in Christian faith in believing that they are from God, in never having confessed to them to her priest, in obeying them rather than the Church, in believing they will get her to Paradise, in believing that they are on her side in battle, in her vow of virginity that she made to them as the surest path to heaven. The visions and her faith in them result in charges of blasphemy, schismaticism, invocation of the Devil, seductive lying, and erring in faith.

These are fairly subjective charges; that is, they are interpretations based on the round-robin logic of "all things considered which are to be considered." If one contrasts them to the endless witnesses at the trial of Gilles de Rais, all of whom testified to lost, murdered, tortured children and to clear attempts on the part of Rais and his magician friend Prelati to invoke the Devil, it becomes clear that Joan's sin is that she has no sin and therefore leaves the Church no room for forgiveness. Quite apart from its desire to be rid of her as a political force, Joan gives the Church, in its own eyes, no option but to punish the sinner for refusing to admit that she has sinned, even (and perhaps especially) if she has not.

Consider, for example, Bataille's description of the charges against Rais—charges to which numerous eyewitnesses attested and to which he himself ultimately confessed: "Gilles was no longer accused simply of having violated the immunity of the Church at Saint-Etienne; he had conjured the Devil, he had cut the throats of children and violated them; he had offered the hand, eyes and heart of a child to the demon" (59). Indeed, Rais had made a pact with the Devil that, with Rais's usual arrogance, had forbidden the Demon from having his soul or shortening his life: "Come at my bidding, and I will give you whatever you want, except my soul and the curtailment of my life."[30] Again, we have a remarkable, if paradoxical, symmetry. If the Apocalypse of John ends with the word *come,* and if Joan dies asking Jesus to come to her, here we have the monster of excess asking in similar language for the Devil to come. In a similar symmetry of opposites, Joan is in constant contact with her voices, while Rais feels himself to be a failure because even the Devil does not respond to his call.

---

30 This note, which was the second one written to the Devil (the first has been lost), was composed in French in Rais's own hand. The "magician" (also conjurer / alchemist / charlatan, and so on) François Prelati, who controlled Rais in the last few years of his life, testifies to the note on 14 October 1440, and to the conjuring that Prelati himself orchestrated (Bataille, *The Trial of Gilles de Rais,* 106 and 207).

Here, however, we are up against another profound difference. Gilles de Rais is part of the book culture: he writes notes to the Devil, asks that his confession be published (in the vernacular, because most people do not, unlike him, read Latin), and is able to read the articles of accusation. Joan, on the other hand, is illiterate. She hears voices, cannot read the articles of condemnation against her, cannot sign her name, must dictate letters, and so on. When Bataille argues that the voice of the mystic, unlike that of the violent sexual criminal, will ultimately be heard, he is referring to the poetry and writings of those mystics. Joan, need it be repeated, does not write; she is silenced. Yet a supplement remains after her death, as if the sins of which she was officially accused were finally unable to overwhelm the "good" that she both seemed to incarnate and, on political grounds, had accomplished for France.

Moreover, her visions remain a supplement as well, as if both undigested and still hovering *in potentia* after her execution. In trouble with the Church because, as we have noted, she belongs to no order and is therefore under no rule, she provides little context for the neutralization of her deviance except as an outsider, a woman. I have already pointed out that beginning in the mid-twelfth century, visions had to be authenticated by the ecclesiastical hierarchy, and more than one critic has held that such demands for authorized visions were largely gendered.[31] Bernard of Clairvaux, for example, had argued that one was not to seek visions of the sort that Hildegard and other women mystics had experienced. These could at best be "corporeal images," lacking in the spiritual and thus unable to represent God. Meister Eckhart continued this view,[32] as did the Fleming Jan van Ruusbroec (b.1293), a mystic of repute in the fourteenth century. Ruusbroec, in his work *The Spiritual Espousals*, strongly warns

[31] For example, Grace M. Jantzen, *Power, Gender and Christian Mysticism* (Cambridge, 1996), vol. 8 in Cambridge Studies in Ideology and Religion.

[32] Visions are too specific for Eckhart, who famously condemns all attempts to "see God" as no different from "looking at a cow." One is really seeing milk and cheese, and so it is all nothing more than self-interest and profit seeking. Thus, Eckhart relegates visionaries of his day as having "a merchant mentality" and visions themselves as posing an obstacle to divine union with God. In his role as director of numerous communities of women, where visionaries were rampant, such a stance against visions must be seen as a gendered, as well as personally doctrinal, hermeneutics. See Oliver Davies, *Meister Eckhart, Mystical Theologian* (London, 1991), 51–68. See also Grace M. Jantzen, "Eckhart et les femmes," in *Voici Maître Eckhart* (Grenoble, 1994), 417–22.

that most visions are dangerous and deceptive, and they come straight from the Devil. For Jantzen, the gendering of all of these dire predictions is evident, if not explicit: "Again, Ruusbroec never explicitly mentions women visionaries; but again, the implication for the gendered construction of mysticism is clear." Those who are not bound by the rules of the Church, argues Ruusbroec in another work, "should rightly be burned at the stake." Indeed, throughout Europe the deviant were burned with alarming and increasing frequency. In other words, the growing suspicion of visions, especially those experienced by women outside Church rule, correlates specifically to the growing power and fury of the Inquisition. The book culture of the Church was cautioning in increasingly strident tones that visions were first and foremost to be seen as dangerous, as illusions produced by the Devil. It is not until the Church loses its political power, much later, that the social construction of the idea of mysticism came to be seen as less dangerous. (Obviously, if religion is no longer viewed as the origin of power and knowledge, the secular state can more easily tolerate, if not thoroughly ignore, various forms of mysticism. The exception to this is of course Soviet communism, which took Marx literally in seeing religion as a dangerous and toxic activity). More to the point, it is a modern idea to see mysticism as personal and private. Thus we return to the earlier claim that Joan is modern in this fundamental way.

THE DEVIL'S GATEWAY: THE MOUTH AND THE VAGINA

Joan is out of step with her time in part precisely because she understands religious experience as private *(occulta)* in nature and inviolably personal. It is not surprising, therefore, given the Church's insistence on community and conformity, and given Joan's equal insistence on an autonomous stance vis-à-vis ecclesial rule, that the articles of condemnation address Joan's visions in six of the twelve counts against her.

Indeed, if one examines these six articles dealing with her visions, it will be noted that all of them contain language echoing that of Bernard and Ruusbroec: visions are the purview of the Devil, unless the Church has been officially sought for counsel and has deemed them acceptable. Joan, in her simplicity, did not know of these theological writings or of their direct "translations" into burnings. She was concentrating on the erosion of the kingdom of France.

The potency of the book culture becomes even more striking if we compare Joan for a moment to Marguerite of Porete, who was burned at the stake by the Inquisition in Paris in 1310. Porete was probably a Beguine, one of a community of pious women who took no orders but lived a life of piety, good works, and chastity in the world. They, too, were suspect precisely because they fell outside the Church's control (they were, however, unlike Joan, part of a community, even if unacknowledged by the Church). But Porete was an intellectual of sorts, a writer who saw the text as a possibility for narratizing the progress of the soul. Her book, *The Mirror of Simple and Annihilated Souls and Those Who Remain Only in Will and Desire of Love,* makes the work of writing into that of the pilgrimage of the soul.[33] Joan had no such concept of "work" or of the soul's progress; she heard voices in the bells and then saw the figures they came from. She is outside the culture of the book, does not know the language of the law or its euphemisms for heresy, and is not aware of the notion of *progress* through the mind for the sake of spiritual growth.

It should be borne in mind that writing is itself traditionally linked to visions. In the Book of Revelations, it will be remembered, John writes (even takes dictation, like Moses on the Mount) to tell all he saw; Jesus commands him directly to write. Derrida, for example, in the work we considered at some length in the previous chapter, takes as evident that the tradition of the apocalyptic relies heavily on the notions of the book, reading, writing, and dictation. After suggesting that the apocalyptic may be "a transcendental condition of all discourse, of all experience itself, of every mark or every trace," Derrida adds, "if the apocalyptic reveals, it is first the revelation of the apocalypse, the self-presentation of the apocalyptic structure of language, of writing, of the experience of presence, either of the text or of the mark in general: that is, of the divisible dispatch [*envoi*] for which there is no self-presentation nor assured destination" (87). Joan is not in this economy of graphesis, even though she has precipitated texts full of *envois* and left the trace of an excess of faith, apophatic in its conceptualization and yet apocalyptic by virtue of

---

[33] See Amy Hollywood's excellent study, *The Soul as Virgin Wife: Mechthild of Magdeburg, Marguerite Porete, and Meister Eckhart* (Notre Dame, Ind., 1995), 87–119ff.

its revelations.[34] But in her experiential context, she is surrounded by academic clerics, and she is not speaking from the same culture: her knowledge does not partake of the court's. She hears and speaks, or she is silent. Her entire experience is determined by speech and sound; all she has to answer the questions is her voice and her voices.[35] Her stance is fundamentally oral; its reception (ironically enough, however) is one of ignoring (rejecting) or stifling all of Joan's concise speech.[36]

The culture of the court, on the other hand, is produced by notated text, doctrine, theological tracts, scribal registers, translations, and citations from Scripture. Gilles de Rais, who could read, spoke Latin, and had an ecclesiastical education, responds to his trial as we have seen with a torrent of words and a demand to be published. Joan responds to her trial and condemnation with silence and, ultimately (according to witnesses) with pitiful cries and lamentations. She does not believe, it seems evident, that she can communicate between these two very disparate cultures.

In addition, she comes to believe it less and less as the trial progresses. Initially, she speaks on what she takes to be the unassailable ground of virginity—a state that her voices commanded and to which she freely consented. Ironically, one of the chief attributes of holy virginity (as we have noted previously), according to the patristic tradition, is silence. The

34 Although Derrida does not say this, it is important to remember that the *envoi* is a textual ploy used by the thirteenth-century Troubadours. These poets often end their verses with an apostrophe to the loved one or to another poet, to whom they explicitly *send* their lines. Thus, the *envoi* is by definition textual, denoting a literature that refers to itself in its production.

35 Much has been written about voice in medieval women's texts. See, for example, Catherine M. Mooney's recent edited collection, *Gendered Voices: Medieval Saints and Their Interpreters* (Philadelphia, 1999). Joan's case is particular, however, not only because she was illiterate and could only speak to communicate her ideas but also because the voice in general is so dominant in her story: the voices she hears giving her instructions, the multitude of voices in the court, and her own voice that she uses to explain her silences—what cannot, in fact, be voiced. One is strangely reminded here of Mallarmé, who uses language to describe the hopeless limitations—of language. Joan's paradox is similar: she uses her voice to explain why she cannot speak.

36 It should also be noted that several witnesses at the Trial of Rehabilitation testified that the questions at the Trial of Condemnation were willfully theologically and intellectually complex, frequently incomprehensible, and rapidly posed, with the constant overlapping and interruptions of questioners' voices. It was as if, these witnesses report, the court did not want Joan to answer lucidly; that she did is all the more astonishing.

Church fathers had, as we know, a great fear of sexuality and of female sexuality in particular. Tertullian, as we have noted, had proclaimed the vagina to be the "gateway of the Devil." The "typical" female is "open"—anatomically she is penetrated by male lust (which she encourages), and spiritually she is open to all the ways of sin. The holy virgin, however, must be closed in all respects, and the Church saw to it that this included every aspect of a virgin's life who was under Church rule. Thus, writers such as Tertullian, Cyprian, Ambrose, Jerome, and Augustine, as one critic points out, "referred to each other's works, built upon each other's thought, sometimes disagreed, but together created a body of thought that established a Christian understanding of many of the issues that shaped Christian society, among them human sexuality and its mirror image, holy celibacy."[37] Or, as Jerome put it, in an argument we have seen before, "as long as woman is for birth and children, she is different from men as body is from soul. But if she wishes to serve Christ more than the world, then she will cease to be a woman and will be called man."[38]

This "man" is closed, with anatomy (the closed vagina) serving to symbolize the life to be led. The female virgin's first attribute is modesty, and this includes silence, being veiled, being enclosed so that she is protected, and shunning touch (the sense that Jerome feared most) and gluttony (it is bad for the stomach to be full; the mouth must be closed, again entailing silence). The hands are to be kept busy and so out of trouble, just as the mind is to concentrate on spiritual things and remain closed to the affairs of the world.[39]

Ambrose professed to be more interested in closure to the world than closure of the body: "The case is going badly when the body has to be consulted for stronger proof than the mind," he wrote, arguing that midwives should not "test" for virginity in young girls. "I prefer virginity made manifest by works of character rather than in the body's enclosure."[40] Yet it is Ambrose who calls virginity a "closed door," a "foun-

---

37 Joyce E. Salisbury, *Church Fathers, Independent Virgins* (London, 1991), 12.

38 Jerome, "Commentariorum in epistolam ad ephesios libri 3," *Patrologia Latina* 26:533. Cited in Salisbury, *Church Fathers*, 26.

39 For a full historical discussion of the ways in which virgins were to be "closed," see Salisbury, *Church Fathers*, 29–31ff. and *passim*.

40 Ambrose, Letter 32, in *Saint Ambrose: Letters*, trans. Sister Mary Melchior Beyenke (New York, 1954), 159.

tain," and a "closed garden." All of the Church fathers refer to the Song of Songs for the metaphor of the garden and the fountain, thus, as Salisbury puts it, "giving biblical authority to their visions of women" (29). In the words of Ambrose, "We ought to realize what praise of it [virginity] the Prophet, or rather, Christ in the Prophet, has expressed in a short verse: 'My sister, my spouse, is a garden enclosed, a garden enclosed, a fountain sealed up.'" He continues, "A rich garden is virginity which brings forth many fruits of rich odor. 'A garden enclosed' [is virginity] because it is shut in on all sides by the wall of chastity. 'A fountain sealed up' is virginity for it is the fount and wellspring of modesty which keeps the seal of purity inviolate, in whose source there may shine the image of God, since the pureness of simplicity coincides with chastity of the body."[41]

The closure of the vagina is echoed by the enclosure of the life and the avoidance of most of the senses. "Modesty," that term that we have noted before and that encompasses all of female "closure," is mentioned over and over again in patristic texts on virginity. The mouth (that analogue of the vagina) also is to be closed, as if the voice of a woman could lead to similar dangers of impurity. Indeed, the only sense that the patristic tradition does not always warn against is hearing. While Ambrose insisted that every sense be "closed," he encouraged virgins to "keep their ears open" to help in acquiring a pure life.[42] Strangely enough, then, Joan's silence, and her voices, fall within what Ambrose considers to be acceptable, even necessary, behavior for virgins.

In his "Letters to Priests," Ambrose emphasizes the notion that the Church itself is a virgin: "And no one can doubt that the Church is a virgin, which, also in Corinthians, the Apostle Paul espoused to present as a chaste virgin to Christ" (334). He explains that those who seek the life of purity in virginity must stand firm "so that no one may undermine you, so that no one can overthrow you." He cites the passages from Exodus and Deuteronomy, repeating the lines "stand thou here with me," adding that one stands by faith and, "that is, you stand with me, if you stand in the Church. The very place is holy, the very ground is rich in sanctity, and abounding in a harvest of virtues. Stand, therefore, in the Church, stand where I appeared to you, there I am with you" (336). Despite Joan's ig-

---

41 Ambrose, "Letters to Priests," *Saint Ambrose*, 333–34.

42 Salisbury, *Church Fathers*, 18.

norance of Ambrose, this passage, I think, most clearly states several fundamental aspects of her faith, and her understanding of the word *Church.* She made a distinction, it will be remembered, between the *"gens d'Église"*—the clerics—and the Church as the purveyor of Mass and Communion. She genuinely seems to see herself as *standing* with that Church, on holy ground, as a virgin consecrated to the faith. It is a simple fact for her: "stand where I appeared to you, there I am with you." She believes this and seems constantly bewildered, less by the intricacies of the ecclesiastic court and its protocols (although that too is the case), than by their constant reference to the Church Militant and its distinction from the Church Triumphant. For her the Church is a holy *place,* a ground on which to stand and on which to speak. She does not understand it, in other words, as a discourse of power, with a hegemony that both defines and condemns her a priori. "Standing firm in your hearts," writes Ambrose, "rout from the Church the wolves which are trying to carry off prey." Ambrose's use of the term *Church,* his understanding of it as a space, is much closer to Joan's.[43] She sees herself as *standing* with the Church and as speaking from the ground it has given her. The court does not; its notion of "Church" is hegemonic—keeper of the faith through what Lacan calls the symbolic.

The problem, to reiterate, is that since she has not bowed to the Church (in her short military career, with respect to her divine encounters, or inside the workings of the trial itself), the place on which she thinks she stands dissolves. Moreover, virginity, the very state she uses to validate her speech as truthful and herself as pure, becomes the site of danger, such that her speech is suspect. The focus on Joan's mouth and its emissions are, then, like a displacement from the unsealed vagina and its "abominations." The court looks to the other facet of virginity (we have spoken throughout this study of the double-edged valence of the condition of virginity) and sees it as a locus of scandal that must be eradicated. Joan becomes herself the "gateway to the Devil." Closed to the court, she will be seen as "open" to sin, a vessel of diabolical arrogance that can easily absorb the unwitting Christian male. Gilles de Rais, who was accused of sodomy and of scorning "the natural vessel of the female" has in this sense never crossed the threshold of the "gateway to the Devil." In shun-

---

[43] Indeed, the French reinforces the spatial concept: to stand is *rester debout* but also *rester sur place.*

ning the vagina, even in having a hatred of it, the excess of Rais is perhaps, horribly enough, more forthright than the serpentine and insidious logic of the misogynist court and its ensuing discourse formation, its ideology of learning, and the texts it produces. Rais plays out the fantasy that the Church unconsciously endorses; and, in contrast to the silencing of Joan, Rais's oratory is permitted, even encouraged. Although both are executed, Rais will die a redeemed son of the Church; Joan, a witch and a heretic whose virginity is either a source of arrogance or dismissed as the lies of a whore.

Parallel to such an ideology, however, is a different book culture—that of classical humanism, which earlier in her career (and posthumously) allowed for the figure of Joan to be depicted in two positive ways: as a warrior maiden in the tradition of ancient Greek and Roman mythology and as a biblical heroine. On the first of these motifs, Marina Warner notes, "To any classically trained reader, Joan immediately and even unconsciously stepped into a category of women made familiar by mythology and history. . . . [A]nyone with any claim to culture at all in the fifteenth century in Europe was familiar with Homer and Virgil and Ovid at least; other texts, in which Diana, the maiden of the chase, and Penthesilea, queen of the Amazons, appear, were also widely known and their stories related and depicted.'"[44] But these models are pre-Christian and famous for their cruelty—hardly the sorts of figures to reassure Joan's judges, bent on condemnation. Nevertheless, humanistic erudition can override Christian paradigms in Joan's age, and the ability to place her in a familiar, if non-Christian, context, accounts for many of the depictions of Joan that were to follow upon her military triumphs, execution, and continuing popularity.

One of the most remarkable examples of casting Joan in this mythological role comes from her contemporary Aeneas Silvius Piccolomini, a poet who was later to become Pope Pius II. His classical erudition was renowned (indeed, he took the name "Pius" to echo "pious Aeneas.") In his memoirs, he defends Joan's attire on both Christian and pagan grounds: she is a virgin and is therefore free to wear men's clothing and to carry "virile arms." He compares Joan to Camilla, the champion of Turnus who fights Aeneas's invasion of Latium. Virgil describes her thus: "Camilla rode armed with her quiver, exulting like an Amazon, through

---

44 Marina Warner, *Joan of Arc: The Image of Female Heroism* (New York, 1981), 202.

the midst of the slaughter, having one breast exposed for freedom in the fight. From her shoulder's level twanged the golden bow, the weapon which Diana uses" (*Aeneid,* Book XII). For Pius, Joan is directly in this tradition: "The girl mounted the most spirited steed; then in her gleaming armor brandishing her spear like Camilla in the tale she made him leap, run, and curvet."[45] The pope who was first a poet sees Joan as the courageous warrior maid conquered by the invaders, but worthy of pity and admiration, like Virgil's Camilla. "When the nobles saw this," writes Pius, "none of them scorned to be commanded by a woman." Although Pius (of necessity, one presumes) whitewashes the Church of its crime and blames the war on the French ("who think hearsay is the same as knowledge" [208]), he nonetheless keeps Joan Camilla-like to the end.[46] It was she "by whose quick wit and untiring effort the French cause was saved." Pius thus emphasizes Joan's intelligence as well as courage, and he concludes that the story is "a phenomenon that deserves to be recorded," although future generations will view it "with more wonder than credulity."

With his frequent recourse to a strategy of *mirabile dictu,* Pius (whose account of Joan is full of mistakes) positions himself as a contemporary Virgil, writing to future generations about the founding of a kingdom. He insists, further, that she was a virgin as well as a heroine: "She bore the flames with unshakable and gallant courage. . . . Thus died Jeanne, that astonishing and marvelous maid, who restored the kingdom of France when it was fallen and almost torn asunder; who inflicted so many heavy

---

45 *Memoirs of a Renaissance Pope: The Commentaries of Pius II,* abridged, trans. Florence A. Gragg, ed. Leona C. Gabel (New York, 1962), 203. Pius's Latin makes clear his stylistic as well as thematic debt to Virgil: *Puella ferociorem ascendit, et ardens in armis, hastam vibrans, saltare, currere atque in gyrum se vetere haud aliter coegit equuam, quam de Camilla fabulae tradunt* (4: 510).

46 Virgil bases the figure of Camilla on Penthesilea (Book I, lines 491–93) and on the Thracian Harpalyce (I: 317), two other figures of courageous warrior maids killed by the invader. As to Pius, he misreads the trial completely, seeing it as he would wish it rather than as it was. The judges, he writes, "could find nothing to correct except the man's dress she wore and this they did not think deserved the extreme penalty." It was only because she swore not to don men's clothes again and then did so, he adds, that she was burned. He appends, however, an afterthought: "It is possible that the English, who had been vanquished by the Maid in so many battles, never felt really safe while she lived . . . and therefore tried to find a pretext for her death" (208). Thus do the executioners become solely "the English."

defeats upon the English; who being made general over men kept her purity unstained among companies of soldiers; of whom no breath of scandal was ever heard" (208).

One can, I believe, argue that the ancients made a *place* for feminine power in their hierarchy of divinities and inscribed it with cruelty (for example, Artemis-Diana), danger, but also courage. There is no such personification of danger as woman warrior in medieval Christianity, unless it is a figure (like Joan's Saint Catherine) fighting *for* Christianity. These are relatively rare, especially since the culmination of their holiness is most frequently passive (if stoic) courage in the face of martyrdom. In other words, the otherness of femininity, and the fear it evokes, is controlled (and vanquished) rather than incarnated. Eve, to name the most obvious, is properly put in her place and punished after the Fall, a succinct and definitive narrative of dominating the feminine. The female martyrs show courage and selflessness, not danger and cruelty. The Virgin Mary is, as we have noted throughout, a woman with none of the female attributes that inspire fear. Moreover, in the stories of martyrs and saints in Voragine and others, the Christian women are above all obedient to their faith and its rules, at the expense of their riches, their comfort, and, ultimately, their lives. It should be noted, however, that in all of Voragine's accounts of female martyrs, the virgins who are about to die are permitted lengthy, didactic speeches, almost as if the female voice were acceptable *après coup*—after, that is, death had sanctified them.

One can venture to generalize and say that Greek mythology factors in, as it were, the fear of woman as a constant, *present* danger that needs acknowledgment and is thus (re)anthropomorphized. Christianity, on the other hand, places the fear of woman, and of her body, within a framework that either domesticates it (women should be under rule or should marry and obey their husbands, and so on) or eradicates it (she who succumbs to her diabolical nature must be burned and excised from the body of the Church and society). These are two very different economies: one of metonymic expression and integration through mythology, the other a metaphorical move marked by repression through "cleansing." But, as Freud notes, that which is repressed always comes back to haunt; surely the figure of Joan has come back to haunt, which is perhaps why she was finally domesticated by being canonized.

Like Pius II, Christine de Pizan in her *Ditié* on Joan also compares her to Camilla.[47] But she includes the second motif, that of biblical heroines. In 1429, the same year as the *Ditié,* three treatises had been written about Joan. Each of these compared her to one or all of the heroines in Hebrew Scripture: Deborah, Esther, and Judith.[48] The first of the treatises, probably by John Gerson, notes that the three biblical figures "obtained salvation for the people of God," as it was presumed Joan was to do. The implication here, not an insignificant one, is that like the Israelites, the French are the (new) chosen people. Fraioli notes that it is not surprising that these texts appeared in 1429, the year that Joan began her mission. The French court, after all, was intent on validating the Maid. Nevertheless, it is significant that, when Joan is to be propagandized as a figure of goodness and salvation, the models that are drawn upon are either from Greek mythology or Hebrew Scripture. Pizan even gives Joan a maternal aspect, nurturing the kingdom of France. Joan is the maiden

> A qui Dieu force et pouvoir donne
> D'estre le champion et celle
> Qui donne a France la mamelle
> De paix et doulce nourriture.

Fraioli notes that Deborah, too, is likened to a mother nurturing Israel: "The valiant men ceased, and rested in Israel; until Debbora arose, a mother arose in Israel."[49]

But when Joan is to be propagandized as the incarnation of seduction by the Devil, we are back to the gateway. This time, it is open to sin, to

---

47 Pizan's earlier work, *La Cité des dames* (1405), which tells the lives of famous women, includes the women warriors Semiramis, Camilla (again), and Penthesilea. Her source for this was Boccaccio's *De claris mulieribus.* By the time of the *Ditié,* Pizan's politics had become much more radical, as we saw in a previous chapter. See *Ditié de Jehanne d'Arc* (Oxford, 1977).

48 For a full discussion of the treatises and these motifs, see Deborah Fraioli, "The Literary Image of Joan of Arc: Prior Influences," in *Speculum* 56, no. 4 (1981): 811–30. See also Dorothy Wayman, "The Chancelor and Jeanne d'Arc," in *Franciscan Studies* 17 (1957): 273–305, which includes the text of Gerson's treatise, *De quandam puella.* One thinks also of a subsequently influenced work, the first part of *Henry VI,* variously attributed to Shakespeare or to multiple authors including him. King Charles says to Joan in that play, "Stay, stay thy hands! Thou art an Amazon / And fightest with the sword of Deborah" (I.2.104–5).

49 Fraioli, "The Literary Image of Joan of Arc," 816. The passage is from Judges 5:7.

Satan, and to the evil temptations of the world. Nowhere in the trial, significantly enough, is there a real question as to whether the voices *exist.* The question is only whether they come from God or the Devil. As Lorraine Daston has noted, until the seventeenth century in Europe, most Christians believed that there was a parallel realm to our own, one of miracles and revelations, that could appear at any moment.[50] The problem was to ascertain their source. Without further "proof" of the source of Joan's revelations, the Church opted for the Devil. "Do the voices have sight?" they ask her. "Do they have eyes?" These are the questions of proof as eyewitnessing, which translates theologically as a demand for sharing the revelations. The court wants to know: Are the voices saints or angels? How does she recognize them? How are they clothed? Are they of the same age? Do they speak together or one at a time? These are revelations, she says, that go to her and to the king of France, "and not to those who interrogate me."[51] The distinction could not be clearer. Joan, who says she has the counsel of her voices "every day," refuses to tell the court more: "I will not tell you any more about it now."

Joan's apophasis with respect, paradoxically, to her revelations, was from the first unmovable and powerless to persuade the court. "You don't have that yet" *(Vous ne l'avez pas encore),* she answers cryptically to yet another question about whether the voices have eyes or possess sight. Her answer could mean both that she hasn't yet given the court that information or that eyesight into another, unworldly realm is something they don't yet possess. And then she adds, quasi-prophetically and certainly wisely, the children's saying that "sometimes people are hanged for telling the truth."[52] The issue of truth could not be more openly destabilized than it is here. The Church's insistence that she swear and her repeated refusal to do so are the marks of a collision of discourses that motivate the trial. But the court has the power, and the accused stands condemned literally (legally) before the fact.

---

50 Lorraine Daston, "Marvelous Facts and Miraculous Evidence in Early Modern Europe," in *Questions of Evidence: Proof, Practice and Persuasion across the Disciplines,* ed. James Chandler, Arnold I. Davidson, and Harry Harootunian (Chicago, 1994), 243–74.

51 27 February 1431; Duby and Duby, *Le Procès,* 55.

52 24 February; ibid., 48

WOMEN POSSESSED

The subject in such a case, already bound by the legal, social, and political hegemony of the Church, is particularly snared if feminine. Indeed, one can argue that there is de facto no female subject in this context. Certeau's work on the text of possessed women in the seventeenth century provides a corollary model for the absent feminine subject. His example stems from his study of the nuns at Loudun, 1632 to 1638, and the documents of their trials before the Church. Because the cases are so extreme, they delineate a moment when the lack of subjectivity in the female speaker is glaringly revealed and when the discourse of the woman herself is indecipherable to her. In the speech of possessed women, writes Certeau, the "I" is renounced, and the space of enunciation reserved for the "I" is replaced by an endless "fluttering" from one proper name to another.[53] Caught as well between the discourses of the Church and of the medical profession, the possessed woman is "doubly lost." Like Joan, such a woman will be lost to her own speech, "because even before the speech can be reformed through the discourses in which it figures by dint of citations, a battery of interrogations has determined all response ahead of time; they have fragmented the possessed woman's speech according to classifications that are in no way her own, but rather those of the inquirer's knowledge. In this respect documents constitute a point of no return" (252).

As with Joan, the possessed woman is confronted with a theological discourse (and, in the cases at Loudun, a medical one as well) that says, "'I know what you are saying better than you'; in other words, 'My knowledge can position itself in the place whence you speak'" (250). Also as with Joan, the possessed woman has to speak "about a so-called ineffable experience which therefore *cannot be spoken about.*" We remember here Joan's attempt to remain within the court's discourse by responding, "I do not have permission to tell you that"; or "Pass on"; or "Ask me on Saturday, then I will perhaps have something for you"; or, more clearly, "You burden me" *(Vous me chargez trop)*. As Certeau puts it, "in established discourse a practice of elocution and a treatment of language trace an alterity that cannot yet be identified with another discourse" (250).

53 *The Writing of History*, 257.

But Joan's answers also betray an important difference with the possessed speech of women two hundred years later. The possessed woman, as Certeau puts it, transgresses discourse because something she does not know is speaking *in* her—indeed, in terms that she herself does not understand. Joan's experience, however, is that something that she knows (or says she recognizes as her angel Michael and the two saints Catherine and Margaret) is speaking *to* her. They are speaking, moreover, not in the indecipherable "flutterings" of proper names that the Church's discourse of demonology will decode, but in French, as she attests, and with a perfectly lucid, if unhappily received by the court, message.

In this difference, as I have suggested, Joan is more dangerous for the Church, for in its eyes she is professing to know better the desire and the very Logos of God than they do. In this sense, her discourse and that of the Church show identical, if clashing, positions with respect to knowledge: both claim legitimacy in their relation to the truth. Her alterity is then more difficult for the Church to assert as demonic, especially since her responses are simple but completely logical. Consider, for example, her response to the dangerous question[54] of whether she knows that she is in God's grace: "If I am not, may God grant that I be so; and if I am, may He keep me there" *(Si je n'y suis, Dieu m'y veuille mettre, et si j'y suis, Dieu m'y veuille tenir)*.[55] This is a voice that, in its stark lucidity, is much harder to counter. It is a voice that itself has taken possession of the divine Logos, since it speaks for, and occupies the place of, the "I" that is to be enunciated by God. Far from being possessed, Joan stands as the possessor and purveyor of enunciation from the Godhead. As Pius II writes of her, "in any case, a girl whose advice was so sensible could not be called mad" (*Memoirs*, 203).

In this regard, we might say that Joan is lagging *behind* her time. Dupré argues that the fourteenth-century nominalists (for example, William Ockham and Nicholas d'Autrecourt) begin to distinguish words from concepts, such that language "ceased to give expression to a Logos immanent within the real. Its task was restricted to referring, extrinsically and

---

[54] Dangerous because if she answers yes, she is guilty of the sin of pride; and if no, she is admitting to be in the state of sin. It has been noted that this response is reminiscent of (but not identical to) a prayer of the time. But this in no way detracts from the sagacity of Joan's response.

[55] 24 February; Duby and Duby, *Le Procès*, 48.

often indirectly, to the real" (104). Words, then, no longer were assumed to "partake in that divine Word through which the Creator secures the essential intelligibility of his creation." This separation from sign and signified means that God's decrees are no longer seen as having an intelligible pattern, so that "we also cease to trust that the eternal Logos secures the basic veracity of human speech" (104).[56] This point is crucial for our purposes, because it explains why Joan is asked to swear many times: quite apart from the possibility that she may be lying (one that certainly looms large in the trial), there is the coeval difficulty that words are suspect. This still novel notion is bearing down on the court. In the words of Dupré, "Henceforth words were to be used at man's risk and discretion without carrying the traditional guarantee that, if properly used, they touch the real as it is in itself" (104).

But for Joan, this concept is bewildering. For her there is a transparency, in Jean Starobinski's sense, between thought and its verbal expression, and even more so between the word of God, which she receives, and its oral transmission. Hence, she cannot comprehend a need to swear more than once, any more than she can the need to answer any given question more than once: "I have already responded to that," she says over and over again; "I have already sworn." For her, language does in fact engage, depict reality. There is no disjunction for her between sign and signified; the sign *is* the signified because she takes Logos literally. Indeed, what we can say is that the disjunction in the trial lies between her language as signifier and the court's interpretation of it into an unintended (and frequently uncomprehended) signified. What emerges in a reading of the trial, however, is the way in which Joan herself begins to mistrust the way her words will be construed. The trial, in other words, gradually places on her the burden of suspicion toward language. It either stifles her voice altogether or insists on the vocalization of what cannot be (or should not be, by her lights) voiced at all.

If Joan begins, then, with a belief in language as vested in the real (thus putting her, as I have noted, behind her time), she ends in a defiant individualism that puts her squarely into modernity. At the opening of the trial Joan demonstrates in her speech the equivalent of *adequaetio rei et intellectus;* by the end she has come to understand the twisted ways of lan-

---

[56] Like Dupré, I am here using *logos* to mean the philosophical sense of the term, such as in Plato, and *Logos* to mean the Christian understanding of it, as the word of God.

guage and its hermeneutical ramifications. She, too, has become suspicious. Consider again, in this light, her response to the judges when they declare her relapsed: "To which she answered that she never understood herself to have revoked the apparitions of her voices. . . . What she had said about them was out of fear of the fire. And if she did revoke, it was contrary to the truth . . . and that she never understood what was contained in the article of abjuration. And that she never thought she had abjured anything."[57] Joan here puts her own words in question with respect to the "truth." She also asserts that she did not understand much of what was said. As a result, she was brought to say things that, if she said them at all, she did not mean. Language no longer necessarily signifies what is intended, and words do not always convey what they profess to mean. This situation, which we take for granted, is one the surprising force of which cannot be underestimated in Joan's era; that is, it comes in response not to Plato but rather to an earlier notion of the Christian Logos that had held that the Word flowed through language to present (not *re*-present) the real. The truth for Joan is inexplicably extracted from speech. The subject, however it may be construed, even if putatively by the court's protocol, is constituted by language. The transparency, by the end of the trial, is gone.

But it is Joan's status as woman, and thus as fundamentally nonsubject, which additionally allows the court to reinterpret her speech within Church knowledge and to say, as the Church will do to the possessed women, "I know what you are saying better than you," and "My knowledge can position itself in the place whence you speak." The text of Joan's trial is indeed a "point of no return"; the questions determine the answers in *inquisitio,* and the Church claims to be a better eyewitness of the defendant's experience than she herself. With her speech caught "in classifications that are in no way her own," this trial of inquisition is a metaphor of the powerless, nonsubject position that describes women at that point and place in history.

Knowledge belongs, then, not to Joan but to her inquisitor. We can safely say that this is true for a woman in fifteenth-century France, even without charges of heresy. Knowledge, and therefore the meaning and intentions of her actions, must always be that of the rigorously patriarchal Church to bless, condemn, or interpret. It is therefore unsurprising that

---

57 28 May; Duby and Duby, *Le Procès,* 173.

Joan turned instinctively to an outside (divine) voice for agency, a voice that had, as the trial minutes read, "always taken good care of her."[58] If she could demonstrate that her actions were born not of her own, personal desire but of the desire to obey holy commands, then her discourse would be grounded and would have agency, even if once removed. In doing lip service to her own desire, in displacing her own voice, no one can question, according to this logic, her right to act. Without such external justification, one that simultaneously erases her voice, her "I" becomes even emptier, phatic. As long as it is not she for whom she is speaking, not she for whom she is acting, she can perhaps circumvent the tradition that, starting with Genesis (3:16), debars her from speaking altogether. As Lacan notes, in a different vein, the speaking subject turns to the other for certainty. Joan turns to a speaking other in order to acquire agency; one cannot say, given her gender, subjectivity.

However, because her inquisitors have already decided that her voices come from the Devil, this agency-as-prosthesis is annulled as well. Moreover, in the texts to which we have referred here—the trial, contemporaneous accounts, fiction—her voice is equally ventriloquized, appropriated, rehabilitated, rescued. In all of these cases, however, even the semblance of an agency, which she had so carefully split from herself, continues to elude her. We began by asking what is the "I" we hear in Joan's trial. There can be no answer to this question since, like Kant's point about asking whether God exists, it already posits a subjectivity the existence of which it professes to question.

The parallel realm in the Middle Ages to which I alluded earlier, that manifestation of the divine that wove itself at will into daily life, has long since been replaced by an internal one. It is most frequently called the unconscious, but it also has other taxonomies.[59] Joan's legislative verbs

---

58 Several Johannic scholars have noted that initially, Joan refers to only one voice. But on 27 February and thereafter, having been endlessly pressed by the inquisitors as to the nature of that voice, she makes it plural and recognizable (into the virgin Saints Catherine and Margaret and the archangel Michael). It is as if by multiplying the voice and giving the ensuing figures specific traits—embodying them—she could placate her captors and thus escape their fatal agenda. In providing ever more details about her voice(s), she is desperately trying to satisfy a probing which by definition has already been determined.

59 See, for example, Julian Jaynes, *The Origin of Consciousness in the Breakdown of the Bicameral Mind*, (Boston, 1976). Jaynes makes a fascinating argument for an older form of human thinking as *non*-(or sub)conscious, needing to wait for an "external" voice to give

conseiller (counsel) and *gouverner* (govern) to describe the externalized mandates of her voices have been supplanted by inner drives, compulsions, and all of their psychological variants. Rather than following a call from "above" through action, we now speak of hysteria as the eruption from "below,"[60] in the unconscious, inscribing itself as symptom on the body.[61] Thus, mutism becomes the option for the woman whose dis-

---

it commands in the face of unforeseen difficulties (accidents, for example). This external voice, Jaynes argues, was experienced as the voice of gods and came from the right hemisphere of the brain, as against the more dominant left side. This voice gradually disappeared and was largely gone by the fourth millennium B.C.E. It was replaced by "modern" consciousness, in which the voice is internalized and consciousness becomes more introspective. For example, as he puts it, one now has the ability to drive a car "nonconsciously," while engaging simultaneously in an animated conversation, and to reason out instantly what to do in the case of an accident. Jaynes contends that the mind of heroes in the *Iliad* is entirely unlike ours because it is bicameral (nonconscious, and awaiting "instructions" from an external voice that is figured as the appearance of a god or goddess when a complex decision needs to be made). The disappearance of the bicameral mind leaves its traces, so that Joan of Arc, for example, is in this scenario the victim of the vestigial presence of bicamerality, and so she "hears" outside voices of divinities, telling her what to do.

60 For a discussion of the ways in which "above" and "below" figure in a topology of the mind for psychoanalysis, see my "Unconscious" in *Critical Terms for Literary Study*, ed. Frank Lentricchia and Thomas McLaughlin (Chicago, 1990), 147–62.

61 Thus, it would be tempting, for example, to decide that Joan was simply schizophrenic, since the hearing of voices is a primary symptom of that condition. There are two major flaws in such a conclusion, however. The first is that it presupposes the mind of the fifteenth century to think like ours—and here I am not making Jaynes's point so much as that of Dumont, "A Modified View of Our Origins," and Arnaldo Momigliano, "Marcel Mauss and the Quest for the Person in Greek Biography and Autobiography," 83–92 in the same volume, *The Category of the Person*. See also Dupré, *Passage to Modernity*, 93–119. The point is that the notion of "person" is neither a monolithic nor an unchangeable one, and it is understood within the parameters it already traces. We cannot psychoanalyze retrospectively onto a period that bears neither our language, nor categories for ailments, nor finally our notion of the individual. On the role of language as a controlling influence on culture, see the work of Basil Bernstein (based here on that of Edward Sapir), *A Socio-Linguistic Approach to Social Learning*, ed. J. Gould (London, 1964), 148. The second difficulty with this view psychiatric diagnosis of Joan is that schizophrenics become gradually more dysfunctional, until they cease (without medication, that is) to be able to function at all. As Jaynes points out, schizophrenics "of every type are much less capable than normally conscious people when they attempt to respond to stimuli" (*The Origin of Consciousness*, 421). Moreover, they lose the ability to narratize, have no sense of time, and are unable to understand a boundary between their bodies and the external world. Joan,

course is already determined by an interrogator who already "knows" the answers better than she does. The most obvious example is, of course, Freud's aphonic Dora.

In hysterics, as Freud notes, writing in turn replaces mutism. Dora's situation and Joan's are, in fact, strangely similar: In both, knowledge is owned by the interrogator, although it is demanded of the interrogated. In both, in an instinctive realization that the subject will be given no hold on her discourse and no recognition *as* subject, the voice is ventriloquized, into the voice of saints or into writing. In both cases, the voice of the speaking woman is canceled either figuratively (she is not *heard*) or literally (she lapses into silence or deferral). Both will try to placate the inquisitor by trying at least once to see things his way (Joan will abjure; Dora will briefly return to Freud). Both will be seen as guilty of relapsing. Thus, Freud will end his partial analysis of Dora with a failure he does not even initially recognize. She leaves. Joan will remain closed as "anathema" to the clerics, who will see to it that her voice is irrevocably silenced. But the Church will have to return to its verdict and, like Freud, try to right a process that it only partially understands as wrong, as incomplete.

In both cases as well there will be a Trial of Rehabilitation, with many other voices explaining how and to what extent Joan was maligned and Dora betrayed, and both misunderstood. Foucault will write that knowledge is generated by the hegemonic structures of power at any given time, not vice versa. Psychoanalysis will rethink countertransference; the Church will rethink its Inquisition. But the issue of the feminine subject-position is still unresolved and, I would say, still at risk. Silence, after all, remains the Virgin Mary's greatest virtue because her motives are within a knowledge that reads them as spotless and because she obeyed. While the shepherds are talking of the birth of Jesus and praising and glorifying God, Mary "treasured up all these things and pondered over them."[62] As

---

on the other hand, plans battle strategies and responds with lucidity and acumen at her trial. Neither of these abilities would be possible with florid schizophrenia. While it is true that she begins to hear her voices at adolescence, typically the time of the condition's onset, nothing else about her behavior matches the presentation of schizophrenia. To classify Joan as schizophrenic says more about our need to be rationally reassured about a fairly incomprehensible phenomenon than it does about Joan. As Pius II put it, "an extraordinary thing happened which after-generations will not believe" (*Memoirs,* 206).

62 Luke 2:19, *The New English Bible.* The King James version is more explicit: "But Mary

misogynists within the Church have frequently noted, the Pauline epistles to the Corinthians and Timothy specifically exhort women to remain silent. In Timothy 2:11–12, for example, we read, "A woman must be a learner, listening quietly and with due submission. I do not permit a woman to be a teacher, nor must woman domineer over man; she should be quiet. For Adam was created first, and Eve afterwards."[63] Joan's silence, on the other hand, is interpreted as disobedience, and her tardy canonization (with its political motivation) has done little to let her voice be her own.[64] Freud, meanwhile, likens psychoanalytic practice to the job of a prosecuting trial lawyer, with the patient standing in the place of the criminal.[65] Revisionists of his knowledge have not altered the position of the analysand as confronting the-one-who-is-supposed-to-know.

---

kept all these things, and pondered them in her heart." The tradition is unambiguous: the *Dictionnaire de Spiritualité* (Paris, 1959), for example, says that during her pregnancy, Mary's lot is "to be in silence. It is her state, her path, her life . . . and her life passes thus from silence to silence, from the silence of adoration to the silence of transformation, her mind and her thought equally conspire to form and perpetuate in her this life of silence." "Silence," 14: 852, my translation. The same article notes that the Koran 19:26 states that "Mary's vow of silence permits her to conceive and to engender the Word" (833). Finally, the article cites Tauler, the disciple of Eckhart, who notes that Mary must be "closed up" from the world in a "place of silence" (847). Once again, the mouth and the vagina are conflated.

63 On this particular passage, and on the notion that women should remain silent in church, see the brilliant pamphlet of the seventeenth-century Quaker Margaret Fell Fox, *Women's Speaking Justified* (1667) from the Augustan Reprint Society (Los Angeles, 1979), no. 194. Fox and her husband, George Fox, published a good deal about the Quaker movement. But it was Margaret Fell Fox who, in her pamphlet, argued that the "Indwelling spirit" was not restricted to males. She read the passage from Timothy as having to do with silence and submission of women in marriage; not in regard to spirituality. In addressing "you dark Priests, that are so mad against women speaking and it's so grievous to you," Fox cites passages from Hebrew Scripture to insist that spirit can be in women as well as men and that women can prophesy and indeed do so in the Bible. Women can, she notes, receive prophetic gifts in the Pauline tradition, a view that Aquinas was to systematize.

64 Throughout the centuries, she has been equally appropriated by Christine de Pizan, Charles d'Orléans, Voltaire, Schiller, Shaw, Twain, Péguy, and, more recently, the right-wing Front National—to reiterate just a few. The staggering number of movies made about Joan, a subject that warrants a book on its own, has been discussed in the introduction.

65 Addressing himself to "future judges and defending counsel" at a law seminar in Vienna in 1906, Freud said, "I must draw an analogy between the criminal and the hysteric.

The female virgin, as I have argued throughout, is perpetually in a state of abnormality and of preexistence, always *in potentia,* hovering on the threshold or gateway (hymen) of complete womanhood. In this sense, too, female virginity is like a metaphor of feminine subjectivity. Paradoxically enough, she will be rendered "complete" by being punctured, when the repression barrier is penetrated. Not yet woman, she also mirrors what complete womanhood is itself: a subject that does not exist as such and thus a monstrosity; a foreigner to male subject agency, a ghost of subjectivity. Or, if she retains the status of holy virginity in the Christian sense, she is, as we have seen, no longer a woman at all. So, too, the feminine voice marks the nonsubject status, silenced or rendered inaudible. Permitted to receive through the ear, hers is the passive role of orifice-as-vessel. Never (even in childbearing) is the woman to be originator or first cause. Her speech, like her womb, can only be the carrier of what is generated by the male, the other. Like the vagina, the mouth can be penetrated, but it can only produce secondarily, by male inception. For woman herself is always a subject to come—like the apocalypse but perhaps, too, in this logic, like the terrifying devil invoked by Gilles de Rais.

Kristeva would overcome this impasse, by seeing psychoanalysis as a natural link to love in the theological sense. "Let us admit," she now writes of the analytic situation, "that it is legitimate to speak of a *subject* when language gathers an identity in an instance of enunciation and at the same time confers to it an interlocutor and a referent."[66] What is the "we" here? If the analysand is female, I for one do *not* admit it. Were the "*je*" of such a subject real in the sense—experiential, political, philosophical—that Kristeva means it, Joan of Arc would have had a very different trajectory. Indeed, Joan's trial exists more in the realm of what the earlier Kristeva called the abject, that which recognizes the fundamental lack of all being, meaning, language, desire and that which, furthermore, the

---

In both we are concerned with a secret, with something hidden. . . . The task of the therapist, however is the same as that of the examining magistrate. We have to uncover the hidden psychical material; and in order to do this we have invented a number of detective devices, some of which it seems that you gentlemen of the law are now about to copy from us." "Psychoanalysis and the Establishment of the Facts in Legal Proceedings," *The Standard Edition of the Complete Psychological Works of Freud,* trans. and ed. James Strachey (London, 1955), 9: 108.

66 *Au Commencement était l'amour: Psychoanalyse et foi* (Paris, 1985), 18; my translation.

Kristeva of the *Pouvoirs de l'horreur* claims that psychoanalysis can only partially grasp.[67]

Kristeva's more recent, psycho-optimistic point on subjectivity is basically no different from that of Emile Benveniste's linguistic perspective. He equally posits a person in the notion of subject and "an interlocutor." In "Subjectivity in Language," Benveniste argues:

> Language is possible only because each speaker sets himself up as a *subject* by referring to himself as *I* in his discourse. Because of this, *I* posits another person, the one who, being, as he is, completely exterior to "me," becomes my echo to whom I say *you* and who says *you* to me. This polarity of persons is the fundamental condition in language, of which the process of communication, in which we share, is only a mere pragmatic consequence. . . . The very terms we are using here, *I* and *you,* are not to be taken as figures but as linguistic forms indicating "person." . . . A language without expression of person cannot be imagined.[68]

But the point is that the "instant of enunciation," even as it uses "I," does *not* confer subjectivity, even as it does not delineate a person if the speaker is a woman. Joan is thus twice echoed: once by the *you* who responds to her "I" and again by the court that repeats her speech in the minutes. But there is no echo as reciprocity, only as fading sound on one side.

Truth appears only when the emission of sound is made an attribute of fantasies, as Irigaray notes reading Plato's cave, or *Hystera.* She adds, "Sound *(phonē)* gives fantasies a character of pure and immediate presence that masks the artificial mechanisms, the reduplications, the repetition-reproduction procedures, to say nothing of the obliterations that *contrive* their elaboration. Sound—taken away from Echo here or elsewhere—indicates the presence of truth, which requires the privilege enjoyed by the *phonē.*"[69] Sound can only act as a "relay station," a detour "that is indispensable in guaranteeing the previous existence of the

67 Julia Kristeva, *Pouvoirs de l'horreur: Essai sur l'abjection* (Paris, 1980), 13.

68 Emile Benveniste, "Subjectivity in Language," in *Problems in General Linguistics,* trans. Mary E. Meek (Coral Gables, Fla., 1971), 225.

69 Luce Irigaray, *Speculum of the Other Woman* (Ithaca, N.Y., 1985), 264.

aletheia, which will henceforth take command of all beings, including voices" (265). But we can follow Irigaray further and reemphasize her point that it is men who lend credit to the *parousia,* in the *polis* as well as in the cave. The ideal of truth legitimizes the metaphors, the "figures used to represent the role of women, without voice, without presence." The feminine serves only to keep up "the reproduction-production of doubles, copies, fakes." To return to Benveniste, there is not a "polarity of persons" in the *I/you* play in Joan's trial. The notion of "person" as generated by the power hegemony does not *admit* as person the speaker who says "I" in the trial. What it does do is reproduce its notion of truth with Joan as metaphor of woman *avant la lettre* and of deviance from the truth. As woman and as heretic, Joan conforms to the horror of the abject: "I experience abjection only if an Other has planted himself instead and in place of that which will be 'me.' Not an other with whom I identify or incorporate myself; but an Other who precedes and possesses me, and gives me being by this possession."[70] In Joan's case, the Church possesses and precedes her, to annihilate the very being it gives her which, once it has been hypostatized, is then loudly rejected. Thus, the trial has not only silenced her voice a priori—Joan is a woman—it also silences her *particular* voice—she speaks from outside the structures of truth and is thus a copy or likeness (metaphor) of evil, wrong thinking, erroneous faith, and so on. I have noted that she had been doubly echoed in the trial, but she is also doubly removed, as metaphor of the metaphor of evil. The auditory *mise en abîme* that removes her voice "here or elsewhere" is echoed conceptually, so that she is figured as the *semblance* of a representation of what was already outside.

Is the female subject perpetually before the horizon of being? Does the female virgin iconize this state in a saturated way? Whose voice do we hear through the transcripts of Joan's trial? Whose voice does Freud give us when he quotes Dora? The heretic of yesteryear, with her external voices, has become the hysteric of today with her muted outer voice paralleled by an inner one, equally unheard. Moreover, silence itself cannot be transcribed into the text of the court minutes, any more than in the case study Freud will write up. Silence is unrepresentable textually, except by its signifier. Like feminine agency, it can only be obliquely inferred, imag-

---

70 Kristeva, *Pouvoirs de l'horreur,* 18; my translation.

ined, and left to float with a signified generated by the power and culture of the time.

In his reverie on language, Heidegger writes that mortal speech must first of all have listened to the command, "in the form of which the stillness of the difference calls world and things into the rift of its one-fold simplicity."[71] Every word of a mortal speech "speaks out of such a listening, and as such a listening." This speaking that listens and accepts, he adds, "is responding." There can be, I think, no better description of Joan's listening than this and no better way of showing how short the judges fell with her—how they neither spoke out of such a listening nor therefore responded. I mean this both literally and also in the way that Heidegger means it: in how the peal of stillness appropriates mortals "by the command of the difference." But there is a caveat, which the philosopher does not consider. "It is held that man," he writes, "in distinction from plant and animal, is the living being capable of speech." This does not only mean that man possesses the faculty of speech. It means "that only speech enables man to be the living being he is as man" (189). Woman, as I am arguing, does not have this enabling and is therefore not such a living being. Her uttering does not break the stillness; in her stillness is heard no peal.

There is a homogeneity to figurings of the feminine voice, as there is to the feminine state of virginity. Caught between the senseless, fading repetitions of an Echo, or the unheeded prophecies of a Cassandra, or again the muffled cries of a Eurydice, the feminine voice is clearly delimited by the myths of the West as that which has no substance and thus no *logos*.[72] To return to Heidegger's terms, her call does not "bring closer what it calls." Her "come," therefore, must always be addressed to another register, to another *place*. As such, the voice of "woman," like her body, partakes of the impossible and therefore, once again, of death.

---

[71] Martin Heidegger, *Poetry, Language, Thought*, trans. Albert Hofstadter (New York, 1971), 209.

[72] It has been hotly contested for centuries as to whether the feminine voice can have logos—that is, whether she can be the vehicle for a divine message. That it can is largely justified by Joel 2:28–29: "Your sons and daughters shall prophesy." Bolstering this view is that the resurrected Jesus first appeared to women. That women cannot use their voices in matters divine is argued by way of I Corinthians 14:34–35 (wherein we are told that it is "shocking" for a woman to speak to a congregation) and I Timothy 2:11–15 (a woman should listen, be a "learner," and keep quiet). The reader is referred, again, to Fox, *Women's Speaking Justified*.

CHAPTER FIVE

FEAR OF FIRE: DEATH AND THE IMPOSSIBLE

> Death in the flame is the least lonely of deaths. It is truly a cosmic death in which a whole universe is reduced to nothingness along with the thinker. The funeral pyre accompanies him in his passing.
>
> —Gaston Bachelard, *The Psychoanalysis of Fire*

> The inquisitors' most severe penalty was death by fire. Technically, of course, the inquisitors, being priests forbidden to shed blood, did not actually condemn anyone to death. They merely "relaxed," or handed over, culprits to the secular authorities, who were expected to carry out the actual executions.
>
> —James B. Given, *Inquisition and Medieval Society*

IT IS REMARKABLE how prone we are to metaphor when fleetingly confronted with the impossible. The impossible here is meant as woman/death. It is this dyad, with its consistent metaphoric cloak, to which we now turn. And it is the murder of Joan that provides a way of attempting to *see* that before which the gaze is continually, and successfully, averted. But all gazes are not alike. If woman is linked with death in masculinist metaphysics (for want of a better term)—a hypothesis that I will argue again here—then the feminine gaze is only partially (or differently) averted, since the fear of women can be aped but generally not experienced in the same way (if at all), from a feminine perspective.

This gendered aspect of the metaphysical gaze is more significant than it may initially seem, for it implies that the impossible is differently, not universally, apprehended—or at least that the gendering of the impossible makes for an *après coup* in feminine thought. Let us begin, then, by assuming the standard pose to address Joan's burning—that is, the position from the perspective of male metaphysics.[1]

---

[1] Whether written by men or women, obviously—the latter as in the "we" of my first sentence in this chapter.

Hegel notes that clear, conscious assurance of certainty has its confirmation in forgetfulness, a declaration that Freud was to second in different language. The soul that has committed a crime, Hegel continues, combines the upper Lethe (absolution) with the lower (death), but "both are forgetfulness" and allow for "peace of the soul."[2] But forgetfulness, or repression, is precisely the averted gaze. I would add, moreover, that it manifests itself as *metaphor*. Freud certainly implied this, and Lacan explicitly asserted it. But I would like to look here at the averted gaze, not first from the point of view of the unconscious but from that of what we might call cultural metaphysics.[3]

Metaphor, after all, is a figure of resemblance *in absentia*. With its literal meaning of "carrying over," its connotations include displacement,[4] transferral, and substitution. This can be read to indicate, of course, a turning away from the original thing, act, vision, and so on. Or it can signify the impossibility of description. Whether used to express an indescribability or to indicate (even if unwittingly) an aversion to a given event, metaphor is an intricate incidence of the averted gaze. As such, metaphor betrays a rhetoric of metaphysics.

Hegel gives metaphor three purposes: to reinforce an effect, to cast off the externality of objects so that the soul can "rediscover itself what is external," and to escape the commonplace by finding affinities between increasingly disparate objects. All of these, it will be noted, partake of what I am calling "the aversion," or turning away. Indeed, as Hegel notes, the human soul "keeps adding image on image to that immediately confronting it," with the result that it remains in its own "tumult," impetuously seeking "to and fro."[5] Irigaray, in a section entitled "Metaphor / Metonymy," more bluntly writes that it is easy to forget (again) that "the whole Universe is

---

2 Georg Wilhelm Friedrich Hegel, *The Phenomenology of Mind*, 2d rev. ed., trans. J. B. Baillie (New York, 1967), 296–97.

3 By "cultural metaphysics," I simply mean those notions that, starting, for example, with Plato, are so pervasive as to be invisible. Derrida has devoted a good deal of his writing to exhibiting these. To name a few: the binary oppositions that pervade our thinking, logocentrism, phallocentrism, and the privileging of *parousia* and *aletheia*.

4 Although for Lacan, for example (following, of course, Roman Jakobson), displacement is metonymic only, I include it in this catalog because metonymy itself can slide into metaphor (as Ricoeur disapprovingly notes) in a move of contiguous substitution.

5 Georg Wilhelm Friedrich Hegel, *The Philosophy of Fine Art*, trans. F. P. B. Osmaston (New York, 1975), 2: 142–43.

already under the Father's monopoly," such that history goes on: "the 'other' doesn't count at all, of course; it only provides the materials. Which are more and more abstract, in fact."[6] Joan's death provides the materials, while commentators add "image on image" that are "more and more abstract, in fact," such that the scandal of her burning is veiled by transferral. The differing (gendered) gaze away from the impossible can only be grasped if a *woman's* death by fire can begin to be rid of its metaphors. Can this be thought?

Here we already encounter a difficulty, one that Paul Ricoeur has approached head on. It is the deconstructionist notion that the paradox of metaphor consists in the fact that its discourse can never be stated outside a metaphorically engendered conceptual network. The paradox is, as Ricoeur summarizes, "of the auto-implication of metaphor."[7] Sharing the *meta,* metaphor is always metaphysics and vice versa.[8] But if to disclose metaphor can only be limited to unmasking the concept, as Derrida would have it, then metaphoricity is "absolutely uncontrollable" and self-defeating, since "the theory of metaphor returns in a circular manner to the metaphor of theory, which determines the truth of being in terms of presence."[9] As such, one is reduced to recognizing the conditions that *"make it in principle impossible to carry out such a project"* as deciphering figures. We will always have the *ur*metaphors of the Sun and Returning Home, as surely as we will never break out of Plato's mimesis machine. Impossibility, in other words, is displaced (substituted) doubly: first onto

6 Luce Irigaray, *Speculum of the Other Woman,* trans. Gillian C. Gill (Ithaca, N.Y., 1985), 353.

7 Paul Ricoeur, *The Rule of Metaphor: Multi-disciplinary Studies of the Creation of Meaning in Language* (Toronto, 1981), 286.

8 This is the same logic, by the way, as that which opens Derrida's "The Purveyor of Truth": that once psychoanalysis posits itself, it will find itself everywhere. It is present, too, in his interpretation of Plato's "machine" for mimesis in "The Double Session" in *Dissemination:* that once this machine is in place, we (Western metaphysics) only change the gears, never breaking out of its model. There are many such defining moments that Derridean logic discovers in its excavations, moments that trap and confine apparently forever and to which, as he insists, deconstruction can only point but never itself break out any more than the incarcerated notions it describes. Thus, as in Whitehead, all philosophy is a footnote to Plato—but as imprinting (in the biological sense, as the duck seizes upon its first viewed object as its mother). It is precisely this economy of imprinting that I am resisting.

9 Ricoeur, *The Rule of Metaphor,* 287.

woman / death; coevally, to that which is more possible to elucidate as impossible: the endless machinery of metaphor.

If this is so, then it is very convenient for, among many other things, the masculinist subject position in relation to that of objectified woman, and we can abruptly stop our study here. Ricoeur himself, however, rejects this deconstructionist stance. It is not metaphor, he concludes, that carries the structure of Platonic metaphysics but rather metaphysics that instead seizes the metaphorical process to make it work to the benefit of metaphysics. He adds, "The metaphors of the sun and the home reign only to the extent that they are selected by philosophical discourse. The metaphorical field in its entirety is open to all the figures that play on the relations between the similar and the dissimilar in any region of the thinkable whatsoever" (295).

My purpose here is not to side simply with one theory, one theorist, over another. Nor is it even a political-existential choice. More than even that is at issue. The point is that this perspective is not a given, ungendered one. For the self-referentiality of metaphoricity is precisely the averted gaze; that is, it stakes out a repetition compulsion, as Derrida's study brilliantly demonstrates, and then proceeds to perform it. At this impasse, the feminine gaze is, if nothing else, productive, in that it does not *see* woman as mystery, enigma, and so forth, and therefore does not naturally partake of the same ontometaphoricity. And lest I myself be accused of partaking in metaphorics, let me be clear here: the masculine "metaphysical gaze" of which I am speaking, while it is indeed philosophically motivated, is above all to be understood literally—the gaze is turned away. The averted gaze, *aversion* from woman, from death, is *not a metaphor;* rather, its turning away is cloaked and hidden in metaphors. And while I do not pretend to "unmask" all metaphor—this would be an absurd claim—I do forcefully claim that I extract myself from metaphoric economy *at least to the extent that it engages gender* and from the conviction that all metaphors are *inevitable,* or unmarked. If my language here partakes of the metaphorical, it is not with the assumption that endless substitution is finally inescapable conceptually, even if it may be so at times rhetorically. Woman has been detained in metaphors of mystery, but the notion that such a prison is inevitable, unavoidable, capable only of being pointed to and at—this is a stance that is inadmissible here, *not* only from the position of willed existential reciprocity, as with Irigaray, for example, but simply from the fact of a different perspective, a different gaze.

Let us attempt, then, to consider how the impossible is veiled when veiling is transferred to images of femininity, for the purpose of thinking the impossible, and the shields we put up before it, without such gendering.

WAITING FOR PAROUSIA WITH IRIGARAY

Irigaray's notion that women do not yet exist is one that I have been arguing as well. But if the malady is similarly diagnosed, I do not share Irigaray's "remedy"—or, in fact, her conviction that it lies in the divine. For Irigaray, it is because women do not have a female god that they cannot access subject becoming. Men, on the other hand, have God as an ego ideal, a projection of ideal masculinity, and thus their subject becoming is "guaranteed." The male of the species, in this account, has monopolized the Symbolic. A woman needs, argues Irigaray in her more recent work, a representation of her own (a goddess) so that she can be mirrored and imagine her own infinite: "Having a God and becoming one's gender go hand in hand."[10] Ultimately, Irigaray wants to hypostatize a "sensible transcendence," one that would provide a reconfigured divinity both transcendent and immanent, spirit and flesh, soul and body.[11] "Why," she asks, "do we assume that God must always remain an inaccessible transcendence rather than a realization—here and now—in and through the body?" The spirit would then impregnate the body "in and through a lasting alliance."[12] Irigaray suggests the image of the placenta as a means of overcoming the binarisms that the male God necessarily produces. The placenta extracts us from the economy of one or two. As one critic of Irigaray puts it, "The One was never a One, not even before parturition; nor was it a Two, the infamous dyad; nor was it really a Three."[13] The

---

[10] Luce Irigaray, *Sexes and Genealogies,* trans. Gillian C. Gill (New York, 1987), 62.

[11] Although I am staying with this translation, I would rather suggest *sensory transcendence,* since the French *sensible* means both "sensitive" and "sensory" but never "sensible" in the English sense. Furthermore, *sensory* insists in English, as Irigaray wishes to do in the original, on the notion of embodiment.

[12] Irigaray, *An Ethics of Sexual Difference,* trans. Carolyn Burke and Gillian C. Gill (Ithaca, N.Y., 1993), 148.

[13] Gail M. Schwab, "Mother's Body, Father's Tongue: Mediation and the Symbolic Order," in *Engaging with Irigaray: Feminist Philosophy and Modern European Thought,* ed. Carolyn Burke, Naomi Schor, and Margaret Whitford (New York, 1994), 363. I refer the

placenta is separate but genetically part of the fetus and so can serve as a model (or *metaphor*) of mediation. The angel is the temporary figure of such a mediation while we "wait" for something to come that has never happened or for it to return. As such, Irigaray's angel is like a figure of annunciation for the time (to come, or to return) when men and women, celebrating their difference, will be able to achieve an ethics of sexual difference. The unembodied angel is the "representation of a sexuality that has never been incarnated, a light, divine gesture (or tale) of flesh that has not yet acted or flourished. Always fallen or still awaiting *parousia*" (*Ethics*, 15). When such *parousia* occurs, a God who is *both* male and female will mediate between the two angels on the Ark of the Covenant. These two new angels will guard as well the (heterosexual) human couple's newfound equality in bodily and spiritual difference, thus halting the return "from sameness to sameness" (*Sexes*, 45). With difference acknowledged, the two angels face each other and wait for the "mystery of a divine presence that has yet to be made flesh" (*Sexes*, 45).

This gender utopia, which I have all too quickly summarized, performs the salutary act of uncoupling patriarchy from divinity, and this is its brilliant and courageous contribution. It is a utopia that also, more problematically, professes to reconnect the human to the divine, a separation that Irigaray insists a previous, ancient time of matriarchy did not admit: "We must not forget that in the time of women's law, the divine and the human were not separate. That means that religion was not a distinct domain. What was human was divine and became divine. . . . Patriarchy has separated the human from the divine. . . . Before patriarchy, women and men were potentially divine beings, which may mean social beings."[14] But "social beings" may in fact be the rub. For Irigaray con-

reader to this excellent collection of essays, several of which I will mention here. The issue of essentialism is analyzed variously by, for example, Naomi Schor, Rosi Braidotti, and Jean-Joseph Goux; the ambiguity of Irigaray's utopian images is addressed by Margaret Whitford, who examines Irigaray's emphasis on the imaginary and argues that Irigaray's recent work, with its turn to love, "explicitly turns its back on the shadows" (29). See also Elizabeth Grosz's discussion of Irigaray's "redefinition" of homosexuality and heterosexuality. While I am to a large extent going in my own direction in my reading of Irigaray, I am greatly indebted to these essays and have profited by their interpretations of Irigaray's complicated texts.

14 Irigaray, *Thinking the Difference: For a Peaceful Revolution*, trans. Karin Montin (New York, 1994), 10–11.

flates what Mary Douglas calls "the two bodies"—the social and the physical—and conflates them without concession. In Douglas's words, "The social body constrains the way the physical body is perceived. The physical experience of the body, always modified by the social categories through which it is known, sustains a particular view of society. There is a continual exchange of meanings between the two kinds of bodily experiences so that each reinforces the categories of the other. As a result of this interaction the body itself is a highly restricted medium of expression."[15]

It will not suffice to say that the divine must be immanent, embodied, rendered material as well as transcendent, when we are living in specific cultural traditions and different historical periods, all of which have in common (in the European West) a patriarchal hegemony that accordingly and variously figures the body. Moreover, there is not, as many critics have noted, *one* body.[16] Furthermore, Marcel Mauss asserts that nothing about body behavior is "natural"—it is all learned through imprinting and must be studied through what he calls symbolic systems.[17] Whether or not this is entirely so, it seems to me that to write, as Irigaray does, of "the body" or "women" is an essentializing stance that mimes the very economy of sameness that her work is attempting to dislodge.[18] Indeed, part of my point in the first chapter of this study was precisely to note the contemporary nostalgia among secular theorists for an imagined "body" that, whole and undivided by Cartesian doubt, somehow once existed, as if outside time or before modern time. Irigaray partakes, then, of

---

15 Mary Douglas, *Natural Symbols: Explorations in Cosmology* (New York, 1982), 65.

16 See, for example, Peter Brown's *The Body and Society: Men, Women and Sexual Renunciation in Early Christianity* (New York, 1988); Kallistos Ware, "'My Helper and My Enemy': The Body in Greek Christianity," 90–110, and also Andre Louth, "The Body in Western Catholic Christianity," 111–30, in *Religion and the Body*, ed. Sarah Coakley (Cambridge, 1997); and Caroline Walker Bynum's *Holy Feast and Holy Fast: The Religious Significance of Food to Medieval Women* (Berkeley, Calif., 1987).

17 Marcel Mauss, "Les Techniques du corps," *Journal de la Psychologie* 32 (March–April 1936).

18 Despite arguments against seeing an essentialism in Irigaray—readings by Whitford and Grosz, as already mentioned, and by Tina Chanter and Penelope Deutscher, for example—I am nevertheless going to argue that in this particular instance, Irigaray is resorting (perhaps unavoidably) to universals. The assumptions underlying such universals, and the ensuing consequences, need critical attention without (one hopes) resorting to reductionism in reading Irigaray.

such a nostalgia herself. For even if we attain the level of sexual ethics, of the two angels, we will still be in a messianic time: we will still be waiting for *parousia*.

The two angels who in this utopic future will guard the Covenant, moreover, will be waiting with us for the mystery of divine flesh to be revealed. The divine as *sensible transcendent,* mediating like a placenta for the Ethical Couple, will mark the space *between* them so as not to return to the "same." With the advent of this better time, we seem to have left veils behind—the one that the first angel temporarily maintained and that Irigaray herself compares to the curtain in the *fort / da* game and to the mediating placenta.[19] The first angel *him*self (for he is still "in the service of the son") is consistently compared to veiling: porous and membrane-like, the angel is transparent. We do not know, however, whether he comes "from beyond the ultimate veil or if he is simply announcing this coming" (*Sexes,* 38). But once the *sensible transcendent* has occurred, and the first angel has left to make way for the two of the Covenant, we come to another veil (the "ultimate" one?). The two new angels guard not only the Ark of the Covenant "behind the temple veil" but also the constant danger of a return to sameness. With the Couple they wait, as we noted, for the mystery of a divine presence that has yet to be made flesh. The divine presence is found "in the place that is left empty between [the two angels]."[20]

This *betweenness* is hauntingly like Derrida's play on *antre* and *entre* in his essay on the hymen, "The Double Session," which we considered at length in a previous chapter. It might also be interjected here that, despite a vocabulary that includes membranes, veils, porous material, placentas and so on, very little about the hymen appears in these more recent angel texts of Irigaray. I would suggest that this is because the hymen, which suggests singularity, or at least a single figure, is not useful in a schema of the Ethical Couple, the union of which is metaphorized by the placenta and mirrored by the two angels. The couple Irigaray suggests is itself surrounded, then, by *metaphors* of veilings. And while it is true that such metaphors have lost their feminine specificity, they have not altered the averted aspect of the gaze. What has changed—no small matter—is that

---

19 In the essay "Belief Itself," in *Sexes and Genealogies.*

20 Irigaray, *Marine Lover of Friedrich Nietzsche,* trans. Gillian C. Gill (New York, 1991), 175.

in the utopic or messianic time Irigaray imagines, the veil is pondered by *both* genders. And yet an *Aufhebung* has nonetheless been performed: even as the difference between the sexes is *preserved*, the Ethical Couple *lifts up* its gaze to the angels and to the mystery of divine presence. At the same time, the impossible has been elided, since the purpose of this better time is to give woman a horizon for imagining the possibility of the infinite. My point, however, is to try to understand how it is that the impossible is figured, where it is that a point cannot be sublated by a fused gaze. I would go so far as to say that, in merging the gaze of the two who comprise the Couple (even though their difference is radically maintained), Irigaray has succeeded in erasing the *otherwiseness* of the feminine gaze, to which I alluded earlier, and created perhaps in spite of herself a new dialectic equally sublated—not through inversion (which she is strong in resisting) or the same but through a joining together of differences that annul binarism but not the uplifting, preserving element of the mysterious *in between*. Once again, the veil serves to affirm the possible, and we wait.

Furthermore, I am not convinced that it is always the case that "we assume that God must always remain an inaccessible transcendence rather than a realization—here and now—in and through the body." If this is so, what are we to make of nuns experiencing stigmata or of Certeau's possessed women in seventeenth-century Loudun? Or of all the early martyrs, for whom the sacrifice of the body *was* in itself a form of transcendence? Or of "holy" anorexia and the endless treatises concerning denying, overcoming, and controlling the body and its appetites, as Foucault has shown (for example, in "Combat de la Chasteté"), among many others? And what of all the treatises on "holy virginity"? And the fact that Christianity preaches a reintegration with the body at the Resurrection? Perhaps Simone Weil formulated the dilemma more starkly: All particular incentives are errors, she writes. "Only that energy which is not due to any incentive is good: obedience to God, which, since God is beyond all that we can imagine or conceive, means obedience to nothing. This is at the same time impossible and necessary—in other words, supernatural."[21] For Weil, the issue is not the body; rather, it is here precisely the impossible—at the level of thought, cognition, imagination. "In and through the body" is not the point for Weil; the problem is in the mind.

[21] Weil, *Gravity and Grace*, trans. Emma Craufurd (London, 1992), 88.

Conversely, an obsession with denying the body is also an obsession with the body, a conviction that the physical body becomes a temple when devoted to God in a concomitant abnegation of the *social* body. The ambivalence in thinking the body is succinct, to take a random example, is illustrated by the seventh-century Climacus, Abbot of Sinai, who worries about the resurrection and imagines his body as a male companion creating any number of contradictions: "He is my helper and my enemy, my assistant and my opponent, a protector and a traitor. . . . How can I escape from him when he is going to rise with me? . . . I embrace him. And I turn away from him. What is this mystery in me?"[22]

The mystery is indeed a murky one, to state mildly the obvious. At least through the late Middle Ages (and thereafter, of course, although perhaps the choreography is less familiar and accepted), the European Christian body is pierced through, wracked, rendered ecstatic, mortified, denied, or glorified by what it understands as its reciprocity with the divine. The divine plays itself out, inscribes itself on, lives in the body—or is thought as performing itself thus, which amounts to the same thing. Perhaps it is in part because this *difference*—between the human and the divine—is performed as existing simultaneously and symbiotically in its radically othered components, that a female god is not immediately necessary for "woman" to recognize herself *as* a self despite the male paradigms. (I am making a distinction here between a *subject* with agency, which—again—woman has never been, and a *sense of self*.) The male God is a *metaphor* of the divine, and women have been too long shrouded in metaphors themselves to take any of them literally. Moreover, Mary (for example), in the European Christian context, offers a viable alternative for ideal-ego mirroring (a concept to which we will return shortly), and this in spite of her nonhuman attributes and the Church's own resistance through the centuries to her cult. Joan's voices themselves will tell her that she is a "fille de Dieu" (daughter or girl of God), thus placing her in an implied genealogy that Irigaray refuses to acknowledge but from which Joan herself clearly takes comfort.

The body may be, as Douglas notes, a highly restricted medium of expression. But it is restricted by the cultural context that figures as well as

---

22 Cited by Ware, "'My Helper and My Enemy,'" 90. Plotinus is embarrassed to have a body, for example. Porphyry, "On the Life of Plontinus and the Arrangement of His Work," in Plotinus, *The Enneads*, trans. Stephen MacKena (London, 1991), cii–cxxv.

judges it. What does not seem to change in this scenario of Western European thought is that the edifice of metaphor is raised at all times (and mainly in a highly gendered way, as we have shown) to veil the impossible and to shroud death—even, finally, in Irigaray, although the gendered aspect is lifted. For in Irigaray we *wait*. As Levinas has noted in his reading of Blanchot, waiting is tied to forgetting. Metaphor itself, as I am arguing here, partakes of forgetting and waiting. Waiting for *parousia* as we profess to do, as Irigaray wishes us ultimately to do while celebrating gender difference, we make certain that the "mystery" hovers without appearing and that the impossible remains firmly *in potentia*.

Perhaps this is why Jean-Luc Marion has suggested that theology need not be grounded in a metaphysics of presence. Ontological difference, he writes, "and hence also Being, become too limited . . . to pretend to offer the dimension, still less the 'divine abode' where God would become thinkable."[23] Indeed, the Christian tradition assumes, in its apocalyptic eschatological economy, that *parousia* will dissolve mystery, and then the concealedness of unconcealedness will be finally unconcealed. But in that tradition, in moments when *parousia* has appeared, it has been metonymized (the burning bush, the visions so bright that the eyes must be averted, and so on). No man, says the tradition, shall look on God and live. Metaphoricity, in contrast and in the waiting, is the veil that protects from *parousia*—that is, the impossible—but it paradoxically veils the impossible so that it becomes possible, apprehensible through metaphor.

Can the subject, imagined as either masculine or feminine, be thought if the impossible is continually veiled so as to appear possible? Can subjectivity confront the impossible? Let me suggest, again, that perhaps it is subject becoming that partakes of the impossible—and that *this* is what needs to be veiled, lest the abyss in Nietzsche's sense reveal a mirror with no ego ideal whatever. More than being the ego ideal for a masculine gaze, God may be the ego ideal for subjectivity itself—the metaphor of metaphor that must not be apprehended directly lest it divulge that sovereignty has never belonged to the subject at all. The veiling of God, then, becomes the protection of the notion of subjectivity. He who gazes upon God goes blind, says the Bible. Metaphoricity in such a context becomes more than a patriarchal game; it betrays a transcendental in Kant's sense: how we imagine that which is not given us to

---

[23] Jean-Luc Marion, *God without Being: Hors Texte* (Chicago, 1991), 45.

know and, I would add, how our wish for an ideal subject formation manifests itself.

But who is doing the imagining? And to whom do the metaphors belong? Clearly, at present, to a patriarchy that more than frequently displaces veiling onto the feminine. If metaphors are stripped away, will this not reveal a new series of veils, the "ultimate veil" in Irigaray's sense? In ungendering the veil, perhaps we can escape *some* of the uncontrollability of metaphors that Ricoeur describes as being at the heart of deconstruction's courageous moves. If nothing else, we are saved from a circular uncontrollability in that we do not *know,* cannot predict, how an ungendered veiling would present itself. Irigaray's vision of the Couple waiting at the Covenant would resolve (at almost every level) the status of women and even make room for imagining a genuine human (heterosexual) love, based on a divinity clearly preferable in its configuration than is our "Good Old God," as Lacan puts it.

But where is death in this vision? And where tragedy? Irigaray's utopic waiting sidesteps the scandal of the impossible, for the vision of a divinity must take account of death and tragedy and of an impossible. As Maurice Blanchot puts it, death ends in being, the origin of man's unhappiness. Through man death comes to being, and through man meaning resides in nothingness. The paradox, he continues, is that we understand only by ceasing to exist and thus rendering death "*possible*" (Blanchot's emphasis); but if we leave being, "we fall outside all possibility of death, and the result [issue] becomes the disappearance of all results."[24]

This paradox described by Blanchot is close to Levinas's point concerning death and its inherent possibility. What I am arguing, then, is that a human cosmology such as the one proposed by Irigaray that does not include death and the impossible must in the end be seen as incomplete because it does not address itself to *being.* In this sense, then, the scandal of death, and thus tragedy, are not only an aspect of being; they are fundamental to any discourse on the divine, on love itself, and, above all, on the subject. As Certeau puts it, death is the problem of the subject.[25] For him,

---

[24] Maurice Blanchot, *La Part du feu* (Paris, 1949), 331; my translation. For a recent examination of Blanchot's notion of the Orphic, see Chantal Michel, *Maurice Blanchot et le déplacement d'Orphée* (Saint-Genouph, 1997).

[25] Michel de Certeau, *The Practice of Everyday Life,* trans. Steven Rendall (Berkeley, Calif., 1984), 192.

the in-between space is the possibility of dying. Death itself, however, is "the point where relations with the meaningless are focused." It is the wound of reason which supports itself "on what cannot be mentioned."[26] Thus, death for Certeau creates a third silence, beyond institutions and language: the silence of the subject.

Irigaray's "remedy" can be taken as a solution to certain social and even theological (certainly ecclesiastical) issues confronting contemporary cultural structures; the social body might well, in this account, modify the categories by which the physical body is known. The medium of expression for the body might well change; gender construction would metamorphose. But the comfort of the Couple elides the tragedy of the self, and especially of the feminine one. It does not take account of death, the impossibility that lies behind the "ultimate veil." To the consoling image of the placenta (neither one, nor two, nor even three), there remains here the unacknowledged problem of zero—that place, as Pascal hinted, that holds the space between the two infinities. But this is not the same between as that which contains the mystery, in Irigaray, of a divinity made flesh.

"Man" is generally read as the number one, the incomprehensible leap from zero that will allow the sequence of numbers to follow. It is to the one, as Irigaray notes in her analysis of going from the "same to the same," that masculinist thought wants to return. Reading Baudelaire's "Correspondance," Paul de Man asks, "For what could be more perverse or corruptive for a metaphor aspiring to transcendental totality than remaining stuck in an enumeration that never goes anywhere?" If a number can only be conquered by another number, and if identity becomes enumeration, de Man continues, then there is no conquest at all, since "the stated purpose of the passage to infinity was, like in Pascal, to restore the one, to escape the tyranny of number by dint of infinite multiplication."[27] But zero, of course, has a special status: as place holder, it permits all other numbers to occur, especially the one. Moreover, zero is the only integer that is not identical to itself; it is a mathematical *symbol.* It stands *between* Pascal's two infinities, marking the place where enumeration and the infinite begin.

Let us consider zero, rather than one, as the place of human subject

[26] Ibid.

[27] Paul de Man, *The Rhetoric of Romanticism* (New York, 1984), 250.

formation, which thus far has been largely masculine. As the place holder between, and as an element *not identical to itself* but allowing for the thinking of "One," zero represents the subject. For the subject builds *his* notion of sovereignty (one) on a disjunction between the totality of subjective thought, on the one hand, and on the impossibility of death, on the other. His status as zero allows for the leap to one and the ensuing proliferation of numbers into the infinite. But such an infinity always returns him to the place between and thus to death. The paradox of zero—the between that at once allows for the endless chain of numbering and the constant return to itself as a nonidentical to itself—is the paradox of subjectivity. It is *both* nothing and impossibility and at the same time something hypostatized as possible through the speculative moves of inference and the logic of the ensuing augmented sequence.

The mirroring of which Irigaray writes, that ego ideal that allows for subject formation, is helpless to render apodictic subjectivity finally to *any* human. Like zero, subjectivity is a symbol that allows for construction but must constantly take into account the disjunction between its being as possible and its death as impossible. To take comfort in proliferation, as Irigaray does (neither one, nor two, nor three, but an endless chain of possibilities), is to forget the other side of subjectivity, the other facet of the circle marking the infinite and the nothingness that is zero.

Gender, and its constructions, cannot be removed from this contradiction since any aspect of gender, from a philosophical point of view (I am not engaging, here, the social aspect of gender), must take the problem of the subject in its tragic contradiction into account. The Ethical Couple gazing on the in between with its mystery is facing, I would argue, the radical incommensurability of thinking the subject. It may be, in fact, that in her lack of a mirroring for an ego ideal, woman is closer to understanding the impossible than is man. She knows, in other words, that the subject is not identical to itself. This is not intended as an apology for the status quo. Rather, I am arguing that the illusion of subjectivity is more easily maintained from the male perspective and more easily veiled. Joan, as a saturated phenomenon *for the spectators* at her execution, illustrates many of these issues in a way that, I will argue, exceeds even the saturated itself.

BEYOND BACHELARD'S FIRE

The scandal of Joan's death (and of any other theater of execution) is the social institution's assumption that the choreographed imposition of death somehow eradicates its impossibility. How, then, to think Joan's death outside (the usual) comforting metaphors? We are already in one by the very means of her death: fire itself is constantly metaphorized. It is one of the four elements, the essence of passion, that which lives by consuming itself, dominant in mythology (Prometheus, the Phoenix, Icharus), and so on. Fire is a metaphor even and perhaps especially in studies that announce themselves as an attempt to examine fire in itself. Bachelard's *The Psychoanalysis of Fire* is a case in point. His interest in fire is grounded in psychophilosophical reverie, one that wants the imagination to be enriched, so that poetry, for example, will rest on the "metaphor of metaphor," if only by a dialectic. More specifically, he wants the poetic image to be activated through metaphors that *decompose* it, that fight against the "egotistical" unity of composition—thus his interest in fire and his coeval conviction that the enormous poetic production of fire images becomes "understandable." At the conclusion of Bachelard's famous study, fire emerges as the best of the image makers, the one that is "most dialecticized" because "[i]t alone is *subject and object*. When one gets to the bottom of an animism, one always finds a calorism. . . . [I]nner fire is dialectical in all its properties, a replica, as it were, of this fundamental dialectic of subject and object."[28] This seems initially like Shakespeare's own metaphor of fire in the seventy-third sonnet: that the poet, like the fire, lies on the ashes of his youth; the fire being consumed by that which nourishes it. The dialectic inherent to fire resides in this paradox, thus yielding Bachelard's subject and object. But these are hardly ungendered in Bachelard. Citing an eighteenth-century alchemist, he notes that fire is frequently the "male principle" that "vitalizes the female substance" (50). Moreover, smoke is feminine because it *veils:* "Need we call attention to the feminine sign attached to smoke, 'the inconstant wife of the wind,' as Jules Renard calls it? Is not every veiled apparition considered feminine by virtue of this fundamental principle of unconscious sexualization: all that is hidden is feminine?"

---

[28] Gaston Bachelard, *The Psychoanalysis of Fire,* trans. Alan C. M. Ross (Boston, 1964), 111.

(52). The "fundamental principle" that femininity is hiddenness genders smoke.

The fire itself, however, is masculine—first because it is warm.[29] Bachelard cites the seventeenth-century doctor Pierre Jean Fabré's connection between fire and semen, hot and cold being masculine and feminine, respectively. Bachelard has forgotten, apparently, that these thermal schemas for gender come from Aristotle, as we noted in chapter 2. But fire is also masculine for Bachelard because it opens the hidden—that is, the organs of the body. Especially masculine is the case of alchemy, which is "uniquely a science engaged in by men, by bachelors, by men without women." In this "strictly masculine society," fire is strongly polarized as well by a sexual dialectic: "This inner, masculine fire, the object of the meditation of the lonely man, is naturally considered to be the most powerful fire. In particular it is the fire which can 'open bodies.' . . . This 'opening' of bodies, this possession of bodies from within, this *total* possession, is sometimes an obvious sexual act" (53).

But such an image exists also outside alchemy. Gilles de Rais, it will be recalled, specifically asked that he be removed from the fire before it had "opened" him—a request that was granted. Joan, on the other hand, is burned until her entrails are "opened." If the fire is seen as masculine in this perspective, in that it opens what is normally hidden (the organs of the body), then it follows that the victim of the fire is feminized. More than asking to be spared after death from the mutilating power of fire, Rais is equally requesting that his manhood be preserved before the spectators of his execution.

None of this is surprising or innocent, in terms of the gender implications. Given the "fundamental principle" of the feminine as hiddenness and the fact that the fire opens the hidden, it is of necessity masculine. From this follows, inexorably, Bachelard's conviction that "we are almost certain that fire is precisely the first object, the *first phenomenon,* on which the human mind *reflected*" (55, emphasis Bachelard's). This reflection in turn awakens in man the desire for knowledge, followed by that for love. Already in this history of metaphors of fire, first cause is aligned with the masculine. Although Bachelard himself refers to many of these asser-

[29] Bachelard's discussion is amplified by the fact that French is a gendered language: fire *(le feu)* is masculine; smoke *(la fumée),* feminine. None of this is conveyed, of course, in the English translation.

tions as "ridiculous," and although he is engaging in cultural psychoanalytic readings of historical documents concerning fire, what emerges is a telling line-up. Fire is masculine and therefore hot, penetrating, positioned as first cause, phallic, and so on. Moreover, it elicits the desire for knowledge and sexual love (read: in *men*). This latter conclusion is Bachelard's own and thus presumably not "ridiculous." Smoke is attached in a way too obvious to warrant discussion ("need we draw attention to it?") to the "feminine sign," changeable like the wind and feminine like every "veiled apparition."

Thus, in Bachelard's famous study on fire, the metaphors are read as interesting historically but ridiculous in their implications. Bachelard's own conclusions, however, *rely* on the very connotations that those metaphors produce. This circular movement, which Freud in another context calls "kettle logic," succeeds in conflating tenor and vehicle, but also legend and the experiential. The "Empedocles Complex," one of the many "categories" of fire that motivate Northrop Frye's laudatory introduction to the English edition, becomes literalized so that "Death in the flame is the least lonely of deaths." It allows the "thinker" a truly cosmic death because "a whole universe" is reduced to nothingness along with him. Thus, the flames overcome death by destroying the cosmos along with the thinker. Death becomes a reverie of the masculine, in which the impossible, through the comforts of primary narcissism, is annihilated through the reduction to nothingness of "the whole universe."

The conclusion of Shakespeare's seventy-third sonnet engages a sorrow that Bachelard's vision erases: "This thou percev'st, which makes thy love more strong, / to love that well which thou must leave ere long." The power in the Shakespeare sonnet lies precisely in the fact that, after twelve lines built on a metaphorical relation between fire and youth, ashes and old age, the couplet leaves metaphoricity behind. Thus, the plainly stated fact of impending death (separation, leaving) has echoes of the fire metaphor (that which is dying burns more brightly = one loves more what is about to be extinguished) but leaves the sorrow unadorned, unsubstituted. Hence, the power of the couplet: the impossible may not be entirely confronted (since, after all, the sonnet imagines more the feelings of the one left behind than those of the one dying), but the irrevocability of death is left to shimmer, even if only as a suggestion, unconcealed. On the other hand, there is nothing to be left behind in Bachelard's study, since the world dies with the thinker. Death, as a consequence, disappears along with loneliness: the veil remains intact before the impossible.

The purpose of this extended reading of Bachelard is not an *ad hominem* attack—on the contrary.[30] The point is how easily metaphor *veils the veil* of that which must remain hidden, how comfortably it allows for assumptions based on substitution, how easily thought and knowledge are appropriated by the masculine. Need we call attention to the feminine sign? That is precisely what must be attempted.

Fire, writes Johnson in his *Dictionary*, is to be inflamed by passion.[31] Here is a hint of another aspect of fire, as Bachelard notes: fire is the dialectic of purity and impurity—impurity because it is sexualized (the passions, Petrarch's burnings, and so on), purity because "it suppresses nauseous odors" (103), although it can leave behind the odor of the body, as Derrida muses in *Feu la cendre*. Bachelard wonders whether the fire of Hell or of the Last Judgment is the same as terrestrial fire. But the critic is clear: "in particular we shall not deal with the theological problem of purification by fire. To give a full account of that would require a very long study." One thing, however, can be said that "suffices," he adds: "It is sufficient to point out that the core of the problem lies in the *contact* of the metaphor and the reality." The fire of Hell or of the Last Judgment is then as if contaminated by the fire on Earth, and vice versa. There is thus an "enormous flowering of metaphors around the primary image of fire." The flowery expressions "used by theology" to adorn "'our brother, the fire,' would merit patient classification" (102–3).

We will retain this notion of Bachelard's—that fire bleeds into different registers and so is diffuse, disseminated, plural. Such contamination seems to encourage metaphoric proliferation. Fire in this reading seems to represent a different dialectic of the pure and impure, then: impurity by contact of metaphor with reality; purity in setting apart a category (such as a heretic, for example) to be expunged from the community so that its contact is effaced. But then we might say that the very aspect of fire when

---

[30] Mircea Eliade and Carl Jung, for example (to name just two), have produced similar studies on the notion of "fire."

[31] This metaphor is ubiquitous. So, for example, Augustine, after he arrives in Carthage, finds himself "in a hissing cauldron of lust . . . caught up in the coils of trouble . . . lashed with the cruel, fiery rods of jealousy and suspicion, fear, anger, and quarrels." *Confessions*, trans. R. S. Pine-Coffin (London, 1961), 55.

used for purification belies itself in its presentation as plural or multivalent, in its economy of contagion.

Even ashes, says Derrida, are but "fire withdrawn," their multifarious remainder doubling the protean aspect of fire itself. Moreover, adds Derrida, with its withdrawal from ashes, fire "again feigns to have abandoned the territory. It still camouflages, it disguises itself under its multiplicity: dust, makeup powder, the inconsistent *pharmakon* of a plural body which no longer cares for itself or has a hold on itself [*ne tient plus à lui-même*]—cannot stay with itself, be for itself."[32] In this sense, too, fire is multivalent since it is at once "virile" and, in its disguises and veils (the smoke, the ashes), presents a metonymic aspect of femininity.

In reading Plato's cave, Irigaray becomes impatient with Plato's internal and external fires: "But fire," she writes, "what is that? A simple body, an elementary substance that can be predicated on the basis of certain qualities." The "excessive power" of the four elements, she argues, must be checked through a rigorous scientific analysis: "They must be put in their place, within a general theory of being so as to lessen our fascination with them" (*Speculum,* 160). What does it mean to put fire in its place? It is, among other things, the opposite view of Bachelard and Derrida, for example. Bachelard's study idealizes imagination, which for him "works at the summit of the mind like a flame" (110). Imagination eludes the determinations of psychology—"psychoanalysis included"—because it is "the true source of psychic production." As such, then, the metaphors produced by the imagination (the "image-maker") must be safeguarded, for they bring us closest to reverie "which delineates the furthest limits of our mind." Poetry, therefore, has a privileged status in this logic, as it does in Derrida, who, while playing metaphor against concept, as Geoffrey Bennington puts it, writes his own poem to metaphor with ash (from which fire has temporarily withdrawn) as both tenor and vehicle in another reverie: "I had first imagined on my part that ash was there, not here but there [*là*] like the story to be told: ash, that old gray word, that dusty theme of humanity, the immemorial image had decomposed itself, metaphor or metonymy of itself, such is the destiny of all ash, separated, consumed, like an ash of ash. Who would still dare to risk themselves before the poem of ash?" (15).

The undertext of *Feu la cendre* plays with the figure of Cinderella, the

---

32 Derrida, *Feu la cendre* (Paris, 1987), 45; my translation.

fairytale of another realm revealing itself to a girl who plays with cinders, ash. But Derrida's text also alludes to Paul Celan and in particular to the ashen hair of Shulamith, that metonymic trope for the Holocaust who leaves the trace of ashes in the wake of her sacrifice. Like Bachelard, Derrida privileges poetry in his read of ashes and of the fire ("no cinder without fire"). Ashes here are the trace of what was and the memory of an annulment "without a phoenix."[33] It is the burning of books and writing as much as of a given body. Dissemination crumbles in ash, letting a place occur: "Nothing will have taken place but the place" (35). In this resonance with Celan and with Heidegger ("a pure place was marked out," writes Derrida), the text of *Feu la cendre* configures a reverie on the trace, on the clearing, and, finally, on Heidegger's notion of *Dichten*. "Pure is the word. It calls for fire." According to Hegel, "Spirit is the flame," to which Heidegger responds that the logic of sacrifice allows (with poetry, with thinking) the "soundless voice" of Being to ring. Derrida disengages, as Ned Lukacher puts it, Heidegger's thinking from this sacrificial logic and turns instead to the trace (without a Phoenix) and to the Other. For Derrida, this is the call of the cinder, of the ash: "That," he writes, "is what is owed to the fire, and yet, if possible, without the shadow of a sacrifice." Metaphoricity cloaks dangerously here as in Heidegger. And it is Bataille, it should be noted, who insists on the suffering of sacrifice (the limit of death on the cross is finally "unveiled" as a catastrophe "in a chaos of light and shadow"). For Bataille, there must be the "shadow of a sacrifice in order to grasp the catastrophe, in order to acknowledge excess as the abyss to which suffering is the necessary path." In this sense, Bataille's work on excess may mark an ethics close to that of David Tracy, who asks that we look without aversion on the moment of suffering in its relation to love with death as its only liberation (death as the impossible, not as the Christian comfort of returning "home"). Catastrophe is seen neither as God nor as nothingness, writes Bataille, "but as the object that love, incapable of liberating itself except outside of itself" ("Sacrifice," 134; see below, n. 34). We must think more about this love that, like fire, must be consumed by that which nourishes it, in the words of Shakespeare again.

Could Irigaray's call for a lessening of fascination in fire, for a demys-

---

33 Derrida is also playing with the other meaning of *feu* in French—that is, the defunct. *Feu ma mère* means "my late mother," for example, so that *feu la cendre* elicits a double death: the fire and the cinders themselves.

tification that would put fire "in its place"—could this be, in this earlier Irigaray of *Speculum,* a plea to leave reverie of metaphor as a concept, or as the concept of a nonconcept, behind or at least to the side? The word *place* in Irigaray does not have Heideggerian overtones, and trace is a logic to be expunged. Nevertheless, this aversion to metaphor may well be a gendered one. "But we are really wasting our time with this show," she writes later after dissecting the cave of Plato with its womb, hymen, fires, paths, and mirrors. But where, in Irigaray's work, is the moment of catastrophe, of the scream of lacerated existence?

Fire is indeed a waste of time. "There is time," as Bataille notes in his essay on sacrifice, not because objects are necessarily destroyed by it "like the *me,* infinitely destroyed by time itself," but because the existence of things is impoverished "in comparison with that of the *me.*" Time projected arbitrarily into an objective region "is only the ecstatic vision of a catastrophe destroying that which founds this region."[34] Time, like fire, is related to sacrifice in Bataille: "The existence of things, assuming the value for *me*—projecting an absurd shadow—of the preparation for an execution, cannot enclose the death it brings, but is itself projected into this death, which encloses it."[35] Sacrifice itself, the ecstatic vision "at the limit of death on the cross" unveils itself as catastrophe letting out the "scream of lacerated existence."

Surrounded as we are by the flames of passion, of ashes, and of poetry (Bachelard, Derrida, Heidegger) and conversely by the call to demystify (Irigaray), let us try with Bataille's vision to inquire into the "real" fire (Bachelard's distinction) this way: The scandal of Joan of Arc's murder is that its fire was definitely not a metaphor, nor were the ashes or the smoke. On the other hand, the burning of a heretic in her context is *in itself a metaphor*—staged as one in the festival of murder, in the spectacle of cleansing, and in the drama of doctrinal triumph that that murder performs.

Bataille alone, it seems, is able to insist on tragedy and its excessive aspect and to consider the *catastrophe* of death on the self. Gilles de Rais's execution, with its solemn procession, endless confessional speeches by the accused, crowds singing and chanting to accompany him to his death,

---

[34] Georges Bataille, *Visions of Excess: Selected Writings 1927–1939,* trans. Allan Stoekl, with Carl R. Lovitt and Donald M. Leslie, Jr., vol. 14, Theory and History of Literature (Minneapolis, 1985), 135.

[35] Ibid.

church music, mourners crying and lamenting, and so on, lent, writes Bataille, "a resplendence that he could never get enough of in his lifetime" (*Gilles de Rais,* 62). Hanged first, he was then burned very briefly so that, as we have seen, the flames could not open his body and entrails. This pageantry was one of expiation, the triumph of repentance, and the reintegration of a penitent son back into the arms of the Church he so movingly endorsed with his death drama. For there to be tragedy, Hegel remarks, there needs to be a crime, and the death of Rais is, in Bataille's terms, a tragic one, despite its resplendence. Nevertheless, great care was taken to see that his suffering and the damage to his body would be minimal.

There was no resplendence in the pageantry of Joan's death, although there was a great crowd. Indeed, one might say that the crime lay not with her but with her murderers, if one is needed to employ the term *tragedy.* Her death can be described in the words of Bataille, from the essay on sacrifices. Time, he writes, is in "common circumstances" as if locked in systems of measure and equivalence. It withers, and with it, existence withers. However, "burning love—consuming the existence exhaled with great screams—has no other horizon than a catastrophe, a scene of horror that releases time from its bonds" (134).

Catastrophe as lived time unbinds it because existence is in excess within the scene of its own annihilation. The horror of Joan's screams are recorded as bringing even the British to tears. More significantly, there is an uncanny reversal of the Crucifixion in Joan's last words. Whereas the last words of Christ are read as the human moment of crying out a sense of great abandonment by God, Joan's last words, those screams of a lacerated existence, were cried out to Jesus, and her gaze was on the cross that one of the priests had gone to get from a nearby church, so that she could see it in front of her until she died.[36] Christ's passion, to which hers

---

[36] The priest was Isambard de la Pierre, a simple Dominican from Rouen who also participated in the trial. His deposition from the Trial of Rehabilitation reads, "Dit oultre plus, que la piteuse femme lui demanda, requist et supplia humblement, ainsi qu'il estoit pres d'elle en sa fin, qu'il allast en l'eglise prouchaine, et qu'il lui apportast la croix, pour la tenir eslevee tout droit devant ses yeux jusques au pas de la mort, afin que la croix ou Dieu pendist, fust en sa vie continuellement devant sa vue. Dit oultre, qu'elle estant dedans la flambe, oncques ne cessa jusques en la fin de resonner et confesser a haulte voix le saint nom de Jhesus." Jules Quicherat, *Procès de condamnation et de réhabilitation de Jeanne d'Arc, dite la Pucelle* (Paris, 1841–49), 5-vol. edition (New York, 1965) of the New York Public Library, 2: 6.

is frequently compared,[37] gives her the strength to endure her suffering; it mirrors the *catastrophe*. Joan's passion is the gift of faith at the moment of the impossible: indeed, witnesses at the Trial of Rehabilitation said that from the midst of the flames, she cried out that her voices had not deceived her. Joan's gift of faith, her "burning love," is screamed, not written, in the horror of being burned alive. It is not, in other words, the "Feu" written in the middle of Pascal's *Memorial* text:

> From about 10:30 at night until about half past midnight,
> Fire
> "God of Abraham, God of Isaac, God of Jacob"
> not of philosophers and of scholars.

This epiphany, which Pascal records in writing immediately after it occurred, was famously sewn into whatever garment he was wearing so that he could feel the document next to his heart at all times and not *forget* the moment. The word *fire* stands alone in this document, with all of its connotations: passion, the revelation of God, consuming (burning) love, the dazzling light of certitude. The word stands alone because its meanings are so inscribed in the tradition that "fire" acts as a mnemonic device in itself—a mantra, reminding Pascal of the event that, while it can be written down, cannot be described. Yet, even the God who is "not of philosophers and of scholars" must be transcribed to be remembered when his grace is felt. Pascal's written *Memorial* thus functions both as a memory trace and as a proof of the hiddenness of God, even within the words marking the representation of divine presence. "Fire" here is the knowledge of the certainty of God—a consuming passion that is dictated, as if by automatic writing, onto the page.

In contrast, Joan's fire (the "real fire") and her cries were recorded by eyewitnesses after the fact. In *catastrophe,* although time is freed (to return to Bataille's notion), there can be no memory, perhaps for the very fact that time is unmeasured—no memory, that is, for the *me* that is lacerated. Death, of course, obliterates memory as well as waiting (*l'Attente l'oublie,* in Blanchot's terms). But Joan is not able to leave the trace of writing fire; we are left only with her cinders (to which we will return)

[37] Especially in the large number of films produced on Joan's life—for example, Carl Dreyer's 1928 *La Passion de Jeanne d'Arc.*

and to witnesses at the Trial of Rehabilitation and letters by contemporaries. Indeed, as Quicherat notes, there is a forgetfulness (or at least a silence) about Joan in the years immediately following her death.[38]

She comes late to her knowledge of death, in part because she believes almost to the end that her voices will save her, will not allow her to burn. She abjures by force, confronted with the stake being prepared for her. But, as we have seen, she recants her abjuration and says that *if* she did abjure (which she had not fully understood herself to have done and which, conversely, she does not fully deny), she did so out of the fear of a horrible death: "everything that I did, I did out of the fear of the fire" *(Et totum hoc quod fecit, ipsa fecit prae timore ignis)*.[39] Is this perhaps the first time that Joan recognizes her body as an agent of mortality? In any case, her Trial of Condemnation can be divided into three parts. During the first (from 21 February to 26 March), she is confident and at times seen as arrogant, so sure is she that her voices will rescue her and that their instructions must be followed.

DEATH IN THE MARKETPLACE

The second part of Joan's trial, from 27 March through 27 May, is one of doubt and confusion. At times she seems to fear that her voices have abandoned her. From 27 to 28 March, the seventy "libels" against her are read, to which she is to respond "I believe it" or "I do not believe it." These are followed by a reading, several weeks later, of the distillation of these libels into the twelve final articles against her. Between 27 March and 23 May, she is admonished twice by the Church authorities. She abjures on

---

38 Quicherat notes that during her victories, many statues and monuments were erected in Joan's honor. After her death, however, to appease those who saw her as a saint and those who did not, *"on imposa silence sur sa mémoire. L'absence de som nom dans des écrits où elle ne s'explique pas, me conduit à cette conjecture."* He adds that in 1433 at Blois, there was a meeting of state at which the "miraculous" military feats of the king were recited from a historical chronicle. The author gives thanks to God, "who had instilled with courage a small company of valiant men to undertake this." On the Pucelle, writes Quicherat, there is *"pas un mot."* Other epistles and chronicles of the time show a similar reticence, and even the poet Charles d'Orléans gives no thanks to Joan who had, after all, saved his lands from the English. See *Aperçus nouveaux sur l'histoire de Jeanne d'Arc* (Paris, 1850), 156.

39 Quicherat, *Procès,* 1:458

24 May at the cemetery of Saint-Ouen in Rouen. There, placed on a scaffold as if to remind her of her fate should she refuse, she is scolded publicly by Guillaume Erard and forced (or, as some claim, tricked) into signing a document of recantation.[40] As the sentence was being read to her, Joan immediately agreed to do whatever her judges wanted: "And after that, as they began to read the sentence, she said that she wanted to hold to everything that the judges and the Church wanted to say and judge, and that she would obey them in all of their demands and wishes. And then in the presence of those aforementioned and of a great multitude of people who were there, she accepted in writing her abjuration."[41] The terms of this document were meant to doom her; Cauchon could not condemn her except as a relapsed heretic. Promising never again to wear men's clothes, it was only a matter of time, given the secular prison in which she was kept and the constant (sexual) threat of her guards, until she returned to them.[42] When she did, of course, Cauchon had his victim exactly where he wanted her.

The third part of the trial comprises the last three days of her life, from 28 through 30 May, the last being the day of her execution. In this period, Joan realizes that her abjuration does not come with freedom; it simply means that she will not be executed but rather left to live out her days in prison on bread and water alone. In this brief time, she begins to reject the court, the judges, and her own abjuration. Never, she claims, "had she understood having promised not to resume male attire." The voices had returned to her on the preceding Thursday and told her that she was in

[40] For various interpretations of Joan's recantation, see Marina Warner, *Joan of Arc: The Image of Female Heroism* (New York, 1981), 140–42; R. Pernoud, *The Retrial of Joan of Arc: The Evidence at the Trial for Her Rehabilitation,* ed. R. Pernoud, trans. J. M. Cohen (London, 1955), 177–82. See also Georges Duby and Andrée Duby, *Le Procès de Jeanne d'Arc* (Paris, 1995), 168; and Quicherat's *Aperçus nouveaux,* 133–38.

[41] Duby and Duby, *Le Procès,* 167.

[42] Joan herself made it quite clear that she had returned to men's clothing in prison as a form of protection from her guards. When asked why she had put on men's clothes, she said, "because it seemed more licit and proper to her to have on a man's clothing as long as she was among men than to wear the attire of women." Duby and Duby, *Le Procès,* 171–72. Cauchon had insisted on incarcerating her in the secular, rather than ecclesiastic, prison. She was to tell him several times that this was unlawful (which it was) and put her in great danger (of rape). Several witnesses at the Trial of Rehabilitation testify to the same explanation: Joan wore men's clothing in prison to discourage the guards from raping and / or harassing her.

danger of eternal damnation for having abjured. She had bowed to the Church to save her life and would, she was certain, be damned for so doing. When she speaks to her jurors on 28 May, it is quite clear that she fears God and damnation more than burning at the stake and that she would "rather die than to be in irons."

Once again, Joan obeys her God rather than the Church Militant, and her pride returns: "And said further, that her voices told her that when she would be on the scaffold, she should answer the priest who would preach her boldly. And added that the priest in question was a false priest and that he said that she had done several things that she had never done."[43] If they keep their promise, she says, of letting her go to Mass and receiving Communion and of being taken out of irons, she will do whatever they order. But she will not deny that she is sent from God, for if she does, her soul will be damned. She says that Saints Catherine and Margaret had told her from God that she had put her soul in great danger by abjuring. The scribe, upon hearing this answer, writes in the margins of the record, *"responsio mortifera":* she has in fact condemned herself in the eyes of the Church with this response, because she claims that God's message is that she will suffer damnation if she obeys the Church demands.[44]

At this point she adds, in the passage we have already considered, that she never thought she had abjured or denied her voices and that if she had, it was out of fear of the fire. On 29 May, the court decides that she is a heretic "and that she must be given over to secular justice asking this justice to treat her more gently than she deserved."[45] The Church did not have the right to execute anyone; they merely "relaxed," or handed over, as Given notes, the heretic to secular authorities. Never, however, did the secular justice go against the Church in this period, so that the secular trial was entirely pro forma (as if the ecclesiastic one had been other than that).[46]

At eight o'clock on 30 May, Joan was taken to the Old Marketplace of Rouen to be "preached." On the miter that covered her shaven head were written the words "Heretica, Relapsa, Apostata, Idolater." A proscenium-

43 Duby and Duby, *Le Procès,* 174.

44 Quicherat, *Procès,* 1: 456.

45 Duby and Duby, *Le Procès,* 175.

46 James B. Given, *Inquisition and Medieval Society: Power, Discipline and Resistance in Languedoc* (Ithaca, N.Y., 1997).

like structure had been built to frame her at the stake, so that, between this plaster structure and the miter, it was difficult to see her even from close up. First, the charges against her were read aloud to her in French; then came the sermon. Witnesses at the Trial of Rehabilitation testified that she bore the sermon with patience and humility. Given by the assessor Nicolas Midi, it took its theme (commonly used for heretics) from the passage from I Corinthians 12:26, "If one organ suffers, they all suffer together. If one flourishes, they all rejoice together." Cauchon's reading of the formal verdict followed, and it, too, concentrated on the limbs of the body. Declaring her a relapsed heretic, Joan was to be rooted out "as a rotten member." Joan was then turned over to the secular authorities, whose judge turned immediately to the executioner and merely said, "Do your duty." There was, in other words, no secular trial, a breach of the law brought to the attention of the judges at the Trial of Rehabilitation. She was immediately burned at the stake without a secular sentencing.[47]

Upon hearing that she was condemned, Joan began to cry and lament in a way so piteous that, as noted, even the British (and, by some accounts, Cauchon himself) burst into tears. She asked the pardon of everyone, even her enemies, and showed herself to be fervent in her faith. The British scholar A. E. Jones takes this to be a second abjuration: "The Rehabilitation tribunal was so pleased to have Joan's piety confirmed in this way that it never seems to have realised that her penitence and requests for the pardon of her enemies meant that she had abandoned her claim to have been carrying out God's instructions and had made a final abjuration."[48] But this conclusion is in contradiction to the testimonies of both Martin Ladvenu and Jean Massieu. Ladvenu had heard her confession and given her Communion on the morning of her death, and he testified that

---

47 Quicherat, *Procès*, 2: 6.

48 A. E. Jones, *The Trial of Joan of Arc* (Chichester, 1980), 237. Jones also believes that it is "unfair" for Joan to have been declared a saint "after having committed herself to a crusade of slaughter against fellow Catholics." He then decides, however, that it is "churlish," given what she suffered for her religious convictions, "to grudge her a distinction which now, presumably, entitles her to greet Saints Catherine and Margaret on equal terms" (304). Jones's entire book is a lesson in scholarship infused with a certain retroactive (English) nationalism, as are many of the French versions, written from the other side. Quicherat is all the more remarkable for his superb scholarship and (to the extent that this is possible) relative objectivity. Indeed, he began his ten-year study as a great skeptic with regard to Joan.

to the end she held to her claim that her revelations were from God and that she had done everything at God's commandment.[49] Massieu, who was at the execution, testified that she cried out to her "felicitous" [*bienheureux*] three saints from the flames. Even though she admitted that there was no angel (as she had previously maintained) with a crown when she went to see Charles—that she, in fact, had been the "angel"—she holds to her story that she really did hear her voices and that "she left it to the churchmen to decide whether they were good or evil spirits."[50] This last piece of testimony is from Pierre Maurice, who in the Trial of Condemnation is virulently against Joan. If we are to discount Massieu and Ladvenu as being overly partisan on her behalf, overly anxious to rewrite the history of Joan twenty-five years after the fact, we must equally discredit Maurice for being biased against her. Also, while it is true that Isambard de la Pierre, in his Rehabilitation testimony, says that Joan was repentant and contrite before her death (which Jones uses for his argument of a second abjuration), he also says that she died as a martyr with the name of Jesus on her lips. This was a sign, he testified, "that she was fervent in her faith in God."[51] She could not, therefore, have been a repentant heretic or a diabolical witch who recanted at the last moment. Isambard de la Pierre, as a matter of fact, compares her to Saint Ignatius and other martyrs "whom we read about."

It is because Joan renounced her voices, claims Jones, that she was allowed to confess and receive the Eucharist. But Duby and Duby claim, citing the Trial of Rehabilitation, that after Ladvenu had heard Joan's confession on the morning of her death, he sent to ask Cauchon whether she could receive Communion. Cauchon gathered the doctors of theology about him and finally decided that she could take Communion and that she should be given "anything that she wants." Manchon concurs with this version. Had she really repented, she would have publicly disavowed her voices on the scaffold, and there would have been a benediction and absolution before the burning. Neither of these occurred; on the contrary, after her confession and Communion, she was declared a heretic and excommunicated. Indeed, compelling evidence indicates that

---

[49] Duby and Duby, *Le Procès,* 282. Although Jones claims that Ladvenu said the opposite (*The Trial,* 240), see the Latin in Quicherat, *Procès,* 2: 158.

[50] Jones, *The Trial,* 241.

[51] Quicherat, *Procès,* 2: 7.

if Joan "disavowed" that morning, it was to ascertain receiving Communion, which she had longed for and been refused throughout the trial.

Let us return for a moment to the passage in I Corinthians 12–14 from which Midi is said to have taken his text for the sermon. Centered on the notion of spiritual gifts, it is here that Paul famously declares Christ to be like a single body, "with its many limbs and organs which, many as they are, together make up one body. For indeed we were all brought into one body by baptism, in the one Spirit, whether we are Jews or Greeks, whether slaves or free men, and that one Holy Spirit was poured out for all of us to drink." Even small organs are important in this single body, for a body is composed of many organs, seemly and unseemly, honorable and less so, frail and strong—hence the line Midi took for his sermon: if one organ suffers, so do they all. For "you are Christ's body, and each of you a limb or organ of it." The initial purpose of this simile turned metaphor is, as Paul himself writes, the building of the community appointed by God. God "has combined the various parts of the body . . . so that there might be no sense of *division* [*schismos,* a tearing apart] in the body, but that all its organs might feel the same concern for one another." There follows the question of gifts: miracles, prophets, teachers, apostles, healing, ecstasy, and interpretation. Love is the greatest gift, however, and prophesy is next. If I do not have love, argues Paul in what is now an overly worn passage, I have nothing—even if I give away all my worldly goods and "even give my body to be burnt." This text of Corinthians, then, is specifically chosen as a corrective for Joan: since she loves the devil, as this logic has it, even the gift of her burned body is useless, since her love is wrong.

But at the same time, this text of Paul's validates prophesy, one of the main reasons for which Joan is burned: "When a man is using the language of ecstasy he is talking with God, not with men, for no man understands him; he is no doubt inspired, but he speaks mysteries. On the other hand, when a man prophesies, he is talking to men, and his words have power to build; they stimulate and they encourage." Prophesy, then, may be useless without love, but with love it serves to build community. Paul is explicit:

> The language of ecstasy is good for the speaker himself, but it is prophecy that builds up a Christian community. I should be pleased for you all to use the tongues of ecstasy, but better pleased for you

> to prophesy. The prophet is worth more than the man of ecstatic speech—unless indeed he can explain its meaning, and so help to build up the community.

Of course, building a (Christian) community is urgent in Paul's time, but Joan was trying to build a Christian nation as well, through the divinely inspired anointment of her king. In addition, underlying her prophecies (that she would lift the siege of Orléans, crown the king, and save France) are all the characteristics of Christian faith as Paul describes them. She communicates to "men," in other words, the specific instructions of her ecstatic reception of visions and voices. Indeed, in her simplicity, there is no need for "interpretation," since the voices speak "French like us" and can be easily seen, she adds, "with eyes from the body." If we stay with Paul's terms, there is a transparency for Joan between the message of the visions and their conveyance or, put in another way, between the ecstatic and the prophetic. In this sense, then, Joan is an example of the kind of prophet Paul seems to endorse. Written all around the line chosen by Midi is a text that, ironically enough, ratifies a figure such as Joan. But Midi manages, by extracting his line out of context, to perform textually the same uprooting of a rotten limb that the fire is to achieve with Joan's body.

Paul's image of the body, however, is meant to be inclusionary, not (at least on the first level) eradicating. Not only, then, is Midi's extraction from the text out of context; it goes against the very tenor of the passage and performs a textual amputation that will be mirrored literally. The eye cannot say to the hand, argues Paul, "I do not need you," nor can the head to the feet. "Quite the contrary: those organs of the body that seem to be more frail than others are indispensable, and those parts of the body which we regard as less honourable are treated with special honour." Cauchon, who uttered the final sentencing, uses the same analogy of the body and for the same purposes as Midi, unsurprisingly. The last words Cauchon said to Joan were to inform her that because of her persistence in such offenses, excesses, and errors, she was declared excommunicated and a heretic, "cut off from the Church like a limb of Satan, infected with the leprosy of heresy; and so that you do not infect other limbs, we relinquish you to secular justice."[52]

---

52 The full passage reads: *te, tanquam membrum Satanae, ab Ecclesia praecisum, lepra haeresis infectum, ne alia Christi membra pariter inficias, justitiae saeculari relinquendam de-*

Obviously, the building of community consists in creating not only a totalizing body but also exclusionary practices. What is noteworthy here, however, is that the same metaphor of the body is used to achieve both of these ends. Just as there is a social and a physical body, in the building of this Christian community there are two bodies as well. First is the single body of Christ, which, in Paul's words, "with its many limbs and organs . . . together make up one body." This body must be protected in its purity from the "leprosy" and putrefaction of heresy by having the rotten part amputated (or, in another cliché frequently employed in heresy sentences, the sickly branch of an otherwise healthy tree must be cut off). What does such an amputation do to the "single body" of Christ and his community? To obviate this contradiction, we are given a second body, that of Satan. This body of evil can be amputated at will, maimed and rendered unwhole to keep the single body intact. Interestingly enough, however, it is the body of evil that endlessly regenerates.[53]

This is the logic of Christian community, then, which by fusing two metaphors of the body creates a catachresis that no amount of finessing can overcome. It is unquestionably the logic of alterity, at the foundation of any community. The sacrificed body of Christ, however, and the eternal goodness of the Christian God are continually confronted with evil as excess, as outside that body. Evil has its own, othered body, there for the maiming, quite literally for the dis-membering. The heretic is executed so as to protect the single body of Christ; but in her death, she is joined to the body of Satan. The killing of Christian heretics claims to perform the destruction of that other body, the one of evil. But evil, too, has its totality, such that no amount of amputation will destroy its reality, and no amount of severing will diminish its power. The heretic, then, stands as the contamination of one body (good) by the other (evil), since she is excised from the first as a contaminant to be purged and grafted onto the second as a way of wounding the body of evil.

Paul's text succumbs to alterity in another sense as well, for it turns out that despite the single body of Christ and the truth of prophesy, to-

cernimus et relinquimus; rogando eamdem postestatem ut, citra mortem et membrorum mutilationem, circa te judicium suum moderare velit. Quicherat, *Procès*, 1: 475.

53 As, it will be recalled, in the Revelation of John, the fiend keeps reasserting himself and his reign, even after he has been subjected to various forms of spectacular destruction.

tality is finally gender-exclusionary. Women are explicitly excised from religious discourse in public. In the passage that Margaret Fell Fox was to spend much time trying positively to interpret, Paul states unequivocally that while it is for prophets to control prophetic inspiration, "As in all congregations [or *communities*] of God's people, women should not address the meeting. They have no licence to speak, but should keep their place as the law directs. If there is something they want to know, they can ask their own husbands at home. It is a shocking thing that the woman should address the congregation." Paul's statement that "You can all prophesy, one at a time" makes clear as well that the inclusive "all" of community firmly delineates what is, to cite Lacan on women again, "not all." Even though we are meant to distinguish between prophesying and speaking aloud in church, the distinction collapses rather easily. In such reasoning it is relatively easy to elide "woman" into that other totality, that of Satan.

Given notes that the Inquisition of Joan's day was trying to create, not uphold, a collective consciousness, and in this he takes direct issue with Durkheim. The latter's model of punishment holds, it will be recalled, that when collective consciousness, that shared universe of moral value, is violated, vengeance will restore public health. But this notion does not fit the discourse of the Inquisitor, because the Middle Ages had no such unified, monolithic moral order: "The Catholic Church and its heretical opponents were engaged in a desperate struggle over the moral constitution of society, a contest turned on such issues as the relation of the divine to the mundane, the spirit to the flesh, and divine authority to worldly power" (72). These are precisely the issues at play in Joan's trial. Moreover, as Given argues, while some spectators at the executions of heretics considered the victims to be evil and deserving of their fate, other witnesses saw the same executions as creating martyrs of the faith who had been wrongly judged. The Christian community in Joan's time still has difficulty in presenting its notion of unity; the mixed reaction to Joan's death amply demonstrates this point. While some in the crowd felt that a limb of Satan was being duly cut off, others were convinced that she had died a martyr's death. Even the executioner, as we shall see later, had serious misgivings about killing his victim. In this sense, the execution of Gilles de Rais was less ambivalent: the crowd cried with him because he had *repented* when it was too late. The order of execution had to be carried out. But scholars are still arguing, as we have seen, as to whether Joan ever finally gave up on her voices, and the unstable valences of her case continue. The witnesses at the Trial of Rehabilitation, some contradicting previous testimony and all attempting to remember events from a quarter of a century before, seemed equally confused on Joan's opinion of her voices at the end, although they all agreed that she was no heretic and died in faith.

We can put these later rehabilitation testimonies aside and conclude (quite rightly, I would argue) that both the Trial of Condemnation and the Trial of Rehabilitation were politically motivated: the first by the English and Burgundian desire to be rid of a powerful figure of military inspiration and diabolical prowess; the second by Charles VII and his followers, determined, as he united the country some twenty-five years after Joan's death, to prove that his kingdom had not been founded by a heretic and a witch but rather a saint and a martyr. We may then assume that the testimony at both trials (and the minitrials leading up to the Trial of Rehabilitation) is at best suspect, motivated by political self-interest and, in Joan's case, a desperate attempt at survival. But if this is the case, which it surely is in part, it simply reinforces my point following Given: that the late medieval Church in France was still trying to *constitute* a community and its power within it, such that the same event could be differently interpreted by members of the same "single body." Indeed, it should be remembered that Joan is initially supported by the Church after her examination in Poitiers; then condemned at her trial in 1431; and finally rehabilitated twenty-five years later. While it is true that Charles had to petition the Church several times before he was granted permission to reopen Joan's case, that permission was nevertheless ultimately granted. The Trial of Rehabilitation, interestingly enough, is quite silent on the issue of Joan's voices; the trial's concern was to ascertain only whether her Trial of Condemnation had been legal. This is a way, of course, for the Church to cover itself, such that it can (and did) simply pronounce the condemnation trial to have been badly handled with respect to ecclesiastical law. But none of this changes the fact that the social valences, and the Church within them, were so unstable that the verdict on Joan changed as the community shifted and as the relationship between Church and nascent state began to be drawn more firmly.

ECCE HOMO

The medieval Christian sacrifices attempt not so much to restore order as to impose it. Thus, it is unhelpful to apply Durkheim in this context or, indeed, the theories on sacrifice of René Girard, who largely follows Durkheim. For Girard, all sacrifice is based on a misapprehension and a forgetting of the initial collective murder that make for community.[54] All religious rituals, argues Girard, are based on the surrogate victim, and all the great institutions of humankind, as he puts it, "spring from ritual." The function of sacrifice is to quell violence within the community and to prevent conflicts from erupting: "The purpose of sacrifice is to restore harmony to the community, to reinforce the social fabric. Everything else derives from that" (8). Following Durkheim, Girard concludes that even capital punishment can be traced back to its "original impulse." "The concept," he says, "can be traced back to spontaneous unanimity, to the irresistible conviction that compels an entire community to vent its fury on a single individual" (299). The victim, in turn, is a substitution for the original murder that lies at the foundation of all societies.[55]

In medieval Christianity, however, there is no such "spontaneous unanimity." The large crowds that form to watch the burning of a heretic are there for a number of reasons, including Girard's notion of vengeance but also much more than that: morbid curiosity, anger, sympathy, chance, fear, holiday cheer, historical interest, obedience to parish orders—to name a few possible motivating factors. The Church did everything it could to ensure a large gathering. The execution ritual was tightly choreographed and added corteges of Church opulence and solemnity to impress its hegemonic power upon the crowd. The final sermon, full of fire and brimstone as well as stern warnings, was addressed to the people as well as to the victim. The acquiescence of secular authority to Church rule underlined the potency of the latter. The script for this drama was always already written, and no amount of contrition on the part of the victim (that unscripted cadenza in the drama) could change the unfolding of events. Only the victim's last words (as in the Salem witch trials) could move the crowd. It was

---

54 René Girard, *Violence and the Sacred,* trans. Patrick Gregory (Baltimore, Md., 1979), 274–308ff.

55 For a critique of this view, see N. Jay's *Throughout Your Generations Forever: Sacrifice, Religion and Paternity* (Chicago, 1992).

considered impossible for the victim to utter the names of God or Jesus if she was a heretic. The last words, then, could change the display of the Church's omnipotence into a travesty of religion.

Hence, when Joan cried, "Jesus!" just before dying, even those who had supported the Church's condemnation of her began to have misgivings. Isambard notes that at the moment of death, when Joan bowed her head, she uttered the name of Jesus "as a sign that she was fervent of faith in God, as we read of Saint Ignatius and several other martyrs." The Church's own definition of martyrdom, then—that the crown of martyrdom is given to those who die for and *in* the faith—nullifies any suspicion or taint of heresy in a victim if she dies showing clear signs of faith. The pageantry and splendor of the event are rendered in such a case suspect in themselves after the fact. Here I am distinguishing between the speech allowed (indeed, requested of) the victim before death—one that, as in the cases of both Gilles de Rais and Joan, elicits great, if resigned, sympathy—and the behavior of the victim at the moment of death. The first instance supports the power of the Church: Christians are meant to feel compassion for the repentant sinner who is going to eternal damnation. The second moment, however, is beyond even the Church's apparent omnipotence. For death does not lie, and even those in the grip of Satan are powerless to feign faith at the end. The moment of death renders the victim a part of death itself; the impossible can utter only the truth. Thus, when Joan cries out, "Jesus!" the crowd turns to the clergy for answers.

We can delineate these two moments even more fully. In the first, when the Church is still in control, death is part of the theater and willfully delimited. After Joan dies, when the Church is still dominating the hermeneutics of her execution, the fire is put out and Joan's naked body is shown to the crowd.

A so-called Parisian Bourgeois of the period witnessed the execution and wrote a journal about his impressions, one that is much cited in the Johannic literature. Significant because the "Bourgeois" is a relatively indifferent spectator (although initially, at least, he believes Joan to be evil and deserving of her fate), the document recounts the burning and the moment after death when the body is on display. First Joan's male attire was removed, he recounts, and she was dressed in feminine garb. Then,

> She was condemned to death by all her judges and tied to a stake on the plaster scaffolding to which the fire was lit. She died quickly and

> her dress was completely burned. Then the fire was pulled away [*et puis fut le feu tire arriere*], so that the people would harbor no more doubts, they saw her totally naked, with all of the secrets that a woman can and must have [*tous les secrez qui peuent estre ou doibvent en femme*].[56]

What are the "doubts" that the people might have been harboring [*les doubtes du peuple*]? That she was a woman of flesh and blood, and not a devil? That she was a woman and not a man? In the great crowd that had gathered, there were at least eight hundred armed men by most accounts, plus many other spectators; several witnesses at the Trial of Rehabilitation testified that "ten thousand people cried." How can "all of the secrets" she possessed as a woman have been seen, especially since other witnesses report that the plaster scaffolding largely obstructed the view of her? One can assume that what is really being said here is that it was evident what genital attributes Joan did *not* have, at least for those closest to the front. With Joan's genitalia facing the crowd, what was in fact displayed was that she was not a man. This was only the last of a series of violations, but it was certainly one of the most heinous.

The story of Joan is replete with various forms of such specula (in the gynecological sense), both physical and conceptual: the frequent checks for virginity that she endured; the probing interrogations of the Church during her trial and of the king's representatives at Poitiers; the leering gazes of the soldiers guarding her in the secular prison, one of whom may actually have raped her; the violation of a sacrament by the priest Loiseleur, who revealed the contents of her confession to the court;[57] even a

---

[56] It is not entirely clear that it was the fire, and not Joan, that was pulled backward because the verb *fut* in this passage relates consistently to her. See Quicherat, *Procès*, 4: 471. For the full text of the journal, see 462–74. There is an English translation: *A Parisian Journal, 1405–99*, trans. J. Shirley (Oxford, 1968), from *Le Journal d'un Bourgeois de Paris*, ed. A. Tuetey (Paris, 1881). Quicherat thinks that this is the work of a single author, probably on the University faculty, and not a "Bourgeois de Paris," as had been traditionally cited. See Quicherat's introduction to the document, 461–62. For another description of this moment in the execution, see the deposition of Riquier, Quicherat, *Procès*, 3: 191.

[57] This information surfaced in 1450 at the inquest. According to Manchon, notary at the Trial of Condemnation, the priest Loiseleur, who was ferociously pro-English, lied to Joan by telling her that he was from her part of the country. He further ingratiated himself to her by telling her bits of "news" from her region (all of which was fabricated). Man-

possible poisoning by Cauchon, who sent her a carp that made her violently ill with fever and vomiting, and the medical probings and bloodlettings she subsequently underwent (against her will) to ensure that she would be in full health for her execution. No part of her body or mind, in other words, was safe from the eyes and hands of the authorities. It is as if all of her *occulta*—mental and physical—were constantly being dragged into the light and violated in the way Buffon was later to condemn as unseemly behavior toward any woman.

Joan somehow represented a threat so profound in her strength as a woman that the darkness that her sex has been given to signify was constantly put in the glaring light of masculine reason. It was done in a manner reminiscent of Lacan's account of the police who, to reassure themselves in a crime they cannot solve, allay their own doubts by subjecting every part of the scene of the crime to mathematical calculations and arithmetically distributed beams of light. No part of the room in question is left in the dark, but the mystery of the crime remains intact. The moment of displaying Joan's dead body before it is unrecognizably charred is the acme of such an obsession with "enlightenment." It is police thought of the same ilk as in Poe's story; that is, there is precisely no thought at all.[58] The uncanny must be rendered canny (we see a variant of this obsession in Freud's own essay), and the mystery of woman must be dissolved in the light of day and its logic. But the fact that it is masculinist thought that has erected woman as irretrievable mystery in the first place is never put into question, and so the mystery remains intact even as it is being (putatively) exposed. Indeed, the modesty that is mandated of a woman in Joan's day (the secrets that a woman "must" have) is elaborately desecrated to show that Joan had no hidden power to reveal, no extrahuman femininity with which to threaten the social order. Femininity is itself on display as paltry, lacking all agency, less than human—a pa-

---

chon testified that he and Bois-Guillaume, the other notary, were secretly put in a room adjoining the one where Joan was confessing. There was a hole through which they could hear what she said. What they could not hear, Loiseleur supplied them with. Quicherat, *Procès*, 2: 10–11.

58 I am referring here, of course, to Lacan's seminar on Edgar Allen Poe's "The Purloined Letter." To the point in this context as well is that Lacan likens the fireplace in the Minister's room to a gaping female sex, such that the entire room as well as its occupant are feminized. The seminar was originally published in *Yale French Studies*, ed. Jeffrey Mehlman, 48 (1972): 39–72.

thetic contrast to Joan's feats of war. What is revealed instead is the mortality of a body that takes its larger mystery—femininity—with it into the ashes, since the same masculinist hegemony that has sought to defuse the enigma is also the one that has established it as irrevocably insoluble and as fundamentally fleeing all light (of reason, of anatomical knowledge, and so on).

In this bizarre inversion of the emperor's new clothes, the Church Militant attempts to cover the secret of its own nakedness (the secret that nothing much remains of it once the pomp and brocade of the vestments have been stripped away) by professing to reveal femininity as a sham; its clothing (whether in the seductive garb dubbed "feminine" or in the utilitarian dress of war classified as the opposite) is the device of its cunning. This is all the more evident when one considers that the crime by which the Church finally "got" Joan was that of cross-dressing. The deeper crime, the unacknowledged one, was that she could so easily succeed in the exploits that masculinity claims as its own, to the explicit exclusion of the other sex.

Much has been made of Joan's cross-dressing.[59] But it bears mentioning here that nothing in the documents concerning her can lead to the conclusion of willful "masculinity" (sartorial or other) on her part. Indeed, Joan makes it very clear that she wore military attire the better to fight in and that she remained in men's clothing during her imprisonment only because she was kept (against her explicit wishes, as we have noted) in a secular prison. The constant threat of the guards was somewhat lessened, in her view, by wearing men's clothes and making herself less attractive to them. Isambard de la Pierre testified in 1450 that Joan, when she was declared a relapsed heretic specifically for returning to men's

59 For recent studies on cross-dressing and transvestism, see, for example, Vern L. Bullough and Bonnie Bullough, *Cross Dressing, Sex and Gender* (Philadelphia, 1993); Rudolph M. Dekker and Lotte C. van de Pol, *The Tradition of Female Transvestism in Early Modern Europe* (New York, 1989); Marjorie Garber, *Vested Interests: Cross-Dressing and Cultural Anxiety* (New York, 1992); Valerie R. Hotchkiss, *Clothes Make the Man: Female Cross Dressing in Medieval Europe* (New York, 1996); and, as mentioned earlier, Bynum's *Holy Feast*. It should be added that although Joan said at her trial that her attire was "the least, the smallest thing," she clearly enjoyed fine clothes. She describes with loving detail several rich liveries and suits of armor bought for her during her military exploits. See, with regard to the importance of cloth in the pre- versus the post- Cartesian "paradigm," Peter Stallybrass, "Worn Worlds: Clothes, Mourning, and the Life of Things," *Yale Review* 81, no. 2 (April 1993): 35–50.

clothing, asked for pardon but explained that "the English had done or had arranged to have done to her great harm and violence in prison when she was dressed in women's clothes." We have noted that Joan thought men's clothing to be a partial protection from rape. Joan held the Church directly responsible for her "relapse," her reversion to men's clothes. She publicly said, "If you, my lords of the Church, had taken and kept me in your own prisons, none of this would have happened to me."[60] To Cauchon, on the same issue, she said, "Bishop, I die because of you."[61]

The Church seized upon cross-dressing as the crime worthy of execution, since when Joan had abjured she had promised never again to dress as a man, and since cross-dressing is condemned in Hebrew Scripture as an "abomination before God."[62] The issue of cross-dressing itself has become one of the focal points of contemporary critical discourse, as queer and feminist theory combines with questions on the subject to display the tenuousness of gender boundary. But I am arguing a different point here: Joan dressed as a man for reasons of *expediency*. Ironically, only a culture that is preoccupied with clothing as gender driven in the first place can interpret entering into battle dressed "like a man" as a necessarily political-gender decision. And only a culture such as Joan's, in which modesty is inscribed in the feminine, will persist on seeing masculine attire on a woman as a sin.

Joan, meanwhile, in all of her testimony extracts gender from her mission. She sees herself as a soldier and dresses accordingly.[63] In this she is ahead of "even" our time; in her radical approach to achieving her ends, she does not privilege gender.[64] It is, then, of great significance that the

---

60 Quicherat, *Procès,* 2: 4–5.

61 Deposition of Br. Jehan Toutmouille, Quicherat, *Procès,* 2: 4: *"Evesque, je meurs par vous."*

62 In the language of the New English Bible (Deut. 22:5), "No woman shall wear an article of man's clothing, nor shall a man put on woman's dress; for those who do these things are abominable to the Lord your God."

63 On 27 February, Joan was asked whether the "voice" told her to put on men's clothes. She responded, as mentioned earlier, that the dress "is but a small matter" and that if God and the angels had asked her to wear a different dress, she would have done so. From the Latin manuscript (Quicherat, *Procès,* 1: 74), "[Joan] respondit quod de veste parum est, et est de minori; nec cepit vestem virlem per consilium hominis mundi; et non cepit ipsam vestem, neque aliquid fecit, nisi per Dei praeceptum et angelorum."

64 Emily Apter, for example, argues in her recent book (which has one chapter on Joan)

Church chooses to undress Joan to "show" her to the crowd, as if what was perceived as the thin veneer of masculinity she had attained with her attire were displayed as more trickery of the devil, so much feminine wiles. As such, then, for the Church of the fifteenth century, woman is always veiled no matter what the gender of her attire. Male attire on a

---

that Joan of Arc is part of the modern pathology of "monstrous subjectivity." To wit: "A drama of the ego, or more specifically, of the nationalized, feminized ego revealed in all its psychic armature." This helps to explain the "historical resiliency" of Joan's legend. Apter compares Joan to Freud's Schreber, who thought he was ordered by God to change himself into a woman. "So," writes Apter, "Joan of Arc effects a sex-change as a barrier against the subject-shattering force of the law. . . . Joan's body hardens into masculinity through war wounds and coats of armor." Apter continues, "This militancy of the ego, delusional, megalomaniac, paranoid, and projective though it may be, becomes objectively 'real' on the sex-crossed body of the subject, endowing the subject with a performative agency of suprahuman proportions. In gendering the 'call' or interpellative moment in the destiny of the subject (nationalizing it in the process), Joan of Arc 'fools' the law into calling its subject by its own name" (46). The result, according to Apter, is that for someone like the fascist Le Pen ("Saint Joan-Marie Le Pen"), Joan has become "the cartoon sign of a freshly bellicose national character whose hubris echoes in the Maid's pronouncements on the last day of her life: 'It was I who brought the message of the crown to my King. I was the angel and there was no other. And the crown was no more than the promise of my King's coronation, which I made to him.'" Therefore, concludes Apter, "The egoism that rings in this repetition of the first-person pronoun tells the story of nationalism's partnership with narcissism; honored historically in monstrous epics of patriotic will" (58).

I will limit myself to only a brief commentary with what I see as the most obvious problems with Apter's analysis. To begin with, in eliding Joan of Arc with the xenophobic and reactionary (fascist, literally) Le Pen and his followers in present-day France—an elision that they themselves, as Apter rightly points out, have both fostered and cultivated—she mimes their ideological gesture. She, like them, conflates the historical Joan with the agenda of the Front National. The following chapter in the present study will deal with issues of nationalism at some length. Suffice it to say here that, if it is true that narcissism and nationalism are joined in contemporary nationalist discourse, it is also the case that neither *ego* nor *state* mean what they do today in fifteenth-century France. Moreover, to use the example of the "angel" is, if I will be forgiven this foray into sentiment, unfair, since Joan made her "confession" concerning the angel shortly before her death at a time when, as the documents clearly show, she was fighting desperately to save her life and was ready to tell the inquisitors anything she thought they wanted to hear. They insisted that she admit there were no angels, so she said there were none. During the months of the trial, however, she was adamant about the reality of her vision of angels. The point here is not whether she saw angels; it is, rather, that to take this moment of despair in Joan's life as an indication of "egoism" and "nationalism's partnership with narcissism" is

woman, by this logic, takes on the attributes of finery. It is, finally, the male attire that is transvestized, as if Joan were seen as a drag queen trying hopelessly to look like a man.

Thus, the question of what doubts are erased in showing Joan's naked body to the crowd is perhaps too profound, even atavistic, to begin to answer. One would have to begin by asking, as we did at the outset of this chapter, why woman has been coupled with darkness and death and continue by inquiring how the fear of death seems temporarily overcome by burning a woman publicly and by bringing into reassuring light all that is *occult* in her. Joan's power is meant to be neutralized by the violation of her modesty *(pudor)*, as if the "purifying" quality of the fire had been insufficient to dismantle the contagion of her menace. It is only after the crowd has ascertained that Joan is indeed a dead, mortal woman that the fire is lit again and a more "normal" death by fire can proceed. Once again, from the "Bourgeois's" journal: "Once this vision [of her naked body] had lasted long enough, the executioner rekindled a great fire under her poor corpse which soon enough was calcinated, with the bones and flesh reduced to ash."[65] Now that her body has been displayed as

---

both anachronistic and historically bizarre. Quicherat puts these words of Joan into a clearer context than does the summary of Joan's words that Apter uses.

But the larger point is that, like many contemporary theorists today, Apter *assumes* that Joan is "sex-crossed." The documents, however, continually attest to the fact that Joan did not consider, as I have noted, gender to be an issue. This seems a far more difficult notion for contemporary discourse to fathom. About the fact that subjectivity is monstrous of ego in contemporary thought, there can be no argument; indeed, it has been one of the topoi of the present book, except that I have been arguing that male subjectivity is the ego; female, the *Nicht-Ich*. That Joan should have wished to "usurp" agency seems fairly normal; that this means that subjectivity *exists* is a notion that I have been trying to undermine throughout. If we wish to talk about "narcissism" at all in this context, let us rather consider (in a nonanachronistic, nonbackformation fashion) that "postmodern" discourse is rife with primary narcissism—that stage in which, it will recalled, the infant is unable to distinguish between itself and the outside world. With primary narcissism one can indeed confuse Joan of Arc with Le Pen as, by the way, the latter would have us do as well. But as Peter Brown's brilliant study *(The Body and Society)* has made abundantly clear, the ancients and, I would add, the people of the Middle Ages are "strange" to us. At best we can "use" them, as I have attempted to do here, as indicators of vestigial beliefs, and as focal points for what I have been calling "nostalgia." Emily Apter, "Saints at Stake: Joan of Arc as National Pathography," in *Continental Drift: From National Characters to Virtual Subjects* (Chicago, 1999), 39–59.

65 Quicherat, *Procès,* 4: 471.

"only" that of a woman, fear recedes, and the Bourgeois himself, strongly anti-Joan as he is, refers almost in relief to her "poor corpse" [*pauvre cadavre*]. Her personage has returned to a recognizable cadre of normalcy. The moment of revealing Joan's sex (in every sense), let us repeat, serves to assert to the crowd that the mystery of woman, like that of the devil himself, will always let down its veil, reveal its disguise, once the Church has reimposed psychic as well as social order. It also served, according to one witness, to show the English that she had not escaped.[66] Here, then, the Church marshals its power and controls the theater of death.

One cannot help but wonder, however, how long is "long enough" for the crowd to ascertain an a priori knowledge that the Church orchestrates. How much specular meditation was necessary for the saturated phenomenon in reverse to take hold? Given that woman is always already mystery, even in the mortality of her death, and that she is never "one," as Lacan has reminded us, it would follow that even after the twin burnings of Joan, there must have been a supplement. And such a supplement, unsurprisingly enough, the story of Joan amply supplies.

As I noted earlier, Joan's death did not match the image of a proven heretic, and immediately after her end, there were murmurings. The "Bourgeois" notes that quite a few people said she was a martyr who had died for the faith, while others said that she deserved to die and had been too long protected. He cautiously concludes, "Thus spoke the people. But whether she did good or evil, she was burned on that day." Only her physical death is certain. But as the years after Joan's execution pass, more and more information surfaces to "prove" that she was devout and probably a saint as well. The supernatural emerges as the inevitable supplement to which I alluded. As Duby and Duby put it, after her death Joan's story rapidly grew as "[t]he inventions of memory and of forgetting quickly evacuated witchcraft. What remained was the memory of martyrdom" (191).

So, for example, the monk Isambard de la Pierre testifies at the inquest of 1450 that the executioner experienced a miracle after Joan's death:

---

[66] From the testimony of Riquier, priest, at the Trial of Rehabilitation. See R. Pernoud, *Joan of Arc by Herself and Her Witnesses*, trans. Eric Hyams (Lanham, Md., 1994), 232. See also Quicherat, *Procès*, 3: 191.

> Item: said and deposed that the executioner, uncontrollably upset, went to see him and Brother Martin Ladvenu. The executioner was struck and overwhelmed by a marvelous repentance and terrible contrition; he was completely in despair, fearing he would never be granted the forgiveness and indulgence of God because of what he had done to that saintly woman. And the executioner said and affirmed that, in spite of the oil, sulphur and coals which he had applied to the entrails and heart of the said Jeanne, nevertheless he had been able to consume or turn to ashes neither the entrails nor the heart. He was as surprised by this as by a miracle of great evidence.[67]

What was left of her charred body was thrown into the Seine (or to the wind, or in the sea, depending on which testimony is read), such that no remainder, no trace whatever, would be found. The Seine was to have functioned as a kind of Lethe, allowing forgetfulness and "peace of the soul," as Hegel puts it. Yet remainders proliferate. At the beginning of this chapter, I noted that forgetfulness is the averted gaze, manifesting itself as metaphor. The unburnable heart (the entrails seem quickly forgotten) of Joan becomes just such a metaphor—at the first level, of her courage, of course. But the heart is also a metaphor that serves to veil the finality and horror of her death. And it is the supplement that equally serves to annihilate annihilation. Finally, the legend of Joan's heart is a prefiguration of the backformation achieved by the supplement of the Trial of Rehabilitation. That trial, which interrogates many witnesses, nullifies the Trial of Condemnation, as if the first judgment were palimpsestically written over, rethought, re-remembered. It emphasizes legend—those aspects that, supernatural and falling outside the economy of the rational, reinterpret the scene of death as one of saintly martyrdom, replete with supernatural signs that the Church at the time refused to see, precisely averting its gaze and ears.

Similarly, Isambard de la Pierre testifies at the inquest of 1452 that an Englishman had seen a white dove fly "in the direction of France" at the moment of Joan's death.[68] The "information" is cited without comment

---

67 Quicherat, *Procès,* 2: 7. Other witnesses also attested to the same.

68 Ibid., 2: 352.

in the articles summarizing the Trial of Rehabilitation but presumably as evidence of Joan's innocence. So, too, it is reported without comment that the flames of the fire spelled out the name "Jesus" at the moment of her death; it is as if the fire itself were called upon to produce the irrefutable text of her innocence.[69] All of these assertions point to continuation; that is, they aspire to a nonfinality in death, as against the mortality so brutally displayed with Joan's genitals revealed to the crowd. But all are, no matter what their status in the historical scene, in fact metaphors. And as has been noted more than once, a metaphysics of presence must, at the very least, be wary of metaphor.

These metaphorical substitutions for death, for stalling the impossible, are literalized as well by the appearance shortly after Joan's death of a "false Joan." According to this theory, Joan would have been *substituted* at the stake with another woman and would have escaped death through this subterfuge. The miter covering her face, the large plaster scaffolding, the confusion in the crowd, the rush to execute her—all would have contributed to deceiving the people into believing that it was Joan who was burned. After her staged death, Joan would have taken the name "Claude des Armoises," having married into that family, and appeared as Joan of Arc from 1436 to 1440.[70] Pierre de Sermoise, a descendent of the Armoise family, has dedicated an entire book to this thesis, arguing by way of family documents that Joan was not the daughter of Jacques and Isabelle d'Arc but rather the illegitimate daughter of Queen Isabeau (mother of King Charles) and Duke Louis of Orléans.[71] King Charles would thus have been her brother, which would explain why Joan was able to recognize him upon their first meeting. Cauchon would have been the instigator of the plot, with, in Sermoise's words, his "Machiavellian skills."[72]

The supplements continue, of course, with the numerous literary variants on the life of Joan. But also with the beatification and ultimate canonization: re-rehabilitation trials. The noise made in all of this is no

---

69 On this point, see Jones, *The Trial*, 237.

70 For the full version of this false Joan, see Quicherat, *Procès*, 5: 321–36. The fact that Claude des Armoises was "recognized" as Joan by the d'Arc brothers is generally attributed to their greed for more of the Maid's glory and gifts.

71 Pierre de Sermoise, *Joan of Arc and Her Secret Missions*, trans. Jennifer Taylor (London, 1973).

72 See R. Pernoud's scornful rejection of this theory in *Jeanne devant les Cauchons* (Paris, 1970), in which she argues that only bad historical research could lead to such a belief.

doubt important at various levels of political and historical intrigue. But the noise also serves to evade the silence (what Levinas calls the innocent suffering) of a young woman whose "crime" was that she acted in the role normally relegated to men and succeeded in so doing. In Levinas, the (inadvertent) feminization of death is explicit at the moment of suffering. Suffering is the impossibility of nothingness, he writes. This is because the structure of pain is prolonged "up to an unknown that is impossible to translate into terms of light." It will be recalled that for Levinas, woman is that being that flees from the light. Light, continues Levinas, "is refractory to the intimacy of the self with the ego to which all our experiences return."[73] Woman is, then, in this logic incapable of such a refraction. Thus, the implication is that her self, her ego, subjectivity itself, are debarred from that "to which all our experiences return." Unknown as she is herself, woman is by this account immediately allied with death: "the unknown of death signifies that the very relationship with death cannot take place in the light, that the subject is in relationship with what does not come from itself. We could say it is in relationship with mystery" (40). United with death as that which cannot take place in the light, woman, too, is a mystery "in relation to which the subject is no longer a subject." Levinas here perhaps unintentionally suggests what I proposed earlier: the nonsubject position of woman, like death, threatens when confronted by forcing an event over which "the subject is not master." It is an event in relation to which the subject is no longer a subject, and, I would add, subjectivity itself breaks down altogether. The dyad woman / death protects from this even when it remains in place as metaphorical. When it is faced, it is immediately "never present." Here is where the analysis must begin, says Levinas, "with the situation where something absolutely unknowable appears. Absolutely unknowable means foreign to all light, rendering every assumption of possibility impossible, but where we ourselves are seized" (41). The moment of Joan's execution may be seen as the event in which woman / death temporarily ceases being metaphorical—that moment when the spectator is at least partially unable to "return the object to the subject." It is the moment where there

Joan's trial goes on, she concludes, "and thanks to the trial we may know her better and thus love her better" (116). But this book was written before Sermoise's more careful study. To his research, Pernoud responds with a more cautious note that until she has more documentation, she will continue to reject the "false Joan" theory.

73 *The Levinas Reader*, ed. Seán Hand (Oxford, 1989), 40.

is an identification with what Levinas calls the passivity of suffering. Or, as Simone Weil notes, "Human life is *impossible.* But it is only affliction which makes us feel this."[74] The moment of execution, then, most threatens the active subject (the spectator) for whom experience "always signifies knowledge, light and initiative." This death that is absolutely foreign to all light is also woman, in that woman reminds the subject of its own impossibility. The male subject here is caught between the choice of a mirror in which he sees himself as Joan, similarly passive in suffering before death, or a *mise en abîme* in the same mirror in which the impossible returns. The only recourse from such a horror is an escape into metaphor, into the protection of gendered othering. The double after all, to repeat Freud's definition, is the ghastly harbinger of death. Paradoxically, it is the stripping of Joan in death, the exposure of her sex, the desecration of her body, that transform the "foreign to all light" into an object of the gaze and into a metaphor of femininity for the purpose of shoring up the masculine subject. With this display of Joan's nakedness, the subject can claim to return to itself, and death and woman remain othered, foreign, unmenacing to the spectator subject.

The supplements, however (the heart, entrails, dove, words formed by flames, even the false Joan), serve as a return of the repressed; that is, the moment of impossibility that Joan's death initiates, quickly covered over though it is, leaves traces nonetheless of anxiety, of something that forgetting has not been able to absolve and that metaphor has not been entirely successful in cloaking. These vestigial traces of the repressed grow until they are, ironically enough, tied to notions of great unity. The fear of death as contagion and the unacknowledged recognition that death may not be so foreign after all will combine to produce a discourse of national unity with Joan as its emblem. Metaphorized to the highest degree, Joan as nation symbol replaces the horror of suffering and the impossible with valiance in the face of adversity. Thus, passivity and the occlusion of self in the darkness of unknowability are inverted into the triumph of individual will. Similarly, the forces that destroyed Joan and gave her nakedness to the crowd are the same that cry for national fusion in her name. In both cases, she is the female figure in the tragedy of the male drama, her own tragedy and suffering usurped for reasons of figuring (and thus neutralizing) the impossible.

[74] Weil, *Gravity and Grace,* 86; her emphasis.

If the social function of representation is to stabilize assumptions and expectations relating to the object or person represented, as Margaret Miles puts it,[75] one can clearly read those assumptions by seeing how the figure of Joan is variously deployed throughout the centuries following her murder. I do not propose to engage such political and social aspects that, in any case, have been excessively charted. Rather, what we will be considering in the final chapter is the way in which "unity"—national unity in this case—is symptomatic of the continuing urgency of metaphor in a masculine subject formation necessarily opposing the impossible. It is in this sense that we will explore the icon of Joan of Arc as symbol of resistance.

---

[75] Miles, *Carnal Knowing: Female Nakedness and Religious Meaning in the Christian West* (Boston, 1989), 10 and *passim.*

CHAPTER SIX

FATHER, CAN'T YOU SEE I'M BURNING?

Next her fall did not cease accelerating, reaching the bottom of abjection's crucible: that stake and that charred carcass before the obscene gaze of the populace. It was level zero, where a benign transmutation was to begin. . . . From then on, her glory would of course burst forth.

—Michel Tournier, *Gilles et Jeanne*

It became clear that she served God rather than the Church, and France rather than the Orleans party. Indeed, the whole conception of France seems to have sprung and radiated from her.

—Winston Churchill, *A History of the English-Speaking Peoples*

AN INITIALLY HOSTILE ENGLISHMAN, it will be recalled, claimed that at the moment of Joan's death a dove flew out of the fire "toward France." This image, upon close examination, reveals the combination of valences that together constitute both the image of Joan at the time and the icon of nationalism and cultural fascination she has become. Let us begin with trying to imagine how that image was understood at the time it was "witnessed."

For what did it mean in 1431 to say that a dove flew out of Joan (some editions report "out of her mouth"; others "out of the fire") toward France? It is a question that, significantly enough, is not asked at the time: everyone seems clear on the implications. Holy Spirit and country conflate in the image of the dove in a manner perfectly comprehensible to the fifteenth-century Christian French mind, but far less obviously to our own. The vigorous division of Church and state that characterizes much of modern Europe and America makes such a suture-less triad almost exotic, and so we examine it with a secular gaze both intrigued and vaguely nostalgic. Such nostalgia, as that for early martyrs considered previously in this study, is again motivated by visualizing a time before division—not, in this case, before Descartes (although his legacy is clearly ancillary) but rather before the compartmentalization of God from country and divine right from legislation.

But in the fifteenth century, the dove is first a symbol for the soul, and saints are occasionally depicted with the dove flying out of their mouths at the moment of death.[1] Thus, one can say that in claiming to see the dove fly from Joan, the simultaneous claim is that her eternal life is attested to—confirmed, despite the Church's dark pronouncements to the contrary. Finality has then been short-circuited: the Maid's soul continues and the miracle of the dove already suggests that she was a saint. If the human being is a composite, a living in-betweenness of body and soul, as the Church father Maximus the Confessor claimed (d. 662), then the moment of death figures the moment of division: the dove flies "home"; the body retains its materiality only. This moment of division, however, is temporary, for the Resurrection of course will reunite what is put asunder by the death of the flesh. The homing qualities of the dove, then, support the implication of its symbolism: the dove will return home, and the soul will be released from its exile on Earth. Complex in spite of its apparent simplicity, the dove image insists on the human soul as out of place; waiting for the moment of return. A type of cultural platonism is revealed here (or Plotinean reassurance)—one so profound as to be virtually invisible to its own culture.

It is worth noting in this context that Jean Anouilh chooses to call Joan a lark in his famous play of the same name (1953). The lark, unlike the dove, flits about aimlessly. Also, of course, it is the subject of a well-known children's song in French, one to which Anouilh is obviously alluding: "Alouette, gentille alouette . . . je te plumerai." [Lark, kind lark . . . I will pluck you]. The slow, cruel plucking of the lark in that song (presumably for roasting) stands as a strong counterimage to the dove waiting patiently to return home. At the end of Anouilh's play, Joan does not die because everyone realizes that she *is* Joan of Arc and that her memory will survive her. Joan will always be remembered, says King

1 Moreover, several saints are traditionally depicted with doves: Agnes with a dove and a ring; David with a dove on his shoulder; Dunstan and Gregory the Great with a dove coming out of the ear; Enurchus with a dove on his head; Remiguis with a dove bringing him chrism.

Charles in the play, "not in her misery of a trapped animal in Rouen, but as a lark in the middle of the sky. . . . The real end of Joan's story is a happy one. The story of Joan of Arc is one that has a happy ending."[2] But this is all a form of *recusatio*. Like the joyous melody of the lark being plucked, the play performs a happy ending that serves only to underscore the reality of her murder. There is double irony, too, in Empson's sense: it is true that Joan's death will be too easily forgotten by way of the brief successes of her military career, all too easily foregrounded as if blocking the execution from view. "Thank goodness that I arrived in time," says Baudricourt in the play, "these imbeciles were going to burn Joan of Arc! Can you imagine?" Anouilh's stage directions call for the play to end with Joan standing "leaning on her banner, smiling toward heaven, as in pictures" (228). "The curtain falls slowly," say the directions, "on this pretty picture from a prize-book."—the kind of book, in other words, that French schoolchildren receive for getting good grades. One might add, the kind of book with images that train the reader's historical vision into seeing Joan as triumphant skylark. The whole play is in itself staged as a play ("We haven't played my coronation yet," complains Charles) with everyone posing for a photograph—a gift to history—at the end. Simulacrum of a simulacrum, the play widens the gap between image and referent, signifier and signified, thought and being. Anouilh's sarcasm could not be more sinister.

The choice of the two birds—the dove and the lark—no doubt says a great deal of what has happened to the belief systems of the two eras: Joan's and our own. The Trial of Rehabilitation, for example, will note the testimony concerning the dove and, as with the unburnable heart and entrails, will do so without commentary. As with Joan's voices, the tacit question will not be whether these events occurred but whether they emanate from the divine. The Trial of Condemnation's firm response to this question will be in a resounding negative; the Trial of Rehabilitation will remain silent. But the notion that these events can in fact be vehicles to a transcendent is never questioned in the late medieval world. Before Kant, before Descartes, the symbol does not represent a symbol; metasymbology is anathema to Joan's world. The divine can manifest itself, and if there really was a dove, then it really was Joan's soul exiting her charred body. *Dasein,* to use a later term, is more tenuous than *Sein*.

2 Jean Anouilh, *L'Alouette* (Paris, 1956), 227. My translation.

I insist on this difference between modern and late medieval thought as a reminder that the implications are fundamental for worldview. *Weltanschauung* must be understood, then, as capable of producing different visions of the same thing, seen with different eyes even if of the same physiological composition. In the fifteenth century of Joan's world, the dove is an instance of transubstantiation; it is above all not a metaphor. In such instances where thought is free of metaphoricity, we can only look again with nostalgia at what for post-Kantian and post-Cartesian eyes must always be metaphorically motivated, always produced by the seductive games of representation. But Kant's quip that just because man cannot imagine anything outside space and time does not mean that either exists can be applied here by analogy: just because we can imagine little of what we think of as divinity outside metaphor does not mean that metaphor is an ineluctable constant in the hypostatization of divinity. It may simply be that consistent metaphoric vision in approaching notions of divinity is the inevitable result of modernity's divides. While the Christian medieval world certainly metaphorized death and woman, as I have noted, in some matters it was able to think divine manifestation as literal—metonymic linkage, clearly, but not metaphoric substitution.

The dove is also the Holy Spirit in Christian symbolism, of course. It is the spirit breathed into the man of clay. Here we arrive at another chasm between present and medieval thought. The passage from Paul considered in the previous chapter insists on Christianity as community, and it is precisely Spirit that makes for the link, avoiding *schismos.* Indeed, members of the Church were *pneumatikoi,* "spiritual." As one scholar of Christianity, John Zizioulas, has put it, "Individualism is incompatible with Christian spirituality. None can possess the Spirit as an individual, but only as a member of the community. When the Spirit blows the result is never to create good individual Christians but members of a community."[3] Zizioulas is here talking about early Christianity, but the strain continues well past Joan's time.

Yet Joan claims Spirit without Church knowledge or supervision. We have noted that throughout Joan's trial the Church labored to represent

[3] Zizioulas, "The Early Christian Community," in *Christian Spirituality: Origins to the Twelfth Century,* ed. Bernard McGinn, John Meyerdorff, and Jean Leclercq (New York, 1986), 27. This anti-individualist strain is present in Greek and Latin Christianity but not in Syriac. See Roberta C. Bondi, "The Spirituality of Syriac-speaking Christians" in the same volume, 153–55ff.

Christian spirituality as community, indeed to control the fashioning of such a community with the Church Militant as supervisor. Part of Joan's dilemma was that she depersonalized herself, on the one hand, presenting herself as the unexpected agent of God chosen to rescue his representative in France, king by divine right. Joan is the personification, in other words, of obedience to God's command. On the other hand, in her privileged "conversations" with divine intercessors, her saints, and in her apparent indifference toward Church authority, she appears very much an individualist. That is, her claim to Spirit puts her personally in the position of mediator between the divine and the Christian as well as political (for want of a better word) community. She alone translates the word of God into military action.

No doubt herein lies part of the reason for which Joan is famously considered the last medieval figure and the first modern one. In her position as personal receiver and interpreter of divine messages, Joan lives the isolation of the prophet.[4] But she is doubly isolated, because she is like a vestigial remnant of a lost prophetic time that the hegemony of the late medieval Church will neither tolerate nor countenance. In this sense, then, she is anathema both temporally and in terms of Church law. The excess of prophesy has no place outside the Church in her time in history, and the singularity of individual thought is nearly incomprehensible for a Church that dictates citizenship within a nascent state it controls, even before it imagines it, by having sole authority over the act of condoning (permitting) through blessing. As Charles Wood notes, with Joan of Arc the end of the Middle Ages began, for "caught up though Joan was in visions of crusading ardour, hers was a voice that heralded different times, times in which the individual conscience would defy the will of the Church, and in which men would begin to declare that the sovereignty of the state could brook no opposition." But Wood qualifies his comment: "Joan's was not the world of Machiavelli and the Renaissance, and neither was it that of Luther," for she died certain of being with God in Paradise.[5] It is precisely this certainty that is epitomized and that simulta-

4 For a study of medieval sainthood outside a hagiographic paradigm and the "everyday life" of the saint, see Aviad M. Kleinberg, *Prophets in Their Own Country: Living Saints and the Making of Sainthood in the Later Middle Ages* (Chicago, 1992).

5 Charles T. Wood, *The Quest for Eternity: Manners and Morals in the Age of Chivalry* (Hanover, 1985), 150.

neously begins to erode at the time of Joan's death. The dove is still seen as one and the same as Spirit, but the time is rapidly approaching when such a vision will be understood as double.

At Joan's death, the dove serves to rechannel Spirit into its proper place, as if the strange new brand of individualism she exhibited needed quickly to be expunged. As a sign of Spirit after death, the dove erases Joan's proto-individualistic stance and returns her safely to the Christian community, thus neutralizing the scandal of her singularity. More than that, the dove erases as well the paradox, from the fifteenth-century perspective, of a female individual. The conundrum of a feminine subject with agency is nullified first by the execution, of course. But the dove grants the other aspect of return to normalcy by blending Joan into a tradition of martyrdom, into which femininity is (too) easily folded and assimilated. On this level, too, then, the dove cancels the scandal of Joan—even to the Englishman who claims to have seen the dove and who beforehand had "hated her marvelously" and wanted nothing more than to hasten Joan's death.[6] The dove, by reintegrating Joan into the Christian community as state, neutralizes her suffering and her particularity even as it elevates her to the status of blessed and probable saint.

The paradox is curious and complex: by "resisting" execution, with the rumor of an unburned heart and a soul in flight for the real home, Joan is reappropriated by the very community that murders her. The rehabilitation is achieved then at every level, including the trial of the same intent. We are left, as more recent appropriations of Joan have demonstrated, in an absurd position. In Simone Weil's words, it is unacceptable to hear the testimony of the murderer concerning the victim. And yet when the Englishman and the executioner testify to Joan's sanctity, this is precisely what we are hearing.

Critical as well in this scenario, however, is the fact that the dove is seen as flying "toward France." It should be noted here that "France" at the time meant the Ile de France and certainly not the Hexagon as we know it. The point, however, is that the dove/soul is going to another home at the same time that it is "returning" to heaven. But where can the dove finally be going, and where finally is "home"? Is France meant to be heaven? Here we have a fascinating conflation of Church and proto-state. Moreover, this conflation that the dove's flight performs is precisely

6 Georges Duby and Andrée Duby, *Le Procès de Jeanne d'Arc* (Paris, 1995), 230–31.

the one that caused Joan such fatal difficulties in her life. How could God have given Joan a military, political message that would pit Christian against Christian? Catholic against Catholic? Surely God does not take sides, and so on. And yet the dove / soul literally takes sides, flying as it does "toward France," thus leading even the Englishman to believe that her mission was warranted and blessed and that the Church and England itself had made a mistake.

Because "France" becomes more of a point of loyalty to Joan than "Christian," we can discern the beginnings of nationalism as we understand it now. The Church has failed, as it were, in its attempt to accomplish Paul's dictum that with Christ there can no longer be Greek or Jew. At the end of the Middle Ages, the Christian community is gradually being replaced by notions such as "France" as against "England." One need only peruse Holinshed's *Chronicles*, for example, written about one hundred fifty years after Joan's death, to see that the idea of nations is firmly entrenched. Holinshed, whose consistently inaccurate account of Joan is followed by Shakespeare (at least one of the authors of *1 Henry VI*), presents her in his *Chronicles* in sharply delineated nationalistic terms:

> In the time of the siege at Orleans (French stories say), the first week of March 1428, to Charles the Dauphin (at Chinon because he was very anxious and concerned with how to wrestle against the English nation), a young wench of eighteen called Joan Are . . . was brought by one Peter Badricourt, captain of Vaucouleurs (afterwards made Marshall of France by the Dauphin) . . . [Joan was] a person (as their books make her) raised up by divine power, solely to succor the French estate which was in great distress at the time.[7]

Holinshed concludes his version of the Joan story by letting readers make up their own minds ("Now judge as ye list"), but his narrative consis-

---

[7] *Holinshed's Chronicles of England, Scotland and Ireland,* vol. 3, *England* (London, 1808), 163. I have rendered the passage into slightly more modern English. For more on Shakespeare's Joan, see David M. Bevington, "The Domineering Female in 1 Henry VI," *Shakespeare Studies* 2 (1966): 51–58; Phyllis Rackin on Joan's cross-dressing seen as supernatural by the English, *Stages of History: Shakespeare's English Chronicles* (Ithaca, N.Y., 1990), 200ff.; Gabriele Bernhard Jackson (who argues that the armed Joan as *virago*

tently refers to "her lovers (the Frenchmen)" as against "the English, who for witchcraft and sorcerie burned her at Rone [*sic*]." He reminds us, moreover, that Paul had noted that Satan can change himself into an angel of light, "the deeplier to deceive."

By 1841, when the French historian Jules Michelet writes his hagiographic account of Joan's life, he understands nationalism in a modern sense, which he sees as beginning in her time. After noting that God chose his virgin warrior from among the most humble of the poor people of France, Michelet adds, "For there was a people [*peuple*], and there was a France. This last figure of the past was also the first of the time which was beginning. In her appeared at once the Virgin . . . and already, the Father country [*la Patrie*]."[8] By this account, Joan personified what was already a unified people of a unified France—clearly a romantic view of the fragmented fiefdoms that comprised fifteenth-century territories putatively under Charles's rule. Indeed, as the Michelet historian Gustave Rudler notes, Joan was motivated by pity for France in her mission, but he adds that there is here a nuance about which one needs to be cautious: "The Father country [*la patrie*] was therefore something quite different for her than it was for her historian: a blend, no doubt, of territories and ideas. But the ideas are here monarchic loyalty and Christian loyalty."[9] Michelet also sees Joan as a figure of transition between two epochs: she is the last figure of the past and the first of a new time. But he does not take into account how closely fealty is tied to regional loyalty and the rights of kings to the order that flowed from such divinely sanctioned feudal power systems.

Michelet was to become less Catholic and somewhat less romantic in his later writings, but it should be noted that for him here, Joan is the conflation of the instrument of the divine and of patriotism. Yet there is a double color to Joan, writes Rudler: the political and the religious. Michelet increasingly deemphasizes the religious and thus "modernizes everything." Citing the great Johannic scholar Champion, Rudler ob-

---

could be seen as a parody of Elizabeth at Tilbury), "Topical Ideology: Witches, Amazons, and Shakespeare's Joan of Arc," *English Literary Renaissance* 18 (1988): 49 and *passim.*; and M. L. Stapleton, "'Shine It Like a Comet of Revenge': Seneca, John Studley, and Shakespeare's la Pucelle," *Comparative Literature Studies* 31, no. 3 (University Park, Pa., 1994): 229–50.

8 Jules Michelet, *Jeanne d'Arc,* ed. Henri Chabot (Paris, 1941; 1987), 118.

9 Gustave Rudler, *Michelet, historien de Jeanne d'Arc* (Paris, 1925), vol. 1, *La Méthode,* 118; my translation.

serves that in the feudal world "what we understand by *Patrie* was always attached to the idea of sovereignty; and the notion of sovereignty was completely tied to the idea of justice" (120). It is in this idea of "paternal justice" that one can find the roots of the modern notion of *patrie.* Moreover, it is in the name of such a paternal justice, continues Rudler, and of an ancient fealty that "Joan protested against the foreign invasion" and that so many people in the countryside revolted against strangers.

Thus, to turn for a moment to Lacanian terms, it did not matter whether Charles had neither the bearing nor the courage of a leader; he was in the place of the Father and as such, in the feudal mentality, assumed the position of the law—what Lacan dubs the Symbolic. This is no doubt why Joan, disappointed as she may have been by Charles's behavior, never ceased showing him allegiance, nor did she question his right as sovereign.[10] Her loyalty is to the role of the chosen sovereign, not to the individual Charles. As Louis Marin puts it, the king is king only in image, but he nevertheless stands in, as king, for that image. The innumerable critics and historians who remain surprised by Joan's loyalty to the flaccid and fickle personage that was the young Charles miss this point, I think. Joan is not responding to Charles as an individual; indeed, as we have seen, the notion of individuality in her time is tenuous at best and far from being ours. For Joan, the right of the sovereign is not to be questioned, since it is put into place by a divine law in a universe ordered by God. The English have no more rights than the Burgundians to overturn that law, for such an overturning would constitute a profound taboo.

---

[10] This is the same argument made by Kristeva to explain the singular power of De Gaulle over the French during World War II: "De Gaulle had understood that regicide peoples were also, and more so than others, orphaned peoples. On his own, he imposed a persona whose aura reached its peak in discourse, as solace for wounded ego ideal and superego. For, in individuals as well as human groups, the ego ideal and the superego, who are our tyrants, nevertheless guarantee identity and regulate actions. He toyed with that potential tyranny of the Ideal, took his chances, but eventually reaped its advantages." Although Kristeva is staying within the tripartite Freudian model and is referring of course to the modern "ego," nevertheless the notion of a paternal Symbolic for "orphaned peoples" resonates with the situation of the French under late feudalism with the figure of an unrecognized (and indeed disinherited) Dauphin. See *Nations without Nationalism,* trans. Leon S. Roudiez (New York, 1993), 70ff. For an uncomplicated but useful approach to the rather perplexing personality of Charles VII, see, for example, Francis Lowell, "The Character of Charles VII," in *Joan of Arc* (New York, 1896), 357–64ff.

The name of the Father, in this fifteenth-century Symbolic, is itself the law.

When Michelet writes, "Joan created France, the *Patrie,*" we might say with Rudler that in Michelet's vision of Joan we find little of Joan but a great deal of Michelet. In his 1853 introduction to the story of Joan, Michelet writes as if in a trance of inspiration: "Let us always remember, Frenchmen, that the *Patrie* for us was born of the heart of a woman, of her tenderness and tears, of the blood which she gave for us."[11] Sixteen years later, in another preface, Michelet will tell us that this notion of *patrie* came from an epiphany; a revelation that occurred during the July Revolution: "In those memorable days," he writes, "a great light appeared, and I saw France." In this remarkable passage, Michelet employs the vocabulary and tenor of Genesis for the creation of *patrie*. Thus, *patrie* has become the focal point of religious imagery and conflates the notion of divinity with that of patriotism. This is, of course, precisely the combination Michelet sees in Joan: "The Virgin . . . and already the *patrie;*" and again: "Yes, whether considered religiously or patriotically, Jeanne Darc [*sic*] was a saint." But as we have noted, Michelet misconstrues (or anachronizes) the valence of those notions in Joan's day—especially since, as Rudler reminds us, the purpose of the July Revolution was to overturn the monarchy which Joan gave her life to defend.

In all of this epiphanal fervor, however, there is in Michelet the curious role of woman. In an earlier version of the same passage, Michelet had written, "The Savior of France could be no other than a woman. France herself was woman: having her nobility, but her amiable sweetness likewise, her prompt and charming pity, at the least possessing the virtue of quickly excited sympathies."[12] The passage, which renders the more religious Genesis analogy into a patriotic rhapsody on women, in its first draft explicitly proposes the figure of Joan as a female Christ.[13] The part that remains of this image is the blood that Joan "gave for us." Moreover,

---

11 Rudler, *Michelet,* 116.

12 Michelet, *History of France,* trans. G. H. Smith (New York, 1848), 1: 154.

13 The comparison of Joan to Christ is a common one. For example, the first full translation of the Trial of Condemnation into English (based on the work of Champion) was, as I have noted, by W. Barrett in 1931. The introduction, by one of the translators, Coley Taylor, states that Joan's trial "has become second in importance only to the Trial of Christ" (vii) and later, "The world has seen nothing like her since Christ" (xii).

at her death, writes Michelet, Joan's contemporaries "recognized in the scene Christ among the Pharisees." Still, continues Michelet, we must see something else in this death: "the Passion of the Virgin, the martyrdom of purity."[14] This "something else" is the woman-ness of Joan that adds to her glory and to her martyrdom.

Indeed, if we return to the fascination with martyrdom that has entered, as I have commented throughout, a good deal of secular "postmodernist" discourse, we shall not be surprised to note that no such fascination is present in Michelet. "There have been many martyrs," he notes with some impatience, "history shows us numberless ones, more or less pure, more or less glorious." There have been martyrs of pride, hate, the spirit of controversy, and the ever-present "martyrs militant" who "no doubt died with a good grace when they could no longer kill." But he adds, "Such fanatics are irrelevant to our subject. The sainted girl is not one of them; she had a sign of her own—goodness, charity, sweetness of soul."[15] Joan, he decides, "had the sweetness of the ancient martyrs but with a difference." The first Christian martyrs were gentle and pure only because they "shunned action," by remaining far removed from the trials of the world. Not so the Maid: "Jehanne was gentle in the roughest struggle, good amongst the bad, pacific in war itself; she bore into war (that triumph of the Devil's) the spirit of God."[16]

Gentle and courageous as the ancient martyrs may have been, they fall short when compared with Joan, who was able to combine goodness (and sweetness, tenderness, and so on) in spite of an active role in the "trials of the world." Clearly, then, what rivets Michelet about his heroine is that she is able to combine saintliness with political action, goodness with warfare, and pity in the midst of the "roughest struggle." Her genius is this ability to maintain "the spirit of God" in the triumph of the devil—war—or, put another way, to live in complete contradiction and to remain good. Such a combination of opposites extends to gender as well. For Michelet, woman is "instinct" and man, "reflection." Woman is able to transform idea into sentiment, and this is her greatness. Joan, however, is for Michelet an androgynous hero, since she is able to have "good sense in exaltation." Her brain, therefore, knows both sexes, and this is the se-

14 Ibid.
15 Ibid.
16 Ibid.

cret of her success."[17] As such, Joan is able to help the "Frenchman" live with paradox and contradiction, and this is her legacy to the men of her age: "The Frenchman, even when vicious, preserved beyond the man of every other nation good sense and goodness of heart" (*History of France,* 154). The old France remained, in Michelet's view, *bon enfant*—that is, good and with the closeness to nature that characterizes children in his view and, more important, women. Over and over again, Michelet reminds us that women remain "closer to nature" because of their reproductive cycle.[18] But "New France" has lost this stance of the *bon enfant,* unlike the Frenchman of Joan's day who "ever remained *bon enfant* [a good child]: a term of small sound, but great meaning. No one nowa-days chooses to be either *enfant* or *bon;* indeed, the latter epithet is considered one of derision." This comment, which Michelet puts into a footnote, reveals the source of his nostalgia: not for a time of prelapsarian divide, for one when men, inspired by women ("The Saviour of France could be no other than a woman. France herself was a woman . . . she remained at bottom closer to nature . . . "), were *bons enfants,* the role Joan of Arc taught them to assume. It is in this sense that we might say that Michelet is a romantic—that is, a romantic in the French tradition: influenced by (even if critical of) Rousseau, mournful of the lost time when unity with nature made for goodness and the corrupt ways of civilization had not yet made irony and "derision" a sign of sophistication. As Anatole France wrote in the preface to his own *Vie de Jeanne d'Arc* (1908):

---

17 Michelet claimed the same dual-gendered mind for himself: "I am a complete man, having the two sexes of the mind." See Roland Barthes, *Michelet par lui-même* (Paris, 1965), 155; my translation.

18 For a brilliant study of Michelet's views on women in general and on the importance of their menstrual cycle in particular, see Barthes, *Michelet par lui-même.* Barthes refers to Michelet as having been "traumatized by blood," and adds, "In Woman, Michelet always sees Blood" (129). One might then view Michelet's frequent references to Joan as "giving her blood for us" as more than a mimetic gesturing toward the Christ story, for Michelet is obsessed with the menstrual cycle and its blood. In his unedited journal, he writes of "the crisis of love which constitutes woman; that divine rhythm which, month by month, measures time for her" (120). It is this cyclical experience of the body that, for Michelet, makes women closer to nature. This life-long conviction was to culminate in 1862 with Michelet's two-volume study on witches, *La Sorcière,* ed. Lucien Refort (Paris, 1952 and 1956). Michelet mounts a moving and poetic defense of the witch, arguing that she wished to know the secrets of nature and that hers was a vestigial form of paganism to which the Church responded with sadistic cruelty and fear.

> From 1841 to 1849, Jules Quicherat, by publishing the two trials and their testimony, opened with dignity an incomparable period of research and discovery. At the same moment, Michelet, in the fifth volume of his *History of France,* wrote fast-paced and colorful pages which will no doubt remain the most beautiful expression of romantic art on the Maid.[19]

For Michelet, the "quickly-excited sympathies" of woman, in particular pity (which Barthes argues is in Michelet the same as love), are what women can teach to men. Women are closer, in other words, to the innocence and emotional authenticity of children. This Rousseau had understood. The quality of pity, it will be recalled, is what Michelet admires almost more than any other quality in Joan.

Michelet's romantic nostalgia in then for a goodness stemming from nature; a goodness that persists despite the corruption of the world: "May new France never forget the saying of the old France: 'Great hearts alone understand how much glory there is in being good!' To be and to keep so, amidst the injuries of man and the severity of Providence, is not the gift of a happy nature alone, but it is strength and heroism."[20] Those who achieve such goodness will ever be "the children of God," even if they stumble occasionally. For Michelet, this was another of Joan's greatest gifts.

Writing at the same time as Quicherat but also Baudelaire and Flaubert, Michelet is, like them, obsessed with the question of goodness in an increasingly industrial world gone increasingly unscrupulous. His nostalgia participates in Baudelaire's and especially in that of Flaubert, which Walter Benjamin saw as *acedia.* "Few people can guess," writes Benjamin citing Flaubert, "how much sadness there had to be to resuscitate Carthage."[21] Michelet's attempt to resuscitate Joan stems from an

---

19 See the preface in France's enormous *Vie de Jeanne d'Arc* (Paris, 1908), 1: 66. The preface gives an excellent overview of the state of Johannic scholarship at the beginning of the twentieth century. Although he describes Michelet's work on Joan as romantic, France, as we will see, has his own brand of romanticism underlying his history of Joan.

20 Michelet, *Histoire de France,* 154. Throughout this discussion, I am specifically distinguishing between what is called romanticism in France and the philosophical concerns of the German *Frühromantik,* of which Friedrich Schlegel was the leader and theoretician.

21 So, too, some sixty years later, A. France will lament modern industrial life. But France's nostalgia will rest on capital as the culprit. France warns that today, as two thou-

equally immense sadness: the "new France" has forgotten the old, and the conclusion of Michelet's study of Joan, "May the new France never forget the saying of the old France . . . ," serves as a melancholic reminder that nostalgia can only appear when its object is already lost.[22]

Michelet's is the nostalgia for lost time that informs the romanticism of such French writers as Lamartine, Vigny, Hugo, and Chateaubriand. It also seeks, in a manner characteristic of the entire French generation of 1848, a return to the exhilarating days of the Revolution (the "real" one of 1789), witnessed by the previous generation. The generation of 1848 is born into nostalgia (as brilliantly demonstrated in, for example, Flaubert's 1869 *Sentimental Education*), and is acutely and painfully aware that the failed revolution of 1848 was merely, as Marx was to put it, repetition as farce.

For Michelet, the late Middle Ages was a time when men were at once virile and open to feminine wisdom, saved from losing their feel for nature by witches and thus receptive to intuition. It was in this climate only that a Joan of Arc could die leaving a legacy called *"le Peuple"*—that is, as Barthes puts it, an absolute for Michelet. *Le Peuple* appears in Joan's day, only to be suffocated by the philosophers of the eighteenth century who were single sexed of mind and thus fell short. The bigendered brain returns with the Revolution, however, which again produces *le Peuple*—bigendered in that it is motivated by the inspiration of both men and women. Thus, Michelet is deeply nostalgic: he longs for the old France of Joan. But like most men of his generation, he also yearns for the days of the Revolution, when *le Peuple* overtook everything, including history itself. As one historian has phrased it, "Michelet transformed the monarchist myth of the king as incarnation of the State into the myth of Jeanne d'Arc as the incarnation of the sovereign French people."[23]

---

sand years ago, we must look to the "laboring masses" to discern a forbidding future. "Every day," he writes, "we see a community of universal labor being organized" (*Vie de Jeanne d'Arc,* 1: 73). For a discussion of *acedia* in Benjamin, see my "Walter Benjamin and the Right to Acedia" in *Hot Property: The Stakes and Claims of Literary Originality* (Chicago, 1994), 128–56.

22 See Marcos Natali's study on nostalgia, "The Politics of Nostalgia: An Essay on Ways of Relating to the Past," Ph.D. dissertation at the University of Chicago, 2000.

23 Susan Dunn, "Michelet and Lamartine: Making and Unmaking the Nationalist Myth of Jeanne d'Arc," *Romantic Review* 80, no. 3 (May 1989): 404. Contrast Michelet's use of *le Peuple* with the same word (in the plural, significantly) in A. France's preface to his

Such a desire for a lost unity, however, is utterly unlike the one we have been tracing: body with mind. That, too, is nostalgia for a lost time but imagined as one when faith could be given through the sacrifice of the body because certainty had not yet been eviscerated by a Descartes or a Kant (to whom we shall have occasion, yet again, to return). This longing for what is imagined as a "prelapsarian" time, as I have been calling it, for a belief in the body as an extension of the mind, is not the issue for Michelet. Rather, he wants to study Joan as "the martyrdom of purity," in whose suffering "the ideal is discoverable, and shines brightly." The body for Michelet serves as a vehicle for ideas. As such, then, it is a metaphor: women are closer to nature because they menstruate and are given a cyclical time by their bodies. Because they also gestate and are "warmer" (*pace* Aristotle), they are blessed with intuition. With all of his intellect, the male is impoverished if he does not combine his reason with the intuition of women. As virgin, Joan was able to do this effortlessly. Her androgyny is not neither/nor, and it is not hermaphrodism; it is, for Michelet, the extraordinary activation of both genders at once in the same mind.

In the "postmodern" texts we have considered, however, the dilemma is how to experience embodiment literally, as precisely not a metaphor. If what has been lost for Michelet is goodness, which female pity (love) best enacted, it is the body itself that has been lost in late twentieth-century musings. The body has become as if its own *Verfremdungseffekt;* that is, there are moments of shock when one recognizes its presence and tries nostalgically to retain that awareness. "And then there are bodies and they have sexes" is a postmodern *cogito* of sorts: I think; therefore, I must have a body. Under what conditions do I know this?

Perhaps, at least in the French tradition, Michelet and his generation begin what becomes the ineluctable procession into doubt concerning existence itself and absolutes (one thinks in particular here of Mallarmé and Nietzsche). The late nineteenth century was to culminate its crisis

history of Joan: "I believe," writes France, "in the future union of [all] peoples." He also believes that the "charity of humankind," which began with the Romans and "was extinguished by so many centuries of European barbarism," has been rekindled "in the greatest hearts of the modern age" (1: 74–75). Here France's firm idealism and forward-gazing stance for the "peoples" of humanity *(les peuples),* combined with his foreboding sentiments about the plight of the working class, highlight all the more Michelet's romantic nostalgia and designation for the French nation, *le Peuple.*

with such famous statements as Kierkegaard's: "Subjectivity is the only truth." The postmodern, late twentieth-century focuses, even as it pushes and dismantles subjectivity, on a proof of being. The search for an apodictic of the body is frequently seized upon as an antidote to disbelief of every variety. It is as if Michelet were still able to construct scenarios of idealism, even if they are always (already) lost. But writers such as Foucault, Certeau, Althusser, Kristeva, Irigaray, Derrida, and so on, are looking for moments of certainty as if trying to remember, or imagine, what conviction of any sort (religious, political, personal) can mean. For Michelet, Joan of Arc can serve as a model of conviction by which to return to a lost glory; for contemporary writers today, Joan is an instance of conviction that is in and of itself sufficient grounds for fascination.

On the other hand, if we consider Voltaire, the leader of the French Enlightenment—that era that we are busily critiquing from the Frankfurt School on—we find that he suffered from no such nostalgia of either variety. I turn to Voltaire, perhaps the greatest of the *philosophes,* because, once again, Joan of Arc serves as a talisman of how different the eighteenth-century mind was from the *acedia*-ridden, late twentieth-century one. Voltaire's mock epic on Joan is famously ribald and outrageous. Borrowing gleefully from Apuleius (Joan rides into battle on a winged donkey that tries to seduce her near the end of the epic),[24] Rabelais, and scatological literature of all types, Voltaire's *La Pucelle d'Orléans* reads as a broad satire of hagiography, social conventions, women, heroic epics, the rustic, and religion in general. The "miracle" of Joan's life in this bawdy work is that she is able to maintain her virginity for an entire year. Indeed, once Joan has met the terms of her contract with Saint Denis—that France would be saved if Joan remained a virgin for a year—she breathlessly anticipates, with great relief, the end of her status of virgin. The text ends with Joan rushing into the arms of her beloved Dunois, the powerful Bastard of Orléans.

Voltaire's text was instantly and furiously condemned, secretly published in distorted form without his permission, pirated, plagiarized, and so on. Nevertheless, as Marina Warner points out, Voltaire realized that

---

[24] In the defense of the kind donkey, it should be noted that its body is taken over by the devil at the end of the epic. Desperate to have Joan lose her virginity, the devil tries this as a means to have Joan break her "contract" (described earlier). Later the donkey, once again itself, explains and apologizes to Joan for the incident.

the crux of Joan's legend was that her virginity was fundamental to her role of savior. Even Michelet, who refers to *La Pucelle d'Orléans* as "the lamentable ribaldry so well-known," ultimately defends the *philosophe*. Voltaire, he writes in a note, "had no real intention of dishonouring Jeanne Darc [*sic*]. In his serious writings he renders her the most marked homage: 'This heroine . . . gave her judge an answer worthy to be held in everlasting remembrance. . . . They burnt her, who, for saving her king *would have had altars* in the heroic times, when men raised them in honour of their liberators.'"[25]

Michelet's citation is carefully chosen, but significant: one of the great leaders of French thought must not be seen as entirely insensitive to Joan's importance in uniting the country. In fact, Voltaire is as outraged that Joan was burned as he is that anybody took her seriously in the first place. In the entry "Jeanne d'Arc" in Voltaire's *Dictionnaire philosophique*, she is referred to as an "unfortunate idiot." The first half of the article lambastes the French for believing that a poor country girl could converse with saints, produce miracles, prophesy, and so forth. "So much for the ridiculous," writes Voltaire, "now for the horrible." He then excoriates his countrymen for having condemned her: because they had the stupidity to take her seriously, they compounded their idiocy by burning the poor girl. They used male attire as a pretext, "as if, in a warrior girl, it were a crime worthy of burning to wear pants instead of a skirt." She cried on the scaffold? Such weakness is "excusable in one of her sex, and perhaps in ours, and most compatible with the courage which this girl had deployed in the dangers of war; for one can be robust in combat and sensitive on the scaffold." All of this, concludes Voltaire, tears at the heart and makes common sense shudder.

In striking contrast to Michelet, Voltaire has his own notion of *le Peuple:* "One cannot imagine how, after the horrors without number of which we are guilty, we dare to call any people by the name of *barbarians*."[26] A "we" the People is still here, but they are scolded by Voltaire, who in a cold rage refuses to brand the other as uncivilized (barbarian) when it is the French whose history is at least as full of acts of cruelty and

25 Voltaire, "Essai sur les moeurs et esprit des nations," chap. 80, cited in Michelet, *Histoire de France,* 153–54.

26 "Jeanne d'Arc" in *Oeuvres de Voltaire,* vol. 7, *Dictionnaire philosophique* (Paris, 1848), 748; my translation.

atavism. Thus, "we" have not earned the right to dub others barbarians, since there is no difference in behavior, only pretension. For Joan of Arc Voltaire has in fact great pity. The judges, he writes, employed sacrilege to be homicidal. And so, "an unfortunate idiot, who had enough courage to render great service to the king and to the father country [*patrie*], was condemned to be burned by forty-four French priests who immolated her under English supervision" (748).

Thus, there is not much difference between Voltaire's mock epic on Joan and his other writings on the subject, including the entry in the dictionary. And this despite Michelet's conviction (which is held by most) that the first is a "lamentable ribaldry" and the second "a most marked homage." In *La Pucelle d'Orléans,* Voltaire makes fun not only of Joan's simplicity (to put it charitably) but also and even more of the populace that is taken in by such mystical absurdity. Moreover, in times of sexual libertinism (which Voltaire maintains is rampant throughout French history), to assume that a country girl can be a virgin is an equally absurd proposition. None of this, however, negates the "horror" of what was done to Joan or the fact that she showed great courage in battle. For Voltaire the case is clear: Joan of Arc is another of countless instances in which superstition has overcome common sense and mysticism has suffocated reason. What Michelet wants—a return to the innocence of childhood—is for Voltaire precisely the problem: man is too often guilty of a preposterous infantilism.

Here, then, is the certainty for which one might be longing. Yet, as we know, the firm convictions of the Century of Lights inspires little nostalgia in contemporary discourse; on the contrary, the Enlightenment is generally that which must be repressed, severed, put behind as a metaphysical security blanket too comforting to be held. For Voltaire there is no mystery in Joan, except for the fact that anyone actually believed in her claims. For Michelet, she is all mystery and, as such, a promise that there can be "an elect" and a glorious future for France. It is not enough to say, as do some critics, that between Voltaire and Michelet threats on France occurred from the outside—threats that made any mockery of Joan out of place and in poor taste.[27] That may certainly explain part of the difference, but it is not enough.

---

[27] See, for example, Marina Warner, *Joan of Arc: The Image of Female Heroism* (New York, 1981): "But in the eighteenth century, the terror of vivisection by an outside power did not exist as it did in the nineteenth, and Voltaire could afford to poke fun" (239). This

Between Voltaire and Michelet lies the French Revolution, that event that destroyed the old order and monarchy that Joan gave her life to save. The shock of guillotining the king is the recognition of his mortality; it is the symptom of a long-festering doubt about the rights of kings, of course. In that sense, we might say that by the eighteenth century, the king had long since stopped being the personification of the image of the king. Put another, more Lacanian way (once again), we might say that for Voltaire, the Symbolic has shifted toward the state and its discourse of authority. But by the time Michelet writes, there is as if a shift from the Symbolic toward an *imago* he calls *le Peuple,* that idealized vision of unity and perfection. It is an Imaginary that, as in Lacan's infant, is doubled: new France looks back at the old and fails to recognize itself in the mirror. Michelet sees his task as forcing that recognition. Within his gender mythology, Joan of Arc emerges as the new Mary, the bigendered mind capable in turn of engendering a new people enriched by both sexes. The fruit of Joan's womb is thus *le Peuple,* on which the new France must always rest its reverent gaze. In a few short decades, we cannot be farther from Voltaire and his Joan.

Nor, however, can we be farther from the postmodernist Joan. Voltaire's brand of certainty, as we have noted—his firm excision of all things mysterious from this story—instills no envy or nostalgia in present-day texts on Joan. Michelet's idealism seems close to pathetic, if brilliant in its analytic historicism. We seem, at present, more obsessed with the mystery of certainty itself. And thus we are back to the dove: to a time not only when, as we imagine it, the symbol actually embodied what it represented (which might serve as well as an ancillary definition of the martyr) but when such a symbol could serve as proof that all was not in vain, that death is not the end, that the body will itself, someday, be reunited with its soul.

What finally interests a good deal of secular postmodernism, then, is what Voltaire ignores: mystery—events in which the uncanny cannot be made canny, and moments when certainty delegates mental hegemonies even as it remains unfathomable. Hence, once again, the dove—but the dove emanating from woman, who is herself a mystery in the Western tradition—heightens the fascination. In such logic, the move away from

is certainly also true; I am merely saying that it alone does not explain Voltaire's approach to Joan.

the well-ordered universe of the Enlightenment will incur a move toward femininity as well. This move is already to be seen in Michelet's romantic rendition of Joan in particular and the feminine as a whole. But in the canonical texts of contemporary critical theory, femininity—like mystery itself—is scrutinized with a nostalgic desire for belief in anything transcendental. Let me be clear, however: the desire is not to return to such a belief but to try to comprehend its possibility. The attempt, then, is to see Joan as she was seen by those who believed in believing, to see the dove as did those who saw it as one and the same as the soul. We seem now to have moved from a fascination with solving riddles (for example, Freud's positivistic move to dismantle the uncanny) to a need for finding riddles that refuse to be entirely deciphered. Joan presents such a riddle, as does femininity from a masculinist perspective. As such, then, Joan is a doubled conundrum in which we find satisfaction. She represents the representability of certainty.

At the same time, however, even contemporary texts avert the gaze from death. If Joan is a hypersaturated phenomenon in this postmodern culture of the West, as I have been arguing from the start, the dove is the excess emerging from what was purportedly final, finished, done with. In her day as well, one might insist, the dove is equally unfinished business: the scandal of Joan's sacrifice was necessary to ensure a resurrection of sorts. As Rais's friend Prelatti puts it in Tournier's novel, Joan will one day be beatified, for "the trial of the fire constituted the ineluctable hinge of such a reversal."[28] A bizarre reversal indeed: the dove is like a return of the repressed, but the repressed here is the belief in justice and immortality and in some kind of supernatural. Simone Weil, it will be recalled, notes that the place of the supernatural is in itself an excess of the impossible. Granted, she writes from her own very particular, nonsecular perspective, but her aphorism is nonetheless postmodern in its resonance and worth repeating in this context: good energy without incentive is good; it is obedience to God. But since God is "beyond all that we can imagine or conceive," this means obedience to nothing. I repeat her conclusion: "This is at the same time impossible and necessary—in other words, it is supernatural."[29]

But if death (that is, the impossible) is cruelly faced in Joan's sacrifice, it is not long before the usual protections from the recognition of its de-

[28] *Gilles et Jeanne*, 109.

[29] Weil, *Gravity and Grace*, trans. Emma Craufurd (London, 1992), 88.

personalizing inevitability return. The heart that does not burn, the dove flying toward France—these are metonymics of Joan herself, somehow overcoming the end and the ensuing sense of futility. As the metanarrative of excess would have it, it is not that Joan returns; rather, it is that she never goes away. The randomness of death, which even the Church's elaborately overcontrolled execution cannot mask, is veiled by the imposition of fate and a willed meaning. This becomes our "necessity," which is not the one that Weil intends.

Joan lives on, such that her legend is really the legend of a *logos* that wills fate into coherence. Goodness, in other words, that most scandalous of all postures, must not be allowed to have been in vain. Thus, the backformations proliferate after Joan's death: from the Trial of Rehabilitation to the beatification and canonization that occur nearly five hundred years later. "She embodied," writes Winston Churchill, "the natural goodness and valour of the human race in unexampled perfection."[30] He adds, "If this was not a miracle it ought to be" (30). And while we are quick to reject the unburned heart and the dove as wishful medieval thinking, the voices have now attained an aspect of excess that consoles us in our very inability to explain them fully.

Part of the present-day nostalgia, then, vests the supernatural in the impossible but flirts with its necessity in Weil's terms; that is, the supernatural, as an excess that eludes knowledge, is like the Lacanian Real—a nonplace caught between the tension of the impossible and the necessary. Vigorously denied intellectually, the supernatural seems secretly to be alluring in secularist musings, and Joan provides the crux for such reveries.[31] Victoria Sackville-West, at the end of her long biography of Joan, is

[30] *Joan of Arc: Her Life as Told by Winston Churchill in A History of the English- Speaking Peoples* (New York, 1956), 45.

[31] I am, as I hope is clear, purposefully excising overtly religious studies of Joan from this aspect of my argument—studies that often combine the mystical with the nationalistic. See, for example, Léon Bloy's *Jeanne d'Arc et l'Allemagne* (Paris, 1915): "La Lorraine de Jeanne d'Arc était, depuis 1870, sous les pieds des brutes, profanation intolérable à Dieu et aux hommes. Où est-elle maintenant, la sainte fille? Qu'est-elle devenue après 483 ans? Elle mourait alors cruellement pour avoir délivré la France des Anglais. Entendrait-elle aujourd'hui des Voix pour débarasser des Allemands notre République sans Dieu?" and so on (39). There is also, of course, the monumental opus on Joan that Charles Péguy produced after, in his words, "seven years of interior battles." For Péguy, Joan is not only patriotism but also the "echo of Jesus," a particular notion of heroism, and the representation of the various stages of human life. Over more than fifteen years, Péguy produced

perhaps the most honest about the problem of the voices. After lamenting the fact that she cannot adopt a "blindly" Christian attitude to explain them, Sackville-West adds that reason alone is equally unsatisfactory: "I have been painfully torn myself. There are moments when I am not at all sure that the religious line of approach may not, in the end, prove right; when I am not at all sure that instinct may not, as usual, be proved to have taken the short-cut rejected by reason. They may both arrive at the same point in the end; only, instinct may be found to have got there first. I am in the unfortunate position of anybody torn between an instinctive reliance on instinct, and a reasonable reliance on reason."[32]

The nostalgia revealed here is the paradox to which I have been pointing: the will to knowledge and, at the same time, the hope that there may be something beyond human knowledge ("the short-cut rejected by reason"). The paradox of reason and instinct that Michelet espouses as the only means to goodness is once again viewed as impracticable. Sackville-West's quandary and her desire for "more" than the here and now are also, it will be recalled, the position of the great rationalist Freud himself. "So after all it's true that the dead can come back to life," he writes, citing "a doctor" (whom he later admits is none other than himself) who confused a woman dead of Graves disease with her sister.[33] Freud's own belief in numerical prophesying, unexplained repetitions, and so on, all point to a need for "fate"—an inexplicable but rational method underlying the madness. Intellectual uncertainty, which Freud dismisses in the essay on the Uncanny and which psychoanalysis itself strains to dispel, if initially unnerving seems ultimately more consoling in its very ambiguities. Like the daemon of Socrates, Joan's voices remain a nexus of intellectual uncertainty, motivating events that cannot be discounted by insanity in either very different personage.

On the other hand, attempts to dissolve the problem of Joan through "scientific" explanation usually leave no end of absurdity in their wake

Jeanne d'Arc (1897), while he was still a student; *Le Mystère de la charité de Jeanne d'Arc* (1910); *La Tapisserie de sainte Geneviève et de Jeanne d'Arc* (1912); and *Eve* (1913), which ends with an evocation to Joan. Born in Orléans in 1873, Péguy was haunted by the figure of Joan throughout his life.

32 *Saint Joan of Arc* (New York, 1936), 345.

33 Sigmund Freud, "Delusions and Dreams in Jensen's *Gradiva*," in *The Standard Edition of the Complete Psychological Works of Freud,* trans. and ed. James Strachey (London, 1955), 9: 71.

and are themselves easily dismissed. When Sackville-West cites Andrew Lang's original article on Joan, one thinks of Hippocrates. At the time Joan began to hear voices, Lang wrote, she was "at a critical age, when, as I understand, female children are occasionally subject to illusions" (351). But Lang is then moved to write what he calls the first "objective English" biography of Joan and changes his mind about the voices. First, he rejects Anatole France's theory that her voices were "an illusion of her heart." About visions and the voices, writes Lang, "we learn nothing when we are told that." Next, Lang rejects his own earlier article: "On this topic I had written a long chapter, but came to recognise that my psychical lore and my inferences might seem as prolix and futile as the 'celestial science' of the Doctors in Jeanne's own day."[34] Lang goes on to cite the "most recent" testimony on Joan, by Dr. Georges Dumas, professor at the Sorbonne and "an eminent neuropathologist": "Practically, and in the right scientific spirit, Dr. Dumas shrinks from the task of 'a posthumous diagnosis.' If the visions and voices always appeared at one side (which, we have seen was not the case, the light was often all round), then Charcot would have regarded Jeanne as hysterical, and subject to 'unilateral hallucinations.' But it is not known that she was hysterical, or suffered from *hemianesthesia* (absence of sensation on one side)." Moreover, "contemporary neurologists attach less importance than Charcot did to unilateral hallucinations in the diagnosis of hysteria" (293). A discussion follows of whether Joan was amenstrual. Lang then returns to Dr. Dumas, who had noted that Joan's voices were *unconscious* thoughts that put her in touch with the divine. This may have been the only role, if any, of "hysteria" in Joan. Dumas concludes that regarding her intelligence and her will, "Joan remained sane and upright." Moreover, "Nervous pathology can scarcely throw a feeble glimmer of light on a part of this soul" (294).[35]

Written in 1908, Lang's comments on Joan's psychic state cover the field of neuropathology, which remains today equally unable to throw a "feeble glimmer of light" on the voices. But Sackville-West, writing a few decades later, ultimately returns to the "safety" of a neopositivistic approach and decides not to speculate. Not only is she "torn," she writes, about trying to explain Joan's visions and voices, but "it is possible, con-

---

[34] Andrew Lang, *The Maid of France: Being the Story of the Life and Death of Jeanne d'Arc* (London, 1924), 293.

[35] Ibid., 294. See also Dumas's comments in France, *Vie de Jeanne d'Arc,* 2: 459–65.

ceivable, and indeed probable," that science will someday clarify these phenomena. In the meantime, we had better wait "rather than waste our time only to expose ourselves to the antiquarian interest of our posterity as yet another example of commendable inquisitiveness but obsolete ignorance" (346). Adopting the same tone as Freud, who insists that every "unexplained" phenomenon will be eventually solved by science, Sackville-West finally puts "instinct" firmly aside, but not before having performed a flirtation of sorts with the possibility of the inexplicable.

Lacan's case study of a certain "Marcelle C." bears mention here as well, by way of a fascinating tangent. Initially authored in 1931 by J. Levy-Valensi, P. Migault, and J. Lacan, the case is part of Lacan's first writings on paranoia. Marcelle believes that she is Joan of Arc, but "better educated and at a higher level of civilization." She is made to guide governments, she says, and to regenerate mores. Her mission is "a center linked to high international and military things" (367). What is interesting about Marcelle, a thirty-four-year-old schoolteacher, is that she insists that she does not hear voices but rather receives a kind of "dictation" from inside herself (her term is "inspiration") that produces a type of automatic writing (hence the name for the case study, *"schizographie"*). She is, says Lacan, as much at a loss in explaining her voluminous writings once they are produced as are her doctors. In one of her letters, she writes that she has been "subjected to the yoke of defense" (which Lacan interprets as a reversal for "oppression"), and she adds, "through *mutism*" (my emphasis). Thus, we have another, later Dora, who equally inveighs against her psychiatric doctors and who prides herself on never having admitted to the domination of a man (366). Lacan, who does a close, philological analysis of Marcelle's texts, notes that she herself frequently refers to herself "in the masculine" (379). Indeed, Lacan concludes that the patient suffers from not only "an intellectual deficit" but also "passionate sthenia—that is, a virility (or unusual strength, which is meant to be the same thing in this context) stemming from "an egocentric tendency" (381). Whereas Freud, to continue the Dora comparison, is blind to Dora's lesbian feelings toward Frau K., the young Lacan equates sthenia with masculinity, even as he notes Marcelle's promiscuous heterosexuality and her "erotomania." But this is the same problem as with Dora: the imposition of medical categories on the female patient with the diagnostic conclusion of egomania. When a woman shows a "strong" subject position, in other words, she is as if *in excess*. There is no doubt that Marcelle is, in fact, an egomaniacal, paranoid, "schizographic" patient. But when she complains of "the morass of sciences into which the doctors have tried to drag her," she is, like Dora, trying to communicate the fact that the gender issue is not being "read" correctly.[36] And *sthenia*, Marcelle's very serious mental illness notwithstanding, is a telling choice of gender determinant: "great strength" is its first definition, but it means "in excess" when applied to a woman.

In 1903, F. W. H. Meyers produces a sympathetic reading of the "real" Joan, placing her in the tradition of Socrates' daemon and concluding that there may be an impulse from the mind's deeper strata "which is so far from madness that it is wiser than our sanity itself."[37] This view might be read as a more charitable interpretation of what Jaynes called the bicameral mind.

Churchill is unperturbed by all of this, since for him Joan is the inspiration of every soldier. Her story survives "the mists of time," and "All soldiers should read her story and ponder on the words and deeds of the true warrior, who in one single year, though untaught in the technical arts, reveals in every situation the key of victory."[38]

The distinguished contemporary French historian Georges Bordonove is more concerned. In his series "Great Hours in the History of France," he approaches Joan's voices with caution: "We are arriving at the shores of mystery. Commentary is useless and attempts at explanation futile. The theories are here merely arbitrary constructions and are worthless. What some call superstitions, hallucinations, is truth for others. The historian establishes the facts and registers the words which were uttered. That is his manner of approaching the creatures he has evoked, with the sole concern of not betraying them. He does not judge as would

---

36 See Jacques Lacan, "Écrits 'inspirés': Schizographie" in *De la Psychose paranoïaque dans ses rapports avec la personalité, suivi de Premiers écrits sur la paranoïa* (Paris, 1975), 365–82. In this reading I differ strongly from Emily Apter, *Continental Drift: From National Characters to Virtual Subjects* (Chicago, 1999), 44–46. Apter (following Lacan) sees in Marcelle a "monstrous feminist agency" and then conflates Marcelle with Schreber and Joan of Arc herself: "Marcelle C. emerges as an enigmatic Joan of Arc of the clinic, as baffling and politically strident as her fifteenth-century forebear" (46). I find this statement in itself baffling.

37 Frederic W. H. Meyers, *Human Personality and Its Survival of Bodily Death*, 2 vols. (London, 1903). Meyer concludes that Joan is not mad and that her motives are pure.

38 *Joan of Arc*, 46.

a tribunal (even though the media cherish the delectable term 'the tribunal of history'); he tries to understand."[39]

What does it mean, however, to try to "understand" when one begins by declaring that we have arrived at the "shores of mystery"? The ambivalence in this age of "posts" (postmodern, post-Kantian, post-Enlightenment, post-Romantic, and so on) with regard to not knowing is striking indeed. Here, for example, is the conclusion to Charles Wood's study of manners and morals in the age of chivalry: "No one can hope to explain Joan of Arc, and possibly we should not try: in mystery lies the secret of her appeal. Yet, even as paraphrased by hostile inquisitors, her common-sense realism emerges with an exceptional clarity that no amount of religious scepticism can deny."[40] Again, we have here the lure of Joan for contemporary thought: her life traces a mystery, obeys it, yet she herself speaks in the "commonsense realism" that the Inquisition had such difficulty entrapping. Her appeal may well lie in mystery, but it is also in her simple logic and in her refusal (her lack of desire) to understand how or why she was chosen. Perhaps, finally, it is this lack of desire to understand, and yet to *feel*, some form of transcendence for which we are truly nostalgic. This state has meaning only in a context that sees itself as nonreligious, even if inquiring into religion—in the texts, in other words, that I have called secular postmodernist. For example, nonknowledge, writes Bataille, communicates ecstasy, "but only if the possibility (the movement) of ecstasy already belonged, to some degree, to one who disrobes himself of knowledge."[41] Is this the way in which "we" are trying finally to rid ourselves of the Kantian legacy and that of the Enlightenment? Could this be the promise of "woman" and of Joan of Arc today? That which means enigma and mystery but that is (seen as) living the mystery without knowledge?

Bataille notes that the sacred is necessary to the world of action and adds, in a Heideggerian move, that this means that the sacred "must all the more withdraw itself from the world, reserve itself, in that it is total."[42] This might, once again, be a description of Joan of Arc. Bataille contin-

---

[39] Georges Bordonove, *Jeanne d'Arc et la Guerre de Cent Ans* (Paris, 1994), 109; my translation.

[40] Wood, *The Quest for Eternity*, 150.

[41] Georges Bataille, *Inner Experience*, trans. Leslie Anne Boldt (Albany, N.Y., 1988), 123.

[42] Ibid., 209.

ues, "In this unintelligible, unrecognizable sacrifice, what is attained, this time again, is the sacred, but in a form so total that one can only enshroud it deeply."

In a strangely similar vein, there is the statement of one of the Papin sisters cited by Lacan as part of his early studies on paranoia.[43] Christine Papin was condemned with her sister, Lea, of a horrible crime in 1933: attacking, killing, and mutilating their female employer and her daughter, in the house where the Papin sisters worked as maids. Lacan ends his essay on the sisters with the following: "On that fateful evening, in the anxiety of an imminent punishment, the sisters confuse the image of their mistresses with the mirage of their evil *(mal)*. It is their distress which they hate in the couple which they drag into a hideous quadrille. They rip out the eyes like the Bacchantes castrated. The sacrilegious curiosity which makes for the dread of man since the beginning of time, that is what animates them when they desire their victims, when they hunt down, in their gaping wounds, what Christine was later, in front of the judge and in her innocence, to call 'the mystery of life.'" This hunting down of the "mystery of life" through gaping wounds is reminiscent of Gilles de Rais; it reminds one of the connection between the "sacred" and sacrifice, of course, but also of an attempt to erase *le mal* through the violent entry into the body, to bring to light what is hidden. Yet the sacred, as Bataille notes, can only remain enshrouded, even as the open wounds seem capable of divulging (something) and even as Joan's naked body was meant to reveal.

The paradox returns, then: what is sacred is always enshrouded, *especially* when it is in "a form so total" for Bataille. But, as I have been suggesting throughout, to uncouple the sacred from the feminine, and the feminine from mystery, might also allow for a clearer sense of how we imagine, and need, an impossible that we are willing to believe in without willing to know (understand) it. But this entails a change (rather than shift) in the Symbolic, so that the taboo would be more of a Pythagorean mental limit, rather than the purview of the father (in *patrie,* in divinity, even in family imagomythology). Such a change in turn entails a revision of subject formation as a notion. For to begin accepting nonunderstand-

---

[43] The story was to inspire Genet's famous play *Les Bonnes.* Jacques Lacan, "Motifs du crime paranoïaque: Le Crime des soeurs Papin," in *Premiers écrits sur la paranoïa,* 398; my translation.

ing may be, in its secular variety, a first escape from positivism, but it also necessitates relinquishing the sovereignty of the subject as male and a reconsideration of subjectivity as in itself a necessary illusion.

The sacred (which in its secular mode might mean something beyond the illusion of the subject) may be that for which "we" yearn, but it must, I believe, be contemplated (engaged with *attention,* in Simone Weil's term, one that Bataille appropriates) with an ipseity unencumbered by gendered notions of mystery. For gender is hardly the mystery; it is rather the dyadic means to attention. This is what Joan of Arc seems to have known without knowing that it was radical, even scandalous. And that is why her condemnation, not to mention the reasons given for it (cross-dressing, false witnessing, misguided faith, and so on), must have seemed far more mysterious to her than the advent of her voices.

INDEX OF PROPER NAMES

www.ingramcontent.com/pod-product-compliance
Lightning Source LLC
Chambersburg PA
CBHW060032030426
42334CB00019B/2283
9780226519821